REVIVALTIME

PULPIT

SERMON BOOK
NUMBER FIFTEEN
C. M. WARD

ASSEMBLIES OF GOD NATIONAL RADIO AG DEPARTMENT, SPRINGFIELD, MISSOURI

Printed in U.S.A.

CONTENTS

Listed alphabetically

CONTENTS

Listed chronologically according to the date preached on the *Revivaltime* broadcast service.

FOREWORD

This edition of *Pulpit* is the fifteenth in the series. But *Pulpit* #15 is not just another book. The words on these pages are more than so much ink arranged in literary style. Those of us who have worked closely with *Revivaltime* Evangelist C. M. Ward have listened to these messages pour out of his soul in evangelistic fervor. They were conceived and born out of a concern to help people find peace for their souls—regardless of creed, color, or condition.

We have listened to these messages as they were delivered, and we have read with gratitude the many, many testimonies of victory from listeners around the world. Some found the Saviour in the very sunset years. Others, who had been backed into a corner by circumstances of life, found new hope and a new reason for living because of this gospel service. The midnight of discouragement was dispelled from still others as the gospel light broke in upon them just in time.

Yes, this is more than a book. It is a volume of hope, help, encouragement, salvation, and healing for those who will peruse these pages in faith believing.

LEE SHULTZ
National Secretary of Radio

The Broadcast Ministry

It's *Revivaltime* . . . across the nation and around the world. . . ." These familiar words are now heard on nearly 700 releases each week, including many overseas radio stations reaching millions in every section of the globe.

The Reverend C. M. Ward, noted evangelist-author, has served as speaker for *Revivaltime* since 1953. The radio preacher's keen and Spirit-guided insight to the Word of God has won him the respect of people of all faiths. And his heart-to-heart gospel presentation receives responses from such foreign areas as Barbados, Panama, the Philippines, the Virgin Islands, Tonga, and Vietnam, as well as a vast audience in the United States.

Former Bible college president, the Reverend G. Raymond Carlson is executive director of the National Radio Department. And Radio Secretary Lee Shultz serves as producer-narrator of the *Revivaltime* broadcast. Rev. Shultz has been instrumental in expanding the ministry of *Revivaltime* by making the recordings of the broadcast services available to prisons, nursing homes, servicemen, and others who do not have access to a radio release of *Revivaltime*.

Radio Department office manager and technical director since 1953, the Reverend C. T. Beem backs his position with first-hand know-how of quality programming experience.

Emphasizing the role of evangelistic outreach through radio, the Reverend Jack Risner, stations director and field representative, is actively involved in adding the *Revivaltime* broadcast to many radio station logs, thus reaching more and more people with the gospel of Jesus Christ.

The Reverend E. S. Caldwell directs the literature offered to radio listeners. This is a vital ministry of *Revivaltime*.

Serving as choir director since 1952, the Reverend Cyril McLellan is an assistant professor of music at Central Bible College, Springfield, Missouri, from whose student body the 40-voice Revivaltime radio choir is selected.

ECHOES

Text: *"Thine ears hear a word behind thee, saying, This is the way, walk ye in it."*

Isaiah 30:21

THERE are *voices*. Everyone has heard them. In the battle before the passing of Arthur, Tennyson tells of the memories in the minds of the warriors:

> "And some beheld the faces of old ghosts
> Look in upon the battle."

You cannot outdistance them, sir! They keep talking to you out of the past. Believe it, parent! "Train up a child in the way he should go: and when he is old, he will not depart from it" (Proverbs 22:6). *There is always that voice out of the past, that "word behind thee," that speaks.*

The songwriter expresses an experience so many of us have shared when he says: "Mother's prayers have *followed* me—have followed me the whole world through." Isaiah states a fact of life when he says, "Thine ears shall hear a word behind thee, saying, This is the way, walk ye in it."

Think back and agree with me that at some crossturning in life, in circumstances which compelled sudden choice between alternatives, and when we were conscious that the choice carried far issues, we chose in obedience to what we can now only describe as an inexplicable sense of premonition, *an unaccountable sense of inner compulsion.* So many times I have felt that strong urging, "This is the way!" And time has justified my obedience to that voice.

This is the voice of *experience,* mister. You don't have to be a mystic. It is as true for the matter-of-fact man. You can discount premonition entirely. You can steer clear of anything that is vague. You can dismiss it as morbid. Yes, you can be the man who says: "The only voice that speaks with authority to me, and says, 'This is the way,' is the voice of reason." *This* text is as true for you. Guidance comes out of the past.

History has something to say. That is why the Bible includes the Old Testament. It has been the voice that has kept Israel moving toward this present hour through almost 2,000 years of dispersal.

When Moses strode up Horeb to rendezvous with his God, he left a nation without a country, a people without a king—a raw, incoherent folk, at the mercy of a thousand chances which might make them merely a mob. What could give such a people cohesion? Scan the parting words of Moses! He tells them to listen to that "word behind" them: "Remember the days of old, consider the years of many generations" (Deuteronomy 32:7). That *voice* has held this scattered people together and now returned them to their land.

By its undying hold upon its past, the race has survived through inquisition and gas chamber; through ghetto and attempts to utterly erase them. That voice of centuries past said to the Jew, wherever he was, "This is the way."

I have read it on a hundred monuments to World War I:

> "Lord God of Hosts, be with us yet,
> Lest we forget, lest we *forget!*"

My tomorrow, sir, is conditioned by my yesterday. I need to remember. Let me share with you something I have learned. I have learned this. The past does not speak by *precedents,* but through *principles.* Coming circumstances, perplexities, temptations, opportunities, will not be as those gone. It is not that the past holds a precedent to dovetail into every experience, and guide in every emergency. That is not it. The ministry of the past is not to provide precedents, *but to vindicate principles.*

New times will bring new things to us. It is a familiar mischief of mankind to insist that the new must fit into some old precedent. Jesus pleaded that new wine should not be placed in old bottles. He observed that things withheld from the wise and prudent are revealed unto babes.

This always disturbs the older generation. The older generation would ride in a horse-drawn buggy. The young find the automobile.

No, mister! We are not saved by *precedent.* There was nothing sacred about a picture that did not move. We are saved by *principle.* Smut is still smut whether it is on a postcard or a movie. Garbage is still garbage whether it is the gay twenties or the long-haired, mini-skirted seventies. Value is always value, and cheapness is always cheapness. The thing to ask yourself is this, "*Am I a person of principle?*" Do you have values, or are you an easy mark?

I will tell you what history teaches. It teaches that false attitudes have been weighed in the balance of experience, and found wanting. *This is how the past becomes God's voice.*

Every year of grace given us is another step in God's great argument for righteousness. I know this. *It will come out the way that Bible in your hand says it will.*

Samuel gave Saul a guideline that Saul should have followed to the end of his days. He said to Saul, not long after he had met him: "Stand thou still a while, that I may show thee the word of God" (1 Samuel 9:27).

Stop and listen! That Bible in your hand, lady, is that unerring "word behind thee" that says to you, "This is the way, walk ye in it."

Let me now mention three factors which give the past the power and the right to speak.

First, *life is a whole.* It cannot be put into compartments. The calendar is an invention of man. The dividing of years is a human device. December 31 did not end something for you, and January 1 did not begin something for you, as far as your life is concerned. The calendar date is not your salvation. A couple of figures have changed but nothing in your life has changed, although you blew horns and sang sentimental ballads. Your life is one piece. Either you make God responsible for your past, or you, yourself, are responsible.

"Whatsoever a man soweth, that shall he . . . reap" (Galatians 6:7), is not abrogated by a new calendar. It will carry over into 1970, mister. Be sure of that! Those accounts are not closed until the final audit. Your life is like a bookkeeper's ledger. Another year simply means that your accounts are "brought forward." You can't ditch your past, mister, by simply throwing the old calendar into the wastepaper basket.

Second, *there is the persistence of personality.* You may turn a new page, but what of the writer? If the new page is to be cleaner, there will have to be a cleaner hand at the writing. If the lines are to be less crabbed, crooked, and uncertain, a steadier hand, and behind the hand a less divided will, will have to be at the writing. No, sir, the next page will be the same unless the writer changes. You need more than a *resolution.* You need a *revolution.* "Create in me a clean heart, O God; and renew a right spirit within me" (Psalm 51:10).

Third, *you and I reckon with an unchanging God.* The things His soul abhorred in 1969, His soul abhors in 1970. God's message has not changed, and will not change. And as long as mankind insists upon a change, there will be this controversy between God and mankind. One or the other must yield.

Dr. Parker said a great thing in his day. He said:

"God will have every wall built plumb. If the wall is not built plumb, it must come down. The sun will not have it. The stars are annoyed by it. Every star that swings itself round the eternal center is offended by things that will not bear the test of geometry. God will have things square, upright, real. If they are not, He will tear them down and throw them away."

Sinner, that is God's truth expressed in the most simple terms.

If the Boss of this universe will not allow maverick calculations—and the astronomer knows this to be true—He will not accept a disordered life. If the Referee of History will not allow rotten cultures and empires of lust and sin to continue—and every scholar knows this to be true—He will not condone a rebellious, proud sinner.

There is a Supreme Authority in the heavens who decrees law and order. *Whatever other accusation you may bring against God, you cannot charge the Almighty with caprice.* There is an exactness built into every fiber, into every item of this universe. Do you think, for one moment, sinner, that you can make your own rules and live the way you please, and get away with it? Not as long as those stars are above you and running on split-second schedule.

You would do well to listen, mister, to that "word behind thee." It is not a silly superstition. It is the voice of experience. Such a voice can be a comfort and a reinforcement to you. It can stabilize your soul. It removes fear. It brings a confidence, "This is the way, walk ye in it."

Tomorrow need not alarm me. The "word behind" me assures me that I can leave the future in God's hands. Yes, I thank God my past comforts me. I have had more than 40 years of proving His faithfulness. I wouldn't want to live any other way.

But to some in this audience, the "word behind"—the past—*is full of menace.* The sense of guilt and shame is a crushing burden. You are never free from it. You know now that you made the wrong turn in the road, even though, outwardly, you are too stubborn to turn back.

There isn't a drunkenness deep enough that can shut out the echo that repeats, "You are wrong." There isn't a stupor capable of scrambling the message that comes from "behind" and finds you, and says to you, "Your life might have been different." There is a *moral beam* in this universe that says, "This is the way, walk ye in it."

One thing you cannot destroy, mister, is *memory*. "In hell he lifted up his eyes, being in torments" (Luke 16:23). And an echo came back to him: "Son, *remember* that thou in thy lifetime receivedst thy good things" (Luke 16:25).

Sinner, God will give you forever to do your homework—to figure it out. But one thing is certain. That "word behind thee, saying, This is the way, walk ye in it," will not change. You will hear it forever and forever.

This is the moment to listen and square your life with the facts. "This is the way!" That is what the echo keeps repeating.

I have this good news for you. "Let the wicked forsake his way, and the unrighteous man his thoughts: and let him return unto the Lord, and he will have mercy upon him; and to our God, for he will abundantly pardon" (Isaiah 55:7).

That is the sensible thing to do at this moment.

A REVIVALTIME TESTIMONY

"I have been listening to *Revivaltime* every Sunday afternoon. Surely if there is a redeeming broadcast in this world, it is *Revivaltime*. *Revivaltime* is second to none. And unless one like Brother Ward has Christ in him, one cannot preach that well!"

ABOMINATION OF DESOLATION

Text: "*When ye therefore shall see the abomination of desolation, spoken of by Daniel the Prophet.*"

Matthew 24:15

THE clue is to read Daniel. Dr. C. I. Scofield said: "The attempt of Nebuchadnezzar of Babylon to unify the religions of his empire by self-deification will be repeated by Antichrist, the last head of the Gentile world dominion."

Dr. A. C. Gaebelein said: "The times of the Gentiles produce a religion which is opposed to the God of heaven." *The picture is in the Book of Daniel.* Let's have a look at it!

Turn with me to Daniel, chapter three. The Book of Daniel sheds more light upon the last book of the Bible, the Revelation, than any other source. There is an *image* in the Book of Daniel, and there is an *image* in the Book of Revelation. The one suggests the other.

Worship of the image in both cases is *compulsory.* To refuse brings about certain death. There is *opposition.* A final, desperate effort is organized to *annihilate* this position. There is *divine intervention.* God is glorified. This is, essentially, the story told in Daniel and repeated in the Revelation. What are the lessons? Preachers call this *learning by type.*

H. S. Miller defines a type. "A type is a literal, divinely appointed person, thing, or event which also has a future spiritual application, and which therefore symbolizes another person, thing, or event."

Generally, you will discover a New Testament *truth* illustrated by an Old Testament *story*. Thus Old Testament stories are more than history. They are *predictions*. They are in the Book of Daniel.

What follows immediately after the reappearance of Jesus Christ is called *the tribulation period*. It is a time of massive trouble. Some Old Testament preachers described it as the "time of Jacob's trouble" (Jeremiah 30:7).

God is ready to resume dealings with Israel. Historical events will swirl around this revived nation again just as they did in Bible times. The most intense struggle since the Garden of Eden will ensue between God and Satan for the worship of mankind. Hell's force will be led by the false prophet. Heaven will find a testimony amid the residue of this much beleaguered people, Israel. The account is not *fantasy*. It is *fact*.

Yes, we can see into the future! I am going to employ the analogy principle. This is the principle under which God embeds truth about Israel, or Christ, or the individual believer in some apparently remote Biblical incident, making such truth demonstrable by an extended series of similarities or contrasts. You can use this principle again and again in reading and studying your Bible.

I am going to look at the story in the third chapter of Daniel to learn what will take place soon as stated prophetically by John in the 13th chapter of the Revelation and subsequent passages.

First, *Nebuchadnezzar set up an image*. It was a literal image. Its dimensions are given. Translated from cubits into feet, the image was 90 feet high, approximately the height of a ten-story building, and nine feet wide. And it may have stood upon a pedestal. It was a *showpiece*. It glittered and dazzled. It was designed to attract attention.

The Revelation states that a future image will appear on earth. "Saying to them that dwell on the earth, that they should make *an image* to the beast" (Revelation 13:14).

Second, *there is a similarity in the mystery of the three sixes employed.* Nebuchadnezzar's image was 60 cubits high, 6 cubits broad, and 6 musical instruments were used to call the people to worship the image. The Revelation tells us about the future event: "Here is wisdom. Let him that hath understanding count the number of the beast: *for it is the number of a man;* and his number is Six hundred threescore and six" (Revelation 13:18). Someday that mystery will be unraveled, but the similarity is there.

Third, *all men were commanded to worship the image.* "Then a herald cried aloud, To you it is commanded, O people, nations, and languages, that at what time ye hear the sound of the cornet, flute, harp, sackbut, psaltery, dulcimer, and all kinds of music, ye fall down and worship the golden image that Nebuchadnezzar the king hath set up" (Daniel 3:4, 5).

The present mystique of the beat, the rock, and the message song, now drawing in the open air more than a quarter of a million devotees at one time, surely points back to Daniel and forward to the Revelation. We are told of the future: "And he had power to give life unto the image of the beast, that the image of the beast should both speak, and cause that as many as would not worship the image of the beast should be killed" (Revelation 13:15).

Fourth, *failure to worship meant death.* Nebuchadnezzar's mandate went like this: "And whoso falleth not down and worshippeth shall the same hour be cast into the midst of a burning fiery furnace" (Daniel 3:6).

Refusal to worship the image of the Antichrist will also mean death. "And cause that as many as would not worship the image of the beast should be killed" (Revelation 13:15).

Fifth, *there is universal acceptance.* Daniel reports that in Babylon: "All the people, the nations, and the languages, fell down and worshipped the golden image that Nebuchadnezzar the king had set up" (Daniel 3:7).

The Revelation says that "All that dwell upon the earth shall worship him, whose names are not written in the book of life of the Lamb slain from the foundation of the world" (Revelation 13:8). *The day of diversified religions is coming to an abrupt close.*

Sixth, *a Jewish remnant refuses to worship the image.* "We will not . . . worship the golden image which thou hast set up" (Daniel 3:18). The opposition will not come from the Protestant sanctuary nor the Catholic basilica. *It will come from the Jewish synagogue.* The Book of Revelation says: "And the dragon was wroth . . . and went to make war with the remnant of her seed" (Revelation 12:17).

Seventh, *the Jew is in trouble.* Nebuchadnezzar "commanded the most mighty men. . . in his army to bind Shadrach, Meshach, and Abednego, and to cast them into the burning fiery furnace" (Daniel 3:20). Likewise the anger of hell is mounted against Israel. Listen to John's words in Revelation! "The dragon . . . *went to make war* with the remnant of her seed" (Revelation 12:17). That seed has survived the butcheries of Pharaoh, Haman, and Hitler. There has always been a "*remnant.*" Satan wants to utterly eliminate it.

Eighth, *there is burning.* First in Daniel—"because the king's commandment was urgent, and the furnace exceeding hot, the flame of the fire slew those men that took up Shadrach, Meshach, and Abednego" (Daniel 3:22).

And the Revelation tells us: "If any man worship the beast and his image, and receive his mark in his forehead, or in his hand, the same shall drink of the wine of the wrath of God, which is poured out without mixture into the cup of his indignation; and he shall be *tormented with fire and brimstone* in the presence of the holy angels, and in the presence of the Lamb" (Revelation 14:9, 10).

Ninth, *the remnant is miraculously preserved.* Nebuchadnezzar bore witness to it in his day. "Did not we cast three men bound into the midst of the fire? . . . Lo, I see four men loose, walking in the midst of the fire, and they have no hurt; and the form of the fourth is like the Son of God" (Daniel 3:24, 25).

Is that a type of things to come? Ponder this! "And I saw as it were a sea of glass mingled with fire: and them that had gotten the victory over the beast, and over his image, and over his mark, and over the number of his name, stand on the sea of glass, having the harps of God" (Revelation 15:2).

Tenth, *the faithful were exalted after their deliverance.* "Then the king promoted Shadrach, Meshach, and Abednego, in the province of Babylon" (Daniel 3:30).

In like manner the Revelation bears this testimony: "And I looked, and lo, a Lamb stood on the mount Zion, and with him a hundred forty and four thousand, *having his Father's name written in their foreheads.* And I heard a voice from heaven, as the voice of many waters, and as the voice of a great thunder: and I heard the voice of harpers harping with their harps: and they sung as it were a new song before the throne, and before the four beasts, and the elders: and no man could learn that song but the hundred and forty and four thousand, which were redeemed from the earth. . . . These are they which follow the Lamb withersoever he goeth. These were redeemed from among man, being the firstfruits unto God and to the Lamb. And in their mouth was found no guile: for they are without fault before the throne of God" (Revelation 14:1-5).

It is an interesting company of survivors with the Father's Name inscribed on their foreheads instead of the name of the Beast.

Thus the foreshadowing! You can learn about one from reading the other. God intends it to be that way. He teaches and informs in this manner.

It boils down to this. *What and whom are you worshiping?*

The choice will suddenly and dramatically be narrowed. There will be no opportunity for religious preference. And lip service will not suffice. The command will be *"Bow down!"* It will be either public adoration or public humiliation.

Only one tiny island of humanity will escape. *The rest of mankind will capitulate.* Where is the "remnant" today? It is in Palestine. A survivor will one more time escape the dragon's wrath. History has introduced us to that wrath. We know what it is.

But, for you, sir—you are not a Palestinian. You have no vested rights outside the grace of God. And when the Holy Spirit is withdrawn from this planet, and the power of the gospel is no longer present to protect you—what will happen to you?

Read it for yourself! "All that dwell upon the earth shall worship him" (Revelation 13:8). That means *you.* Only Christ can save you. But His offer is good *now*—not *then.*

So, your choice amounts to this as time runs out—Christ or Antichrist. When time runs out, there'll be no choice.

A REVIVALTIME TESTIMONY

"I am only 15 years old and have been saved about nine months. I am a Lutheran, but it was through an Assemblies of God minister and his wife that I came to make my decision for Christ. In them I saw what I had been looking for for quite a while.

"I stay up until 10:30 p.m. to listen to *Revivaltime* when everyone else is sleeping. It is then that I can pray and grasp every word.

"Praise God for your ministry, Brother Ward. It means food for a hungry saved soul."

A RADIO INVITATION

New and more detailed signs are constantly challenging our attention toward the will of God for man and this planet. It is so important to bow and say: "Thy will be done in earth as it is done in heaven." *I ask you to make this moment that great moment when you surrender yourself to Jesus Christ.*

God's Word is filled with detail. God has entered many contracts with many inhabitants of earth. *That is why Bible study is so important.* Suddenly, you ask: "Why is history taking this turn?" Then, you discover that it is turning to comply with the will of God documented centuries ago in the Book called the Bible.

Be at peace with God, sir! It is the delightful and secure way to live. Your home will be different. Your family will be different. Your health will be different. *Get rid of your sin problem!*

"Lord Jesus, I kneel on behalf of those at this long, long altar. I pray for inward peace. I pray for release from guilt. I pray for broken fetters—deliverance from alcohol, narcotics, tobacco, undisciplined temper, lust. *I pray for victory.*

"I pray that these lives shall be Spirit-filled and Spirit-employed. I pray for great joy to be manifest among us—a spirit of resurrection emphasis.

"I pray for personal needs to be met—for income to appear where there seems to be no sign of income, for jobs to open. I pray for the healing of sick bodies. I pray for the salvation of wives in this audience who have resisted Thy gospel. I pray for Christ to be exalted and glorified among us. Amen."

PERILOUS TIMES

Text: *"In the last days perilous times shall come."*

2 *Timothy* 3:1

I BELIEVE the text could easily be read, "In the last days *revolutionary times* shall come." Probably no other half century in history has involved such cataclysmic change.

There have been two world wars. There has been a world epidemic of influenza that still threatens from year to year. There has been the greatest political upheaval of all time—the Communist Movement. This planet has experienced the worst outburst of anti-Semitic hatred in history. We live in the shadow of the most deadly invention of all time—the bomb. The sex revolution and the crime wave threaten society. Israel has returned to the family of nations. *I believe you and I have a right to identify this day with Paul's text.*

Add to what I have said, the "breakthroughs" of the past half century! We have applied radio, television, radar, and sonar to everyday uses. We have split the atom, broken the sound barrier, sailed under the Arctic ice pack, pumped oil from ocean floors, irrigated deserts, and visited the moon. Daniel says that in "the last days"—described by Paul as "perilous times"—"knowledge shall be increased" (Daniel 12:4). I cannot doubt the significance.

These are hazardous times. They are times without clear delineation. The cry and demand are for peace while taxes snowball for war. We try to turn off prosperity, and make poverty a national issue. We place the Bible on our stamps, and kick God out of our schools. We license the man who sells liquor, and we jail the drunk. There are more educated clergy than ever before, and less soul-saving dynamic. Existence has become a mine field. Look with me at some of these *"perils!"*

First, there is *the philosophic peril.* Basically it is an acceptance of man as his own originator. I become responsible to myself alone.

It is willful thinking. Paul tabs it when he says: "Who changed the truth of God into a lie, and worshipped and served the creature more than the Creator" (Romans 1:25).

Your very *skin* must tell you there is a Creator. It clothes your raw flesh with an attractive covering. It repulses enemies that attack your body. They are bacteria, dust, too much sunlight, too much heat, and too much cold. Your skin eliminates poisons by *breathing* and *sweating.* Your skin acts as an "air-conditioner"—warming you in the winter and cooling you in the summer. Its sensitive nerves keep you in touch with the outside world, and warn you to withdraw your hand when you touch a hot utensil, and cover your ears when it is bitterly cold outside.

Your skin is composed of *two layers*: the upper, or outside, called the *epidermis,* consisting of a layer of living cells that replace the outside cells which are dead and which are constantly worn away by abrasion. The outermost cells are "keratinized" (cornified), and this gives them resistance to wear and tear without giving pain to the body. These "dead" cells are a *buffer* between you and a hostile world, and yet the layer of dead cells is not too thick, otherwise you would not be warned of real dangers such as fire.

The lower layer of the skin is the *dermis,* the skin proper. In contrast with the partly dead epidermis, the dermis is a highly complex arrangement of blood vessels, nerve endings, connective tissue, and various useful glands. Because of the functions of the dermis, our bodies are "homoiothermic"; that is, *they have a constant body temperature.* That temperature is 98.6 degrees. Beneath the dermis is a layer of fat, which varies with the individual. This acts as *insulation,* and also *protection.* It lessens the force of a blow on the body from the outside.

What Infinite Mind could have planned such details! *Someone* has a personal interest in you. That skin is yours. Your fingerprints are personal. Your footprints are different. Your skin markings on the palms and elsewhere are individual. They belong to you, and to you alone.

I want you to think, young man! Monkeys have long hair so that their babies can cling to them as they jump from tree to tree in the forests. God made man and woman practically hairless that mothers might know they are to cling to their children, and care for them with a tenderness and love that animals do not know. Yes, we live in a day of philosophic peril!

Second, there is *the financial revolution.* Grandfather's principles are out-of-date. We are involved with "deficit spending" and planned inflation. Taxes are moving us toward the complete socialized state. Hell has surveyed the road to dictatorially controlled "buying and selling." "That no man might buy or sell, save he that had the mark" (Revelation 13:17).

The only real credit a nation possesses is the willingness of the citizen to be taxed. Rapidly we are reaching the point of no return. When enough citizens rebel, it will mean national bankruptcy and the fertile soil for dictatorship. The greatest tragedy is this. The New Economy provides less and less incentive to work. And work is God's provision against total moral apathy.

A man was made to take pride in his work—to strive for excellence. Isaiah knew this. He said, "Yet surely my judgment is with the Lord, and my work with my God" (Isaiah 49:4).

Months ago when I interviewed Mr. Walter Knott of the famous Knott's Berry Farm Enterprises in Southern California, this old-fashioned Methodist said to me:

"Mr. Ward, I believe God left this planet with enough work

to do, so that everyone—regardless of his profession—can leave some little sign of progress behind. I have tried to do this with these California acres. Mrs. Knott and I found them unimproved, desert acres. We have nourished them and built on them and opened them to the public for their pleasure."

Yes, we are in the midst of a financial revolution!

Third, there is *a revolution in the arts.* Best sellers sprinkle their pages with obscene, four-letter words. The comedian solicits applause by association with the crude and the rude. The competition seems to be—who can suggest something filthier than the other. The apostle John identifies it on the last page of the Bible, "He which is *filthy,* let him be filthy still" (Revelation 22:11). Jude recognizes this as a last-day peril. He says: "Likewise also these filthy dreamers defile the flesh, despise dominion, and speak evil of dignities" (Jude 8).

Content is sacrificed for shock. When you look at the stage and the screen—when you listen to the bleat and the bang euphemistically called music—when you view the undress and the slop called style—you are forced to one conclusion. This world is *sick.*

Young woman, Hollywood has a sad page. You should read it. Jayne Mansfield was decapitated in an automobile accident near New Orleans. Marie McDonald died of acute drug intoxication. Marilyn Monroe took her own life. Carole Landis committed suicide over an unrequited love affair. Lupe Velez perished in the same fashion. She was carrying another woman's husband's child. Linda Darnell became the victim of liquor and perished in a Chicago fire. Ann Sheridan was a cancer victim. All were billed by the world of fun and frolic as sex symbols. "And the world passeth away, and the lust thereof" (1 John 2:17).

Fourth, there is *the educational peril or revolution.* God is not on the side of ignorance; to the contrary, "Add to your faith . . . knowledge" (2 Peter 1:5). Note a provision Peter observes! Before you add *knowledge,* you should add *virtue.* The passage reads, "And to your faith virtue; and to virtue, knowledge."

The essence of education is *character.* Knowledge without character can produce a culture of super-criminals. "The fear of the Lord is the beginning of knowledge" (Proverbs 1:7).

I have long ago underlined the passage of Proverbs 22:12 in my soul: "The eyes of the Lord preserve knowledge; and he overthroweth the words of the transgressor." God is *for* every technical advance, and *against* every perverted use of it. The film can be either used to instruct, or it can carry a salacious appeal.

The "behaviorist" and the "permissive" schools have sown to the wind. Now we are reaping the whirlwind in our youth. We are in the midst of social revolution. The welfare of the student has been sacrificed for experimentation.

One of our governors had a wise thing to say recently. He observed that campaigns by liberals to make such things as marijuana and abortion legal are immediately followed by business opportunists who push the sale of these by vivid merchandising and advertising campaigns.

There are many additional "perils" I might name—revolutions in the status of women—in the choice of adventure and pleasure—in automation—in theology! It's all topsy-turvy. Paul tells the Corinthians: "If the trumpet give an uncertain sound, who shall prepare himself to the battle?" (1 Corinthians 14:8). It is not easy to find your way in the midst of "perils."

No, Dad, it is not the same world! No longer can you buy a dozen eggs for ten cents, or get a wool suit for five dollars. But one thing has not changed. *Sin is still sin.* No change of philosophy, no change of economy, no change of style, no change of learning have eliminated sin. *Personal failure is written everywhere.*

The outline of political realignment is visible. Israel, regathered, has become the focal point of strife in the Near East. The "Colossus of the North" is no longer the meandering mind of an ancient prophet called Ezekiel. The play that is going on among Arabic peoples—jockeying for a power position—makes you read seriously the description of Daniel about the "King of the South" and the part he is to play in the last drama. The nations of western Europe, through the instrumentality of the "Common Market" are in the fetal stages of the revival of the old Roman political concept.

This is the moment, mister, to think about *escape*. God is telling you what He told Lot, "Escape for thy life; look not behind thee!" (Genesis 19:17).

God offers you, and your family, a way out. *You cannot reverse the trend.* "This know also, that in the last days perilous times shall come." But you need not be caught and dragged down in the undertow.

A REVIVALTIME TESTIMONY

"If on a rare occasion I should miss the broadcast, I then read one of the sermons *Revivaltime* has sent me. I have all the sermons from the past year and have them stapled together in book form. I read at least one sermon every day. I've read and reread all the literature I have received from *Revivaltime* in the past year.

"Brother Ward, if you could have known the two different me's, you could see the difference since I have been saved and guided to the Saviour through *Revivaltime!*"

FIRE

Texts: *"He shall baptize you with the Holy Ghost, and with fire."*

Matthew 3:11

"For our God is a consuming fire."

Hebrews 12:29

FIRE has been a sacred symbol since time immemorial. In Rome the sacred flame was guarded by consecrated priests and vestal virgins. Were it to be extinguished, all executive and national affairs were suspended. It had to be rekindled, either from lightning, or from the concentrated rays of the sun.

The foreign ambassador had to walk by the holy fire before he could be received in the council of state. The Slavonic and Teutonic bride had to bow before the holy fire as she entered her new home. The Red Indian sachem would walk thrice around the campfire before he would give his counsel or confer with his public visitor. The twelve Grecian tribes brought their twelve firebrands to Theseus, and were consolidated into the State, and their sacred fires were combined in the Oracle of Delphi. Persian fire worshipers looked upon the sun and the flame as sacred things, and it was unpardonable profanity to spit in the fire or commit any impropriety in the presence of these holy elements. The Olympic Games begin when the torch has been carried across land and sea to the chosen site of the international competitions.

Fire is a very important symbol in God's Word. It is a reminder of God's transcendent glory, and the power of His presence. Fire is the most valuable physical force with which we are acquainted. The sun is the power force for our planetary system. In miracle ways this energy has been stored in vast coal mines. We have harnessed it and made it work in a thousand different ways, from the atomic bomb to modern transportation. Without electricity we would still be groping our way out of the Middle Ages. I think of this line again and again while involved in modern business, with electrically driven machines which can out-think man, "Our God is a consuming fire." *God is the source of all forces.*

God plans this force to be utilized in the believer. The Day of Pentecost made this a practical, everyday reality.

For long years in the history of the natural world flames revealed in sky or volcano were objects of mystery, uncertainty, and almost dread. Mankind realized there was force, but mankind did not know how to use it as a servant. Science has changed fear to respect.

In like manner the child of God knew the mysterious flashes from another world spoke of miracle, but the child of God did not know how to receive and adapt such miracle to his everyday walk. Moses and Elijah record such fire. The Burning Bush and Carmel are turning points in the Old Testament narrative.

Jesus brought a *change*. Any disciple can enjoy, and should expect, "these signs shall follow" (Mark 16:17). Christ has placed "the fulness of the Godhead bodily" (Colossians 2:9) at the believer's disposal.

Mister, without God's manifest presence, your religious profession is a charade. It is meaningless. Israel traveled only as the Presence traveled. It was the Shekinah glory in the midst of the Holy of Holies that made God's people "more than conquerors."

In all the sacrifices and offerings fire was an important element. The *paschal lamb* was roasted in the fire and eaten by the people as a symbol of Christ's flesh prepared for us and ministered to us by the Holy Ghost as our Living, Sustaining Bread.

The *sin offering* was carried without the camp and burned with fire, as a symbol of our sin upon Jesus and consumed by the Holy Ghost outside the pale of our consciousness, so that we have nothing more to do with it, but simply to lay it on the Lamb of God and leave it with Him.

The fire was never allowed to go out in the Camp of Israel. *Thus the ministry of the Spirit of God is absolutely necessary.*

The *peace offering* was associated with fire. It was a type of our communion with God. The fat and the inwards were given to God. They were consumed on the altar; the shoulder and breast were given to the priest and eaten by him. *Only the Holy Ghost can maintain this sense of communion.* It is a life without friction—God having His part and the believer strengthened to enjoy his mission and ministry.

There was the *meat offering.* It was fine flour baked in the fire, mingled with oil and frankincense, and free from leaven and honey. It pictured the ministry of Jesus Christ to the believer, nourishing and feeding the believer by means of the Spirit.

It is one thing to feed upon the truth. It is another thing to feed upon Christ. The difference is just the same as if you should attempt to feed upon raw wheat instead of prepared bread. *Only the Holy Spirit can make Jesus real to you.*

Another wonderful glimpse is the use of fire in *the ordinance of the red heifer.* This ceremony represented Christ our Sacrifice, slain and consumed for us on the altar of God. But in the burning of the heifer there appear the scarlet wool, the cedar, and the hyssop leaves, *representing something which is to be consumed, along with the death of Christ.*

The scarlet wool represents our sins. The cedar represents our strength. The hyssop represents our weakness and the clinging element in our nature. *These things are to be crucified with Christ.* This can only be done with fire—in the power and ministry of the Holy Ghost. I can *consent,* but I cannot *implement.* I am not equal to the task of self-crucifixion.

There was something additionally interesting to this particular offering. Even after the death of the heifer, the fire was to be preserved and made perpetual *by the preservation of the ashes.* By pouring water upon these ashes a lye was created, a very acrid, pungent, burning substance. This liquid was used as a symbol of *purification* when anyone in Israel had contracted any sin or defilement whatsoever. Thus the Holy Spirit constantly cleanses the believer from pollution absorbed from the things with which we live.

Fire was everywhere in Israel's culture.

Mister, it is the same today! The Holy Ghost is the power of God in our work. Hell cannot extinguish it any more than multiplied barrels of water could fizzle the flame that devoured Elijah's witness at Carmel.

It is a fire, sir, that delights in the hardest places and the most difficult undertakings. You need not fear to claim this power for even the impossible! Summon the mighty Spirit of God to the difficulties you face. Elijah believed that the fire would make a way. He was not disappointed.

Israel's false and presuming priests learned a lesson. They dared to offer strange fire at the altar of God. The fire of God consumed them. Ananias and Sapphira presumed in the New Testament. They substituted make-believe for reality. It did not pass God's judgment.

Make no mistake about it, careless professing Christian! This cleansing agent is in the Church. *Water* may and does make the *exterior* acceptable. *Fire* moves into the *interior.* It penetrates. There are a lot of ceremonies that can make you an acceptable church member. But what are you inside? Only the Spirit of God detects that.

Thank God for this holy spark! It quickens. It gives life.

Never forget it for a moment! *You are born again of the Spirit.* Jesus said it categorically. "That which is born of the flesh is flesh; and that which is born of the Spirit is spirit" (John 3:6). *You need something more than your flesh.* Paul said, "It is the Spirit that quickeneth" (John 6:63).

It takes more than trimming trees and plowing the soil. It takes power to germinate the seeds and produce the fruit. The Holy Ghost breaks the fetters of fear and sorrow. The Spirit of God kindles the love of God in the heart.

The church is simply a corporation without this energy. I have this simple faith, folk. I believe the same God who energizes the earth and its fullness, energizes His Church. It would be as foolish to assume that a peach tree can produce peaches without life, as it is to assume that a human being can produce godliness without divine energy.

The same God who can hold each planet in its course *can hold me on course.* Believe that, church member! The same God who stores combustion in a lump of coal can infuse me with the power described in the Book of Acts. Science turns to this unlimited force to drive the wheels of progress. Why doesn't the Church use the same common sense? *The truth is, we have divine resources at our disposal.*

Mr. Believer, turn toward the Sun of Righteousness! Expose yourself to Him. Suddenly your life will be *ignited.* Christ is God's *eternal flame.* When you touch Him you are motivated. Your life suddenly blazes in the midst of a community of darkness and death.

"He shall baptize you . . . with *fire.*" God send this warmth into our midst!

A REVIVALTIME TESTIMONY

"I am a regular listener to *Revivaltime*. This broadcast has completely and miraculously changed my life. Praise God I am saved!"

SLIPPERY

Text: *"For thou hast delivered my soul from death, mine eyes from tears, and my feet from falling."*

Psalm 116:8

WINTER is a season in so much of the world *when it is easy to fall.* The danger is slipping. A bit of ice, skidding, unseen dips increase the risk. Many a person has suffered a nasty tumble. It becomes a season of broken hips and collarbones. The need for the exhortation "Watch Your Step" becomes apparent.

It is always that kind of season for the soul. All of us live within the shadow.

"In an upper room at Pompeii a family of eleven died together. In the cellars of a noble villa eighteen women and children lay with their heads covered as though asleep. Near a garden gate a group of men had been emtombed with bags of money and other valuables they had tried to carry away. One held a key in his hand. . . ."

That was the year A.D. 79 in Italy. The month and the day when Vesuvius erupted were August, the 24th. *Peril caught and claimed hundreds of Pompeians.*

But the man in my text claims *deliverance and protection.* Is it possible? Is there an "Operation Safeguard"? Accident insurance can soften the blow, but it is not insurance *against* accident. It is insurance *for* accident. I want protection from the evil that pursues me. "Lead me not into temptation, but deliver me from evil" (see Matthew 6:13). That is my prayer. *Is such protection available? Does it work?*

The testimony of Paul and Silas says it works. They were delivered. They had been thrust into the maximum security cells of the Philippi prison. "Suddenly there was a great earthquake, so that the foundations of the prison were shaken: and immediately all the doors were opened, and every one's bands were loosed" (Acts 16:26).

The testimony of Hezekiah says it works. He was a dying man. Disease had a conqueror's hold upon him. "In those days was Hezekiah sick unto death" (Isaiah 38:1). Even the preacher thought he would die. "Isaiah . . . came unto him, and said unto him, Thus saith the Lord, Set thine house in order: for thou shalt die, and not live" (Isaiah 38:1).

It is discouraging to have the preacher talk to you like that. You have a choice, mister. You can either die, or do something about it. "Then Hezekiah turned his face toward the wall, and prayed. . . . Then came the word of the Lord to Isaiah, saying, Go, and say to Hezekiah, Thus saith the Lord, the God of David thy father, I have heard thy prayer, I have seen thy tears: behold, I will add unto thy days fifteen years" (Isaiah 38:2, 4, 5).

God has extended a blank check to you. Here it is! "Call upon me in the day of trouble: I will deliver thee, and thou shalt glorify me" (Psalm 50:15). That is for you, my friend.

In a word, God's business is *salvation.* It provides full coverage. It cancels the *past.* "Thou hast delivered my soul from death." It comforts the *present.* "Thou hast delivered my feet from slipping." It compasses the *future.* "Thou hast delivered mine eyes from tears."

It is a terrible thing to drag out your life under condemnation. A sinner is on *deathrow.* The electric chair is the lake of fire. "And whosoever was not found written in the book of life was cast into the lake of fire" (Revelation 20:15).

I do not blame you for seeking psychiatric help. That sense

of guilt is enough to make you sweat. It is enough to cause sleeplessness. It is enough to drive you to drink and drugs.

It is not an *analysis* you need. You need *forgiveness,* a pardon. I don't need to tell you that you have broken God's laws. That is what is making you feel so terrible. You know it. Staying away from church does not help. It makes you feel worse.

You need the good news that came to me and changed my life. "He that heareth my word, and believeth on him that sent me, hath everlasting life, and shall not come into condemnation; but is passed from death unto life" (John 5:24).

That is what the writer of this text means when he says, "Thou hast delivered my soul from death" (Psalm 56:13). It is an escape that no psychiatrist on earth can provide. You hear this choir sing it so often because it is true:

> "No condemnation have I in my heart,
> He took my sins away, . . .
> His perfect peace He did to me impart,
> He took my sins away."

Then the writer of the text rejoices in *the keeping power* of the Saviour. "Thou hast delivered my feet from slipping." That is what frightens the sinner at the altar call, "What if I were to slip?"

Let me tell you, sir! There is something more at that altar for you—a lot more. Many a "Lazarus" who has been raised from the dead, is still *hampered by the graveclothes of the old life.* I am afraid too many of our churches leave their altars unmanned. The word to the Lord's helpers is this, "Loose him, and let him go" (John 11:44).

Many a new convert needs to be *"loosened."* He has been raised, delivered, saved by the power of God. That convert needs the ministry of friends. Many a Paul cries: "O wretched man that I am! who shall deliver me from the body of this death?" (Romans 7:24).

He feels shackled to a corpse. That old carnal nature wants to dictate how, when, where you should live for Christ. It says Sunday school attendance is enough out of a budget of a week's time. It says like Pharaoh to Israel: "Go, . . . only ye shall not go very far away" (Exodus 8:28). It says, "Don't give up everything!" It speaks the disobedient, compromising language of Saul of Israel: "But Saul . . . spared Agag, . . . and all that was good, and would not utterly destroy them: but every thing that was vile and refuse, that they destroyed utterly" (1 Samuel 15:9).

That is the voice that whispers to the convert that perhaps cigarettes, secret societies, a friendly game of cards can be used to good advantage. Saul put it this way to Samuel. He said, "I kept them to sacrifice unto the Lord."

It is one thing, mister, to be delivered from the *penalty* of sin. That is *forgiveness.* It is another thing to be delivered from the *power* of sin. That is *cleansing.* Remember! "He is faithful and just to forgive us our sins, and to cleanse us from all unrighteousness" (1 John 1:9).

Professing Christian, you won't make much headway until those "graveclothes" have been cut away. This is a great word. "Thou hast delivered my feet from slipping."

Do not be afraid! There is plenty of keeping power. "Fear thou not; for I am with thee: be not dismayed; for I am thy God: I will strengthen thee; yea, I will help thee; yea, I will uphold thee with the right hand of my righteousness" (Isaiah 41:10).

I love that promise, "I will uphold thee." That means He takes my hand. I can walk surefootedly. He will guide me past the pitfalls. Any adversary will think twice before attacking me and my big Brother. Haldor Lillenas, that great Christian gentleman with the Nazarene Fellowship, wrote:

"When I am tempted He walks beside me,
When I am weak He can make me strong;

> When I am burdened I feel His presence,
> Keeping, sustaining me all day long."

What about the future? Yes, there is a promise! "Thou hast delivered mine eyes from tears." Not until eternity will God "wipe away all tears from their eyes" (Revelation 21:4). Until then I am *kept,* but I must live in the *presence* of sin. I must live where the front page and the network report and the demonstration remind me daily of heartbreak, disaster, failure, and horror, and death.

Yes, I experience *sadness!* How could it be otherwise in such a world with our hospitals, our jails, our casualty lists, our funerals, our detention homes, our divorces? But salvation promises something better, when "there shall be no more death, neither sorrow, nor crying, neither shall there be any more pain: for the former things *are* passed away" (Revelation 21:4).

The prospect is dazzling. It taxes the imagination to conceive a pattern of living without marital tragedy, without announcers intoning traffic fatalities, robberies, and political shenanigans. "Former things are passed away" (Revelation 21:4).

Today we weep over our own failures and over the sins of others. We suffer loneliness. We feel heartsick when we see our nation slipping down into the gutter of godlessness and unbelief. We grow numb at the indifference.

I find relief in tears. It provides an overflow. Jeremiah wept. Joseph wept. Paul wept. Christ wept. You have wept this week. Don't apologize! You don't need to. You and I weep because we would like it to be different.

I wish that body wouldn't age, wrinkle, bend, and crumble. I wish streets would stay paved, washed, lighted, and shaded with trees trimmed and beautiful with immaculate grass and pretty shrubbery. I wish taxes could be lowered. I wish incomes could be raised. I wish poverty could be eliminated. I wish narcotics did not exist. I wish I could never feel anger again, nor jealousy, nor contempt. I wish there were no blind. I long for a world where children can have strong legs and healthy minds.

Yes, I cry! I cry for "new heavens and a new earth, wherein dwelleth righteousness" (2 Peter 3:13).

The text I have used for this message precedes immediately a passage you will recall. "I believed, therefore have I spoken: . . . I said in my haste, *All men are liars*" (Psalm 116:10, 11). The Revised Version reads, "All men are *a lie*."

This is a sweeping indictment. Their lives are untruth, false, vanity, unreliable. But you know fine people on your street! You know neighbors who move in the best circles of society.

Let me ask you! "Do they belong to Jesus Christ?" Christ is the *Truth*. Any person who hasn't any room for Jesus hasn't any room for Truth. John says as much in his letter. "Who is a liar but he that denieth that Jesus is the Christ? He is antichrist, that denieth the Father and the Son" (1 John 2:22).

That is a fearful charge to make against fine, respectable people. I would not dare make it. I would not dare say your generous and well-behaved neighbor is living a lie. But God makes it. *Without Christ their lives are a lie.*

They profess a righteousness they do not possess. They expect a salvation—an entrance into heaven—they will not obtain. Like Cain, they believe a holy God will accept "the offering"—the fruit of their own efforts. They claim a peace they do not have. They exhibit a goodness they do not own. They publicize a supposed relationship to Jesus Christ that He will deny. "And then will I confess unto them, I never knew you: depart from me, ye that work iniquity" (Matthew 7:23).

You can change that lie. *You can stop pretending.* You will find all the answers in God's salvation. "Whosoever shall call upon the name of the Lord (that is Jesus, sir) shall be saved" (Romans 10:13). Place your faith in Christ.

FALSE STARTS

Texts: *"Thus saith the Lord of hosts; Consider your ways. Ye have sown much, and bring in little."* *Haggai* 1:5, 6

"Is the seed yet in the barn? yea, as yet the vine, and the fig tree, and the pomegranate, and the olive tree, hath not brought forth: from this day will I bless you." *Haggai* 2:19

NOT many people know Haggai, the preacher, one God set forth in the Old Testament record. He ministered to his nation with a younger colleague, Zechariah, a mystic and a poet.

Haggai was a matter-of-fact, plain-spoken man. Both, the older Haggai and the younger Zechariah, vividly reflected in their utterances the views and temper of their time. All that is known of Haggai must be gathered from the two short chapters of his message. *This man just got it said without ruffles of speech.*

What were the times? He faced a movement that had made an enthusiastic start and had *stalled.* Haggai's problem was how to get the movement started again. Years before Jerusalem, the pride and joy, had fallen. A humiliated nation had been reduced to despair and carried away into exile. We marvel, as we look back, that a dispirited people did not wholly lose their individuality as a nation; that they were not completely erased. Who and what might arouse them? They seemed finished for all time and purpose.

You catch the pathos and the morbidity in the 137th Psalm: "By the rivers of Babylon, there we sat down, yea, we wept, when we remembered Zion. We hanged our harps upon the willows... How shall we sing the Lord's song in a strange land?" (Psalm 137:1, 2, 4). There was a sense of deep melancholy—a frustration—complete and shattering disillusionment. They simply weren't any good. Circumstances had trounced them. *They wallowed in failure.*

God reached them through His chosen speakers, *Ezekiel* and *Isaiah.* They declared that the power of the captor would be broken. They didn't *argue* it. They *declared* it. They stated that Babylon itself was doomed. They were right.

Cyrus the Persian padlocked Babylon's ambition. Belshazzar had been a *scourge* to the Jews. Cyrus became their *patron.* They were freed to return to the homeland and aided from the royal exchequer. It seemed as though happy days were here again.

A real movement was born. Revival was in the air. Thousands turned their backs on material comfort and personal prosperity in a Gentile world, and turned their hearts and faces toward the barren hills of Judah. They were off to "fight the good fight of faith."

It was an era of deep, religious spirit. Hope was high. Zeal and joy and unselfishness characterized the movement. Speedily the work of restoration was begun. An altar was raised. The sacrifice was established. Foundations were laid. It was exciting and filled with promise.

Suddenly the flame died. A good start became nothing more than that—just a good start. Their spiritual ideals proved insufficient against stern realities. There were extenuating circumstances as usual. Bad seasons came and impoverished them. Disease thinned their ranks. So a status quo set in. It seemed impossible to move away from dead center. They were beaten in mind and spirit.

Self-seeking set in. Worldliness and luxury motivated the stronger and the more durable among them. *Attitudes changed.* Suddenly it was smart to come to terms with the times, and to make the best of it. Wainscoted houses mocked the dreary beginnings of the temple. The bare foundations of what had been chosen to epitomize faith and revival, barely showed above the weeds.

You wouldn't have recognized the movement. Ideals were forgotten. Confidence and faith disappeared. The more provident among them grasped what they could for their own comfort. The rest were sorry for themselves. It all became a contagion for stagnation, out of which arose moral pollution.

Believe me, sir, when men lose faith, when impetus subsides, when the cause is no longer thrilling and foremost—men ask, "What is the use?" The next step is to come to terms with the times—*to follow instead of leading.*

The golden opportunity threatened to slip away irretrievably. The favorable break in history, the Cyrus hiatus, threatened to pass without being fully redeemed. The promises of Ezekiel and Isaiah seemed out of step with the times. A decadence settled over the movement. *No one believed very much any longer.*

Suddenly God spoke. He always has. He always will. He chose this elderly man, Haggai, for His instrument. He was a man of unvarnished tongue. There is no glamour to his preaching. He employed no dramatics. He waded in with authority and without consideration of how it might affect his popularity or his place in history. He was content to be God's man alone. He called people back to the fundamentals. He faced his task with dogged determination. He was a disciplined man set to reactivate a disciplined people. He could be, as Stanley once said of Arnold, "heroic without romance."

He faced a drab situation. The old man rose in the atmosphere of indifference and said in the shortest possible terms what he felt he had to say. He said it to the smug and to the callous. He said it in language impossible to misinterpret. He pointed his finger at people who had abandoned their pioneering for bonuses that an Anti-God system offered. He bridled at the squalor of self-seeking. It is one of the most powerful initiatives in Old Testament record.

And God helped this elderly brother. Yes, He did! He would have long been forgotten without that help. It is hard enough to *start* a people, as Amos, Hosea, Micah, and many others have discovered. No movement is easy to inaugurate. But Haggai volunteers a vastly harder enterprise. He sets about to redeem a false start—to get something that was worthwhile *going again* He sets about to energize sluggards and turn them into soldiers. He campaigns to replace melancholy and indifference with sinew and determination.

It is a colossal task anytime and anywhere. It is tantamount to making a living soul out of dust. *Creation* needs but a breath of the Eternal. *Redemption* needs a Calvary. It is always tough, mister, to recuperate, to rebuild, to get going again.

Haggai is one of those seldom-sung heroes without a halo. He doesn't measure his conviction or his mission against applause, or a gallery, or compensation. He is simply dedicated to awaken something dormant.

How does it work today? There is a parallel. How many bright beginnings lie sterile at this hour—how many in your own story! How many ideals in your own soul have dwindled? How long have you been treading water—just keeping your head above the point of no return?

There were earlier experiences. You can recall earnestness, zeal, strenuous pursuit. They complain against the indifference, discouragement, and disenchantment that have taken you out of circulation. *Why don't you even try any longer?* What has evaporated in your soul?

Think back to the moment when you were aroused for God! Remember that glorious sense of emancipation. There were laughter and excitement, a spirit of homecoming. You had left exile and you knew it. *It was the thrill of an escapee.* I know.

It was a time of projects to be carried through by sheer enthusiasm for Christ and the kingdom of God. You and I were building that truly inner sanctuary, the real, indestructible church, in which the Spirit of God exalts Jesus Christ. *I wouldn't trade a movement for the best denomination on earth.*

Where are you today? Is your salvation nearer than when you believed? How long have you been becalmed? When and where did the doldrums seize you? The external semblance may deceive for a moment, but inside, mister, you are hollow, evacuated, lifeless. A great evangelist once said: "It is almost refreshing to have to do with a man who has never professed Jesus Christ before." It's something to deal with the newly converted before discouragement and disillusionment and difficulty set in.

Haggai describes what he faced: "Ye have sown much, and bring in little; ye eat, but ye have not enough; ye drink, but ye are not filled with drink; ye clothe you, but there is none warm; and he that earneth wages, earneth wages to put it into a bag with holes" (Haggai 1:6). "Consider . . . since the day that the foundation . . . was laid, consider it. Is the seed yet in the barn? yea, the vine, and the fig tree, and the pomegranate, and the olive tree have brought forth" (Haggai 2:18, 19, ASV). It is a picture of frustration, emptiness, and dissatisfaction. It is a disappointment that can paralyze.

What has cooled you, mister? How soon, after you started so well, did rigor mortis set in? Have you ever asked yourself, "*Why?*" Does the public ask about you, as they ask about so many, "This man began to build and was not able to finish"? Do they whisper, "You were running well, who did hinder you"?

We have the record back in the generation to which Haggai ministered. Perhaps the same erosion has taken place in your spiritual experience.

First, *the task was harder than they dreamed.* The romance

faded quickly. Suddenly it was hard work. They could not endure hardness. Rough going discouraged them. They looked like winners on the practice field. It was different when the game began. Don't let any denomination deceive you. It will take all your manhood and all your womanhood to say with Paul: "I have fought a good fight, I have finished my course, I have kept the faith" (2 Timothy 4:7). The weak ones fall by the wayside.

Second, *they prospered in material things, and physical, material comfort took the fight and the "go" out of them.* Soon, it came down to this. Their houses were the best, what did it matter whether the temple was finished or not? They were making money, and who could ask for anything better than that? Where was there a better "heaven"? Emerson once said about money: "The worst of money is that it often costs so much."

Third, *the Samaritans sneered at them, and they grew ashamed.* They had to live with the outsider, and religious enthusiasm was not "the thing" in their set. So, they were *muffled.*

Run down that old-fashioned checklist in your own life as I bring this message to you. Were you a better Christian when you had a humbler home and cheaper furniture? Have you let criticism and worldliness rot your ideals, so that you feel it beneath you to do what you have once been proud to do? Take a long, hard look at yourself!

You can get going again! You should start with this service.

Haggai accomplished it for the generation he faced. The false start was redeemed and the frittered opportunity retrieved. He summoned those before him to move out of their slackness and softness. He asks them to face the facts, and be done with pamperings and self-excusings. He asks them to build muscle again. Suddenly there was an awakening. Something *stirred.* "And the Lord stirred up the spirit of Zerubbabel . . . the governor of Judah, and the spirit of Joshua . . . the high priest, and the spirit of all the remnant of the people" (Haggai 1:14).

That is the key! *The spirit must be stirred.* That is where mischief begins, lady! Something dampens the enthusiasm that makes you want to. The new start will be worthless, if it is not from inward sources. You cannot put on an act. Haggai got these folk back to God, and that did it. There was a touch that rekindled all they had once felt. They experienced the *passion* that had lain dormant.

No, a fresh start is never easy! If you are waiting for some crest to sweep you out into the mainstream again, you will wait for a long time. You will have to take inventory of yourself. I will tell you this. When you decide you are going to get back into the race, no matter what it takes—not asking or desiring what is easy or pleasing, but only what is right—you will feel the moving of His Spirit upon yours. I promise you that.

God help you to shake yourself free from the nausea that immobilizes you! This crowd that Haggai faced had become victims to a mental hazard. "This new temple will never be like unto the old—so, no matter how hard we try, we'll never make it anyhow, and if we do, it won't count for much." That's the devil's lie, mister—*his slander.* God hasn't called you to be an "also-ran."

Haggai gave them the answer. He said that God would make their unpretentious house *greater in glory* than the former. Give God your best, lady, and He will fill it with grandeur.

So, get up and get going again! There is every possibility of being a winner. Jesus Christ intends to make you that. He is always Victor, and He isn't going to change that because you have trusted yourself to Him. He has coached, developed, guided, and crowned millions of champions—*overcomers.*

Haggai told his nation: "God will be better to you than at your beginnings." What are you waiting for? Get going again!

NOT YET

Text: *"Mine hour is not yet come."*

John 2:4

THIS must be the answer to many petitions. It is the nature of man to demand how, when, and where. It is hard for us to understand there is another Party even more involved than ourselves.

The same Providence that initiated Paul's rescue on the Mediterranean shores of Melita from a broken Roman merchant ship might have saved him from the typhoon that tossed him up and down the Adriatic, or for that matter canceled the custody altogether as he stood before Festus and Agrippa. Many of the church must have prayed that way for the apostle. Now we know there was a greater design. "Thou must be brought before Caesar" (Acts 27:24).

The same God, who overnight, elevated Joseph from a forgotten political prisoner to price czar for the empire, could have spared the son of Jacob the kidnapping terror, the character smear and years of imprisonment. But would history have been the same? "Thou shalt be over my house, and according unto thy word shall all my people be ruled: only in the throne will I be greater than thou. And Pharaoh said unto Joseph, See, I have set thee over all the land of Egypt" (Genesis 41:40, 41).

Christ addressed this text to His mother. It is a picture of every mother who intercedes. The element of rejection is always there. It is more than saying "please." It is more than informing the Lord. *It is falling in step with another world.*

There was embarrassment. A marriage was falling to pieces before it had decently started. The Creator was there, and Mary felt the agony and frustration of failure. "They have no wine" (John 2:3).

She expected Jesus to do something about it. That's what a Saviour is for, isn't it—*to save*—to erase our mistakes? She believed He was equal to the need. She was anxious for Him to use His power. It could all add to a great testimony.

It is never easy to face the "what have I to do with thee" in your soul. There are times on your knees when you feel you are trying to convince an enemy rather than a friend.

One thing Mary learned. She could not direct Christ's ministry. And if she could not, then my distraught, interceding friend, you and I cannot. Anxious parent, I know how upset you are about a child of yours. That is understandable. Nevertheless, you cannot tell God what to do.

He could not supply the wine just because it was the natural desire of His well-meaning mother. He had refused to make bread from stones for Himself when He hungered. There isn't any *magic,* parent. *A price is always involved in a release and redemption.* What you seek must be found in Calvary. You must stake your claim there, or you cannot stake it at all.

"Not yet" does not mean *never.* Mary learned the same lesson the Syrophoenician mother learned. The first step is always *anxiety.* You are troubled about your son. You are troubled about your husband. God understands. *But anxiety is not faith.*

Ringing the alarm is necessary, but ringing the alarm won't put the fire out. After you have rung the alarm, you exercise *trust.* You place your trust in the Fire Department. You do not inform the department what route to take, what equipment to bring, or how to tackle the blaze. *Those are decisions aside from and beyond your control.*

There isn't a thing you and I can do to change the "not yet."

This isn't fatalism. It isn't the attitude of "what's the use?" That would be letting the building burn without ringing the alarm. *It means that you and I adjust to God, rather than demanding that God adjust to us.*

Martha's sister, Mary, learned that lesson. Mary thought Jesus Christ was late. "If thou hadst been here, my brother had not died" (John 11:21). Word had been sent to Him during the sickness. The sisters "sent unto him, saying, Lord, behold, he whom thou lovest is sick" (John 11:3). An unusual thing took place. "When he had heard therefore that he was sick, he abode two days still in the same place where he was" (John 11:6). *How can God wait when you and I are in a hurry?* That is the excruciating pain of every intercessor.

Never forget this beautiful paragraph! "When Jesus therefore saw her weeping, and the Jews also weeping which came with her, he *groaned* in the spirit, and was troubled" (John 11:33).

> "Jesus knows all about our troubles,
> He will guide till the day is done.
> There's not a Friend like the lowly Jesus,
> No not one! No not one!"

Oh, yes, He *cares,* mother dear. "Jesus wept." He said to Martha, who felt it was all over, "I *am* (not I *was* or *will be,* but I *am*) the resurrection, and the life: he that believeth in me, though he were dead, yet shall he live: . . . Believest thou this? She saith unto him, Yea, Lord: *I believe*" (John 11:25-27).

That is what He is waiting for—*trust.* If He didn't care, all our asking would be in vain.

Do not let the empty water pots discourage you. "It is not for you to know the times or the seasons, which the Father hath put in his own power" (Acts 1:7).

To the spectator, the patriarch Job's case seems unreasonable. A humanitarian would have intervened at once. It is the most tantalizing, tormenting 41-*chapter delay* in all literature. In chapter after chapter the answer is "not yet."

You would think when his financial assets were wiped out, that would be enough to bring his family to God. You would think when his wife and personal friends upbraided him, that would be enough to bring his family to God. You would think when he lost his health, that would be enough to bring his family to God.

It had been his daily intercession that disturbed hell. There were ten children. Affluence and wealth had made them careless.

"His sons went and feasted in their houses, . . . and sent and called for their three sisters to eat and to drink with them" (Job 1:4). Job felt a burden for them. He "rose up early in the morning, and offered burnt offerings according to the number of them all: for Job said, "It may be that my sons have sinned, and cursed God in their hearts. *Thus did Job continually*" (Job 1:5).

That kind of praying disturbs hell. *And it leads you into the roughest kind of combat with unseen forces.*

Victory is important. But how you win it is even more important. "So the Lord blessed the latter end of Job more than his beginning: for he had fourteen thousand sheep, and six thousand camels, and a thousand yoke of oxen, and a thousand she asses" (Job 42:12). There were also the same number of children, "seven sons and three daughters" (Job 42:13). They became his crown of rejoicing. I'll read it to you.

"And in all the land were no women found so fair as the daughters of Job: and their father gave them inheritance among their brethren. After this lived Job a hundred and forty years, and saw his sons, and his sons' sons, even four generations" (Job 42:15, 16). *It took some trusting.* "Though he slay me, yet will I trust in him" (Job 13:15). Parent, are you that *yielded* to the divine will?

The Blessed Mother learned to trust Jesus implicitly. She left the time, the method, and the circumstances to Him. She had this confidence—*He would intervene.* She expressed that conviction to the servants, "Whatsoever he saith unto you, do it" (John 2:5). She got out of the way, and that is a big lesson. And it turned out just like it did for Job. The wine was better at the last than it was at the beginning.

Frances Ridley Havergal wrote:

> "Ask not how, but trust Him still;
> Ask not when, but wait His will;
> Simply on His word rely,
> 'God shall all your need supply.' "

It isn't easy to live with the "not yet." *Waiting is the most difficult task in life.* It wasn't easy for Isaac as Abraham and he trudged their way to Mount Moriah. To Isaac's question, "Where is the lamb for a burnt offering?" (Genesis 22:7), Abraham could only reply, "My son, God will provide himself a lamb" (Genesis 22:8).

It wasn't easy for Caleb and Joshua. They had to mark time in the wilderness for 40 years while a disobedient, rebellious generation was erased.

It wasn't easy for Hannah. "The Lord had shut up her womb" (1 Samuel 1:5). The record says that "her adversary also provoked her sore" (1 Samuel 1:6). The tension increased until "she was in bitterness of soul, and prayed unto the Lord, and wept sore" (1 Samuel 1:10).

It wasn't easy for David. There were long, long years dodging Saul's madness. Would the kingdom ever be his? When would the promises of God be fulfilled? General Abner, David's guerrilla chief, reminded the vacillating elders of Israel: "Ye sought for David in times past to be king over you: now then do it" (2 Samuel 3:17, 18).

It wasn't easy for Esther. The infamous plot of Haman encircled her. That story is one of the greatest "cliff-hangers" of all time. There is a confrontation between evil and good; between right and wrong, that is massive. *History would be written as a result.*

It wasn't easy for Jairus, the ruler of the synagogue. His beautiful teen-age daughter was dying. The Great Physician seemed to digress. "There came from the . . . house certain which said, Thy daughter is dead; why troublest thou the Master any further?" (Mark 5:35). To which Jesus replied, "Be not afraid, only believe" (Mark 5:36). No, it is never easy to *wait.* But you and I cannot change the determinate counsel of God's "not yet."

You and I must live with this. "Commit thy way unto the Lord; *trust also in him;* and he shall bring it to pass" (Psalm 37:5). The trusting is the hard part.

There is another side to it, mister. God waits for us. He *waits* through long years of heartbreak. What if He didn't wait, sinner! What if God demanded answers, our yes or no, as quickly as we demand them? *What would have happened to you in your sins?*

Many a time our prayer might have been: "Lord, have patience with me, and I will pay thee all" (Matthew 18:26).

When? That is the question. Ralph Carmichael has put it in a beautiful new song of invitation:

"Time after time He has waited before,
And now He is waiting again
To see if you are willing to open the door,
Oh, how He wants to come in!"

The moment is set. It was at Cana. "Draw out *now.*" Search your heart. Ask yourself as the altar call begins, "Is this God's moment for me?"

THE REDEMPTION OF THE BODY

Text: *"To wit, the redemption of our body."*

Romans 8:23

PAUL always included the *body* in the experience of salvation. "Know ye not that your body is the temple of the Holy Ghost" (1 Corinthians 6:19). That was his position. "Ye are bought with a price: therefore glorify God in your body" (1 Corinthians 6:20).

He felt that victories were won or lost in his body. "I keep under my body, . . . lest that . . . when I have preached to others, I myself should be a castaway" (1 Corinthians 9:27).

He said, "Christ shall be magnified in my body" (Philippians 1:20), and again: "I pray . . . your whole spirit and soul and body be preserved blameless" (1 Thessalonians 5:23). *These convictions are conclusive.*

Christ regarded His body as a *temple*. John 2:21 says, "But he spake of the temple of his body." One thing is certain. *The experience of salvation must be manifest.*

Christianity is nothing less than the power of life. It is an increase of *vitality*. It is an enlarged capacity for living. It makes you *effective*. I have read again and again this statement of Jesus, "I am not come to destroy, but to *fulfil*" (Matthew 5:17). That is what Christ wants to do with you.

The new birth is not *repression*. It is *expression*. I say this with all the conviction of my soul. In Jesus Christ, sir, you will realize the greatest possible fulfillment. The supreme emphasis of Jesus was upon life. That is the impulse He awakens. "I am come that they might have life, and that they might have it more abundantly" (John 10:10).

When I believe that, I must believe something else. Such expression employs my body. The Creator has ordained my body to be the authorized organ of expression. My body must carry that life. *It must fulfill Christ's redemptive will for me.*

The plan is not debatable. "The Word was made flesh" (John 1:14). God flowed through a body. He found the maximum expression in a body. God employed flesh. Never forget that! The body must always be an important part of true religion.

The New Testament *glorifies* the body. It is sacred. It is redeemed to be the channel of holy things.

The Incarnation says it all. Paul tells Timothy, "God was manifest in the *flesh*" (1 Timothy 3:16). The miracle of new birth makes that divine process possible again and again. That is the difference between believer and unbeliever. God is either manifest in you or absent in you. That is the simple answer as to whether or not you are saved.

When I believe this, I can promptly dismiss two items.

First, I can dismiss *dualism.* It is still quite common to talk of man as a double creature. This assumes that your body is the hereditary enemy of your spirit. And strength for this assumption is often gathered from the translation, "our *vile* body."

I have never found my body to be vile. My body has been good to me. I know the purpose of the passage is to afford an antithesis to the next word about "His *glorious* body." There has never been a question in my mind that I could not use a *better* body. I could, and I long for one.

God means the body to have a place of dignity. The gospel brought a new viewpoint. There was the class who allowed the body to master them. Then there was the class who determined to master the body because they despised it as essentially low and degraded. *The gospel disagreed.* It brought respect and dignity for the body.

Before, men desiring to be good, despised the body, because they knew not its real powers and its functions, nor its real relationship to themselves. Your body is meant to help you be a great Christian. You cannot isolate some department in your life and post "no admittance."

Second, then my body is meant to be an organ for the Lord's expression—*a temple.* Music is of the musician's soul. That is where it begins. It is born there. But he dies with all his music in him if he does not train and discipline and command his body to become the instrument of expression. The marvelous melody of redemption is born within a soul.

God is a Spirit. God sought *expression.* So in due time "the Word was made flesh" (John 1:14). Similarly, my body is the vehicle to express the glorious fact that God is resident. No, mister, you cannot live dual lives—one in the spirit and one in the flesh.

I will tell you this. Every sin of the flesh is a sin of the soul first. "Out of the heart of men, proceed evil thoughts, murders, adulteries, foolishness, blasphemies, the evil eye" (See Mark 7:21, 22).

Sin is not a physiological question. If it were, you could submit to surgery and have it removed at a hospital. Its remedy is not at a drug store. "We wrestle not aginst flesh and blood" (Ephesians 6:12).

The answer is not *asceticism.* Asceticism says that the body is evil, that it must be punished. Scourge the flesh, that the spirit may thrive. Yes, I recall the Master saying: "Pluck out the offending eye. Cut off the offending hand." I also remember the Master telling about the empty house, clean and sterile, to which returned sevenfold more devils than were driven out.

That is a salvation attempt by *eviction*. It is heroic but discouraging.

The plain fact is this. *No man can save himself*—no matter how much you cut away—no matter how many devils you evade.

Salvation is not ascetic. Jesus came eating and drinking. So, what does the New Testament teach?

First, *it does teach the supremacy of the spiritual.* When Jesus defined life it meant more, vastly more, than material existence. Life, to Jesus, meant the fullness of man's powers—*the completion of man's possibilities.*

The cardinal fact about man is that he is a spiritual creature. He is more than animal. He does not live by bread alone. He is profited nothing if he gains the whole world and loses his soul. His problems cannot be totally answered at the grocery store, the clothing store, the amusement park, or the campus.

There is a *thirst* that pleasure cannot quench. There is a *hunger* that wealth cannot satisfy. Paul describes the greatest of all human tragedy—a life ruled by the flesh. He shouts it to his world, "To be spiritually minded is *life*" (Romans 8:6).

Second, the New Testament teaches that *the body is meant to be the instrument of the spirit.* That is the divinely designed purpose of my flesh. It is designed for the fullest expression. *God wants to reveal Himself in and through me.*

My business, then, is to see to it that I present to God the very best possible instrument. If this passion, or that appetite, frustrates the purpose of God in me—at that moment I am under eternal obligation to cut off, or to cut away, that hindrance. *The New Testament makes my body obedient to God's will.*

In addition, the body is not only the vehicle of the spirit, *it is the opportunity of the spirit.* Through the body every art, every science, every invention have been realized and implemented. The body has been an arena to determine what is wrong and what is right—what is valuable and what is refuse

—what is progress and what is reactionary. Through the things that he has suffered and felt in his body he has come into the *mastery* of the things that made him feel and suffer, so that now they do him service. Thus man's victory over polio and man's impending victory over tobacco.

The body is a grand jury that renders a verdict. The body will sift the evidence, and tell you what is eternal and what is superficial.

How can I put all this into practice?

First, I must say by my day-to-day acts that the eternal is supreme. I accomplish this objective by *plain living* and *high thinking*. There is a vulgar display of affluence that is increasing—that says how much I need to grab this side of the grave and how little I really believe lies ahead. It is the most militant form of denial, of atheism. It shouts that there is really nothing on the other side, that it is all here and now.

Parents, that is what your stress on physical comfort is teaching your children. You are preaching down everything a New Testament evangelist upholds. I must take every practical step available to me to make my body subservient to my spirit. I sidestep it when I loll in luxury and pamper the physical. "Thou fool, this night thy soul shall be required of thee: then whose shall those things be, which thou hast provided? So is he that layeth up treasure for himself, and is not rich toward God" (Luke 12:20, 21).

Remember this! The *mere athlete* is a pitifully incomplete person, not to speak of a pitifully incomplete Christian. There is more to you than your muscle. Young person, keep a sense of proportion! Preachers, some of you have improved your golf scores to a greater degree recently than you have improved your preaching. That is a mistake.

In the scale of destiny brains weigh more than brawn, and *character* weighs more than both. I still believe what I recited as a lad, that the chief end of man is not to break records, but to build character and to glorify God.

All of us can permit our bodies to commit *soul murder.* I can take pride in my assets—my automobile, my knickknacks, my yard, my library. Suddenly I become a lover "of pleasures *more* than" a lower of God. The danger expressed here is in that four-letter word, "more." I begin placing legitimate things—things which in themselves are not sin—*ahead of God.*

That leads to soul murder. I suffocate my soul "in the abundance of . . . things" (Luke 12:15), which I may possess, and which have begun to possess me. They make the ears deaf, and the hands unready for the needs of this planet, and the claims of God.

In Frederick the Great's biography there is a good peckaboo into this truth. Frederick said: "How could I fail to win at the Battle of Rosbach? My opponent, Soubrise, had seven cooks and one spy. I had seven spies and one cook."

Watch the proportion of things! The Master had this word for all of us. "What I say unto you I say unto all, *Watch*" (Mark 13:37). *It means constant vigilance.*

Drop your guard for a week, for a month, and suddenly you will discover you are no longer attending the midweek Bible study. You are surprised that you are sleeping in on Sunday morning instead of going to Sunday school.

The first duty is to grow a soul. Second, it is your business to keep your soul as well dressed as you can. May "the very God of peace sanctify you wholly; and I pray God your whole spirit and soul and body be preserved blameless unto the coming of our Lord Jesus Christ" (1 Thessalonians 5:23).

Let the presence of Jesus Christ in your life *transfigure* you. Luke gives this account. "And as he prayed, the fashion of his countenance was altered, and his raiment was white and *glistering*" (Luke 9:29).

The word "glistering" means to *sparkle*. That is what I want to happen to my body and outward effects. I want my soul to find such completeness in God that my whole person will *sparkle*. Calvary demands my body.

A REVIVALTIME TESTIMONY

"With eagerness I anticipate the *Revivaltime* broadcast. It was only through this medium that I was able to lead a dear and faithful friend to the *Revivaltime* altar call. It was like a magnet. My friend accepted the altar call unquestioningly."

BENAIAH AND HURAI

Texts: *"Benaiah the Pirathonite, Hurai of the brooks of Gaash."*
1 Chronicles 11:31, 32
"A wise man, which built his house upon a rock."
Matthew 7:24

YOU have heard it said, "It takes all kinds to make a world." And any lineup for baseball, football, or basketball presents a strange list of personalities. Here are two, Benaiah, and Hurai, who found their way into an Old Testament program.

A man is not responsible for his name, but he is responsible for what men think of when they call him by his name. We are extremely image-conscious these days. The whole story is told in this brief line, "Benaiah the Pirathonite, Hurai of the brooks of Gaash." That is the summary which appears in the divine record.

These are names of army men who made up the bone and muscle of David's fighting forces. The great Economist didn't waste many words on Hurai–*five words to be exact*–"of the brooks of Gaash."

For many years Jack Dempsey, the great heavyweight, was followed by this line, "the Manassas Mauler." President Andrew Jackson was followed by this line, "Old Hickory."

Hurai had his house in Ephraim, by the torrents that sometimes swept down the mountains of Gaash, and he was known by his location. Side by side is the name "*Benaiah* the Pirathonite," which means that he had his home at the fortress of Pirath. The custom of *nicknames* is sometimes indicative. These men were best known in the army of that day by these descriptions

—the one as "of the fortress"—the other as "of the brooks."

In a land where the water supply counts for almost everything, to be located by mountain brooks, which one day may be fierce destructive torrents and the next dry channels, is unsatisfactory. A mountain torrent is fickle. It depends upon storms rather than springs, and has no depth in itself. When you most need water, it has none to give; when you do not need it, it threatens with an uncontrollable deluge. It is romantic but unreliable. You may build a mill by it, but your wheel will either stand still for lack of power, or be swept away by too much of it. You are always caught by extremes. It has nothing between drought and drowning.

There are lives in this world like that. I daresay Hurai was a good fighting man. When he was up, he was really up. There were times when he could look like a world beater, the greatest prospect to ever appear on the horizon. Better to be the absolutely dependable Benaiah of the fortress. It may not be as glamorous or colorful, but it is unfailing in time of need.

Now I want to turn this contrast toward you, sir. Is your life an "on-again-off-again-gone-again" record of "hit-and-miss," or is it a record of dependability? Do you act on impulse, or on principle? Is your life being left to the mercy of circumstances, or has it strength within itself that can defy these? *What is being written after your name?*

Fordham University, many years ago, had a front line on its football team that became known as "the seven blocks of ranite." How does your office tag you? Every one of us are on a "shakedown cruise" here in this life on our way to eternity. Impulse, emotion, passion, may carry you through for a while, but they are too fickle for the real demands of life.

Saul is an example. He was an eye-catcher. No youth of Bible record seemed to have more promise. Great hopes centered in him. He was goodly to look upon and generous of instinct. He seemed on his way to all-time greatness, to an enviable place in God's Hall of Fame, the eleventh chapter of Hebrews.

But he fell, and dragged his throne with him, because he had fed his life from the flashy torrents of passion and feeling, and had never dug deep that his life might be fed from the great wells of God. All the poverty of his life was revealed under the severe test of life's great demands. He didn't have what it took. There weren't any inner resources. He needed wisdom, but he whined like a spoiled child. He needed the courage of godliness, but appealed to fools who could only tickle his fancy. The torrents were not there when he needed them. He couldn't find the driving power when victory was in his grasp. I hope that story isn't your life, mister.

I will tell you this. There is something quite as serious as to be a *king*—it is to be a *man.* Mister, I advise you to aspire toward a citation that says: "Behold, the man."

There was a Youth in Galilee, upon whom came presently, as upon Saul in his day and measure, the challenge and strain of His life's task. And in those three years of public life under pressures and constantly changing conditions—there was revealed in this young Carpenter unfailing resources He had made His own, and round which He had built His life in the 30 years of obscurity. *They sustained Him when the world, the flesh, and the devil tested Him.*

There is always this contrast. You will find it on the street where you live, in the office where you work, in the school you attend, and in the church where you worship. The lesson is this. You need something more than impulse. You will never make it on surface energy alone. You are going to have to find something deeper.

There are long stretches of life that must be lived successfully where there is no great excitement to spark you. Have you tapped the springs below that will provide the necessary flow for your welfare in these dry seasons of monotonous duty?

Take your intellectual life? What is going on there? What

are you feeding your mind? Are you building a culture on flashy bits, smatterings here and there, a hodgepodge of unrelated trivia? What you feed, you become. "For as he thinketh in his heart, so is he" (Proverbs 23:7).

Are you spasmodic, perhaps going long spells at a time without touching anything worthwhile? You can't develop a first-class mind that way, sir. You will build a comic-book character out of yourself. There will come a moment in your life when you will reach for inspiration, and it won't be there—no David, no Solomon, no Paul—not even any Shakespeare, or Charles Dickens, or William Henry Wadsworth. *It takes time and effort to develop a life that is strong.*

So many build by the brooks, morally, as well. They sink no great convictions. Their lives are superficial, built on the feeling of the moment. They do right when they feel right. They pray when they are in a tight spot. They tithe when they need help.

Our Lord made church attendance in Nazareth a *custom*—"as his custom was" (Luke 4:16). Paul left a record, whether at a restaurant or in a revival—"a conscience void of offense toward God, and toward men" (Acts 24:16).

And spiritual life must be measured by the same rule. Do you feed it from *without,* or from *within?* Does it depend upon sentiment, or association? Is your only source of motivation the big meetings—the area-wide campaign with its massed choir and spectacular full-page ads?

Yes, be thankful for such things! I am. But count them incidental, a few extras that pass your way. Don't depend upon these occasional gushes. Find your security in Jesus Christ. Fasten to that Rock! Big-name evangelists come and go. Then you are not left high and dry, at the mercy of some torrent you hope will pass your way again. Build your soul on the great steadiness of a persuasion that fortified Paul—"I know whom I have believed, and am persuaded that he is able to keep that which I have committed unto him against that day" (2 Timothy 1:12). That will hold you, lady!

Look with me for a moment at this man Benaiah the Pirathonite. He rooted and grounded his life. He chose a fortified place. *He built to last.*

The Master Builder had this same concern. He practiced what He preached. *He asked others to build their lives as He built His.* "A wise man, . . . built his house upon a rock: and the rain descended, and the floods came, and the winds blew, and beat upon that house; and it fell not: for it was founded upon a rock" (Matthew 7:24, 25).

The religion of Jesus Christ is proof of what *survives.* It has survived apostasies, popularity, negligence, torment, liberalism, and legislation.

The tragedy of *shallowness* is always before us. A woman can be on the front page of our newspapers and magazines, and ten years later almost forgotten. An athlete can be the toast of Broadway one year and an also-ran the next year.

As this message draws to a close, I ask you a personal question: "What kind of religion do you have?" I am not referring to Jewish, Catholic, or Protestant. In my humble opinion, there are three types of religion which are at the mercy of the tests which reveal and destroy. They are the *conventional*—the *aesthetic*—the *emotional.* Each can crumble under the test.

Beware of the *easy acceptance!* It offers shortcuts. It scoffs at any real excavation. The Bereans passed that kind of religion by. "These were more noble than those in Thessalonica, in that they received the word with all readiness of mind, *and searched the Scriptures daily,* whether those things were so" (Acts 17:11).

Then there is the religion that is more anxious about how it *looks* than how it *stands.* The robed choir doesn't give a two-bit piece about what it sings as long as they look gorgeous and sound dramatic. So much of religion today is for *show.* That is where the money is spent—but scrape beneath the surface and there is nothing.

A public figure in Samaria wanted that kind of evangelism. "There was a certain man, called Simon, . . . to whom they all gave heed, from the least to the greatest, saying, This man is the great power of God. And to him they had regard, . . . And when Simon saw that through laying on of the apostles' hands the Holy Ghost was given, he offered them money, saying, Give me also this power, that on whomsoever I lay hands, he may receive the Holy Ghost" (Acts 8:9-11, 18, 19).

Mister, a religion that is only an embellishment isn't strong enough to take you through. And there is that religion that is more intent upon *impression* than *stability.* It is the kind that can let you jump high and live low. It never gets to your *will.* Jesus described it. "Some fell . . . where they had not much earth: and forthwith they sprung up, because they had no deepness of earth" (Matthew 13:5). *These three types of religion invite disaster.*

Christ invites you to put the truth as it is in Him to the test—"Whosoever heareth these sayings of mine, and doeth them, I will liken him unto a wise man, which built his house upon a rock" (Matthew 7:24). Jesus says to you: "If My religion is what I say it is—test it under the toughtest conditions. If it cannot sustain you, then you are under no obligation." That is the offer heaven makes to you.

What God insists upon, mister, is *reality.* He won't give you a passing grade on play acting. You can't pretend and ask for credit. He asks you to pass the test—to compare His salvation with every other panacea offered. Jesus Christ of Nazareth is not embarrassed to make that offer. He believes there isn't a storm big enough to destroy His gospel.

The house that we build cannot stand by its own strength. It must have rock beneath it. You may surround yourself with

Christian habits, enlist Christian associations, prefer Christian atmosphere. But you may have nothing beneath all of that. You have never personally tied in with Christ.

You need more than Christian *architecture.* You need Christian *foundation.* Your will has to be Christian. Your nature has to be Christian. How *deep* does it run with you, or is it only a pretty Sunday decoration? Are you, yourself, a *doer?* That is how Christ put it. That takes any profession you may have out of the cloudland. It brings it right down to Monday morning.

The Rock will keep you if your trust and conviction rest upon it. Find that strength in Jesus Christ now.

A REVIVALTIME TESTIMONY

"It is a joy to write and let you know how much I enjoy *Revivaltime.* The broadcast caused me to buy a tape recorder so I could tape the program.

"I am from Barbados, in the West Indies, and I enjoyed *Revivaltime* while there. Brother Ward preached a sermon one time that so touched my heart I could not sit or stand until I knelt down and gave my heart to Jesus."

THE SEARCH OF A DARKENED MIND FOR MUSIC

Text: *"Provide me now a man that can play well."*
1 *Samuel* 16:17

Many a shipwreck speaks eloquently. The pride that once was is still there. *Saul was never an ordinary man.* He had been deemed the likeliest and fittest man in all Israel to be king.

He had a *charisma* about him. There were noble bearing and powers of enthusiasm that could kindle others into action. He could bring the stands to their feet.

Like a magnet, he brings me back again and again to read his life. He lived it as though he wanted to get through it in a hurry. You can walk slowly on to that battlefield in the gray of the morning and see what is left of such a promising life—a discrowned corpse, a self-murdered man lying on a moor, a grinning skull on the gates, a suit of riven armor at the shrine of Ashtaroth, a headless skeleton hanging on the wall of Beth-shan.

Listen to the lament! "The beauty of Israel is slain upon thy high places: how are the mighty fallen! Tell it not in Gath, publish it not in the streets of Askelon; lest the daughters of the Philistines rejoice, lest the daughters of the uncircumcised triumph. Ye mountains of Gilboa, let there be no dew, neither let there be rain, upon you, nor fields of offerings: for there the shield of the mighty is vilely cast away, the shield of Saul, as though he had not been anointed with oil. . . . How are the mighty fallen" (2 Samuel 1:19-21, 27).

A tragedy has means of teaching. *What can this man's defeat teach me?*

If you will accompany me, we will look into the story when the clouds have gathered, and night, which never lifted, begins to settle on Saul. The darkest day in this man's life is the day when he began to find it intolerable to live with himself.

He was possessed of tremendous drive. The secret of his undoing was that he never turned the key to the direction of those powers to God. He insulted and defied the Spirit of God. A man can do this. But when a man does—that man opens his life to another spirit which he can never dislodge. Remember that!

The Spirit of God abides with us at our consent. He is never an intruder. He does not reside a dictator. He blesses, sanctifies, and strengthens the will toward righteousness.

> " 'Tis done, the great transaction's done!
> I am my Lord's, and He is mine;
> He drew me, and I followed on,
> Charm'd to confess the voice divine.
>
> "High heaven that heard the solemn vow,
> That vow renewed shall daily hear.
> Till in life's latest hour I bow,
> And bless in death a bond so dear."

But once evil has entered, it will snatch the will and absolutely dominate the life. Saul drove out the Spirit of God. Then he could not drive out the hell which came into rule when God went out.

Gloom settled upon Saul. He became afraid of himself. He could not escape from himself. He sits a king, yet he is a *prisoner*. His soul is fettered. He cannot dispel the despair that wraps his life. When "the light that is in thee be darkness, how great is that darkness!" (Matthew 6:23). You live in a dungeon, mister. It will take everything you can do to retain your reason.

You can trace this tragedy in Saul. *It began with an uncompromising temperament.* That can be fatal mischief in your life, boy! All of us arrive on earth with strains in us that need to be detected early. There was a strain of melancholy in Saul. He permitted it to harden into permanence. There was in him an elemental brute violence, and he made no fight against it.

I will tell you a solemn thing, lady. *You cannot escape your soul.* And that soul can either be heaven or hell, and that is where you have to live. Saul, unfortunately, emphasized the negative in his life.

There was another side he could have pushed. He had brave, reverent, kindly, and generous qualities. They were enough to have made him an overcomer, had he chose. He never did. There is no sign nor hint that he ever sought to win any grace which was not naturally his. The quality of moral strenuousness is missing. If it didn't come easy, he quite trying.

That attitude toward life, sir, carries the seed of disaster. Rot sets in early. There was either an inability or an indisposition to handle himself.

As the story opens, he is described as "a choice young man" (1 Samuel 9:2). There is no improvement from that point. He is as good as he will ever be right then. "From him that hath not shall be taken away even that which he hath" (Matthew 25:29). You cannot mark time, sir! When you stop trying to move forward, you begin to slip backward.

Saul is that kind of person who says despondently and defiantly: "What do you expect? It's not in me. I wasn't born that way. So, why don't you leave me alone!" He won't struggle against the bad. He accepts his limitations, and that is the end of it.

I want to sound this out in this service. Limitations do not determine destiny. They can and do locate our field of conflict. *I know where I must make an effort in my own life.*

Jesus set forth an individual who never tried to improve. He was a disappointing and unprofitable man. He had been trusted with a talent, and the hope was that he would make that talent grow. He didn't. *He covered it and did nothing.* Afterward he whined in self-pity.

He was a man who had become paralyzed by constantly indulging exaggerated feelings about himself. He began by magnifying his own disabilities. He dwelt upon them until he became so sorry for himself that he couldn't work.

Examine his defense. He asserted that there was a grave and impossible disparity between the demands made upon him and the assets he possessed. He was servant of a master who expected to reap where he had not sown.

Jesus denounced this whining culprit as a rogue. He is revealed as an unscrupulously lazy man. He would not rouse himself. He would not use what he had. It was easier for him to contemplate what he didn't have. He thought folk always expected too much from him. He develops a fierce self-righteousness. Everyone else is out of step.

Others, during the same time, have gotten the job done—been successful. Only he is a failure. But he will not admit it. He takes refuge in blaming someone else for his troubles. He denounces the condition. If it had been another time, in another place, under other conditions, it could have been different.

He is a man with a grievance, for a grievance has become necessary to his self-complacency. He can never understand why he should ever be blamed for something he never really wanted to do anyway. Saul had this root of mischief in his life.

Second, *lacking moral drive, he became offended with those whose life and counsel suggested a nobler way.* He never lacked for good advice. There was a time when he said, "Bring unto me the prophet." That had been forgotten. Now he says, "Provide me now a man that can play well."

He no longer wants to hear the truth. He wants the theater —to insulate himself in the make-believe. He wants those who will tickle his fancy and make him forget reality—who never prick his conscience or disturb his soul sleep.

It is always the same. When you drive away the truth, you will fiddle for the rest of your life. It is always easier to play than to face facts. A prophet will tax your thinking, trouble your conscience, and cut too deep for comfort. Without a preacher, mister, you will lose your way! The ministrels of life may soothe and charm. It takes the prophet to discipline your life and improve it.

Paul describes the crowd. "They will not endure sound doctrine; but after their own lusts shall they heap to themselves teachers, having itching ears" (2 Timothy 4:3), And "lovers of pleasures more than lovers of God" (2 Timothy 3:4). They worship sport. They love the temporary thrill. They are always seeking "a man that can play well."

It is an appeal to the physical senses for relief for a disturbed conscience. The sensuous, the aesthetic, the comic, the superficial are a cover for the real, gnawing need buried deep within.

Saul wanted to lull the pain. He was looking for a Pied Piper that could relieve him from hell's rats closing in on him. He wanted to laugh and dance and fritter away the moments, and forget, for an hour, his awful failures. He needed "a man who could play well." He wanted to be carried all the way from fact to fancy.

I can find it on the street where I live, and so can you. The search every Sunday is for "a man who can play well." They have turned from the Church and the Sunday morning service, and the voice of God, and now they seek refuge in "the man who can play well"—the football or basketball scene. They search the dial endlessly for anything that promises to scatter the black horde of fears, misgivings which infest their souls.

You cannot satisfy the soul with the tickling of a sense.

You need a deeper remedy. You need to meet your God and relate to Him. That is the only way to stop the ache. Your inner self is saying to you, "Lead me to the rock that is higher than I" (Psalm 61:2).

You need Someone better than yourself, greater than yourself for sanctuary. You won't find that refuge on the stage, or the screen, or the ball park, or the golf course. You are a lost soul—as lost as Saul—when you cry, "Provide me now a man that can play well."

When you omit God, you rob your life of a fellowship for which you are created. Sin has penalities which touch your health, your position, and your possessions. But even more deadly is the darkening of the mind and the weakening of the will.

Every day you feel the spoil going on. You smell it. You hear the deterioration. You are a witness to your own ruin. You watch the loss of self-respect. You ask yourself, "Where is my honor?" You become more rotten by the hour. So you search for a troubadour who can blot out the shame you feel for an interval.

A thousand generations before you have sought for deliverance from this world's minstrels. So many of you think that if you can get away, leave the big city, and return to the simple life, you will find peace. That is folly. *You carry your problem with you.* You cannot find your salvation in Nature. Nature will mirror your exact self. The quiet and simple will only raise the sound level of the condemnation you carry within.

Where can you find a relief? *There is no place to go.* You are cornered. You sense that you are going down and out; that you are *beaten.* You may hear the last few notes before the lights go out. The minstrel is gone, and finally you are eternally alone.

TEMPERAMENT AND CHARACTER

Text: *"Till we all attain . . . unto a fullgrown man, unto the measure of the stature of the fulness of Christ."*
Ephesians 4:13,A.S.V.

TEMPERAMENT is that individual peculiarity of organization by which the manner of acting, feeling, and thinking of a person is permanently affected. We start with it. *We did not make it.* We are not responsible for it.

Character is an engraving. It is what we ourselves carve out. The engraver is not responsible for the quality of the plate he is given to work upon. *He is responsible for the lines he cuts upon it.*

Temperament is the natural groundwork of character. They interact upon each other.

The ancients spoke of *four* distinct temperaments. There are endless combinations. The four they spoke of are these—*sanguine, despondent, choleric,* and *phlegmatic.* You and I are by birth one of these, or some combination of these. What are our chances in life? What can we do about them? It is these questions Paul answers.

The sanguine may keep and enlarge all the good qualities of his temperament, and *add* to them solidity. The despondent may keep his gravity, but discover a wellspring of optimism. The choleric may sanctify his audacity and add wise judgment. The phlegmatic may keep his sureness and add will to its weight. He may still be slow but he can be decided. Paul says that in and through and by Christ every human being can *grow.*

God places *variety*. Don't quarrel with that. It is not our business to try by any process to make ourselves like another whose starting point is different than my own or your own. *Don't scrub out your personality*. Redeem it and determine to refine it until, under God, you are the complete man or woman. That is the point Christianity makes.

First, *recognize that what we are is ours to handle in the interests of what we may be*. Make yourself a franchise of Jesus Christ. He exercises the very best management of human lives obtainable. The record of His successes in the lives of men and women is without serious competition in the history of the human race. Life without this divine energy has missed its meaning. When you make fun instead of character, the goal of living nobility vanishes.

To every stage there is always *entrance* and *exit*. You enter with temperament. You exit with character.

What is character? Paul put it this way. He prays that what is lacking may be "filled up," or as it is translated "perfected,"—that his life may attain a *completeness*. Only God knows what it takes to "fill up" or "perfect" your personality.

Human nature balks. It wants to be left alone. So often you hear it: "Who wants to be made over? Can't you take me and love me just as I am?"

James agrees with Paul. He says that life requires a discipline. He says the goal is, "perfect and entire, wanting nothing" (James 1:4). Jesus put it most daringly. "Be ye perfect as your Heavenly Father is perfect" (see Matthew 5:48).

There is no place for *mediocrity* in the Christian program. When God drew an earth picture, the tabernacle in the wilderness, and later Solomon's Temple, the dimensions and design were perfect. I have always loved this line which says: "A man's reach must exceed his grasp, or what is heaven for?" That is the purpose for this short residence between two eternities. It is to become full-grown—"unto the measure of the stature of the fulness of Christ."

Paul talks about this constantly. He described it in another passage as growing "up into him in all things, which is the head, even Christ" (Ephesians 4:15).

To be "in Christ," Christian, means *incentive.* You aren't finished when you sign a personal worker's form. That is the *beginning.* There are new experiences in Jesus Christ constantly.

God extended toward mankind the best and loftiest scale of measurement, His Son, Jesus Christ. I find I fish better when I am in the company of a master fisherman. I discover I preach better when I review the work and ministries of my peers.

When a lion masquerades in a donkey's skin, that isn't *modesty,* mister. That is *imbecility.* What kind of a person are you, when you try to lower yourself instead of raising your sights; when you aim to be worse than you were the day before, instead of better? So a wise and a loving God let *perfection* dwell among us. When the Holy Spirit grants me a revelation of Jesus Christ, I feel a surge and an urge.

That is what happened to quite an emotional man, with a very dominant personality, Simon Peter. He was as good a fisherman as they came on the Galilee. But when he saw a Carpenter do a better job than he had ever done in his own chosen field of fishing—saw Him fill a net until it burst with fish, when he, himself, had directed a company all night in the art of fishing and caught nothing—he said: "Depart from me; for I am a sinful man, O Lord" (Luke 5:8).

The fact is this. Christ can help you do what you are attempting to do, better. That is what God wants to prove to you, sir, by a personal experience with His Son, Jesus Christ.

There is no living without *ideals.* This generation must rediscover this truth. Material prosperity, in itself, is not enough—not nearly enough. Nor are worldly success and advancement enough! These things carry peril in their promise.

Let me tell you this! Many a man and many a woman has had to accept *less* from life—less prosperity, less success, less advantage and advancement than they sought, *and they have been eternally grateful to settle for less.* They have found greatness and satisfaction in spots of obscurity. Their dreams have been disciplined by duty. My mother was a marvelous evangelist, but she settled for a kitchen and raising a family.

It isn't preacher's talk when I tell you that no person can place his soul in prison and ever find completeness. You have to see beyond the horizon to feel complete. I can't permit my immediate surroundings or circumstances, the nearby, to dictate my motives. I will not muddle my life like the man who said: "What shall I do, because I have no room where to bestow my fruits? . . . This will I do: I will pull down my barns, and build greater; . . . And I will say to my soul, Soul, thou hast much goods laid up for many years; take thine ease, eat, drink, and be merry" (Luke 12:17-19). Within 12 hours he was dead.

Your soul, sir, tells you that you are built for eternity. Christ stands with you and points the direction.

Make sure of this! Jesus is a *Disciplinarian.* He is a demanding Coach. He asks for perfection. You cannot hope to play on His team and not show *desire* and *improvement.* He asks that a man be "transformed" by "the renewing of his mind" and aim, not only toward "the acceptable or good," but toward "the perfect will of God" for his life, (see Romans 12:2).

You won't get much encouragement from the world system around you. The world couldn't care less about how much I read and search the Word of God. It is in love and pursuit of other things. It values gold more than character—comfort more than self-respect—ease more than duty—popularity more than conscience—liberty more than righteousness.

There are always those who don't make it. "Demas hath forsaken me, having loved this present world" (2 Timothy 4:10). That is the worst possible dropout. The man who recorded the defection of Demas had spent thoroughly tested years on land and on sea, obedient to what he called "the heavenly vision"—his magnificent obsession. *That vision never lost its gleam for him.*

Look at the team Christ put together while in Galilee—the *twelve*. He kindled a flame in these men. He baptized them in His Spirit. That divine energy wrote the Book of Acts. Only Judas capsized. He jettisoned his soul for the softer way. Less than 24 hours later, he eternally regretted it. He saw with rare clarity what he had forfeited. He could not live with a cheaper Judas. Once he, like Demas, had "set his affections on things above" (see Colossians 3:2); and he found he could no longer abide "things below." They tried and failed.

Do you think, professing Christian, that you can return to the world and succeed where they failed? "Having once tasted," that is the way the writer to the Hebrews describes it.

When you retreat, when you abandon the ideals Christ has initiated in you, it means that you submit to be governed by what you should control. It means a loss of self-respect. You won't want to look at yourself in the mirror. You can't stand yourself. Judas couldn't. It means divided allegiance. You try to become a double agent. You drag on with a sense of betrayal. You make your life hell on earth.

Yes, you can become discouraged! From the starting point to the goal seems such a long way. From the raw material to the finished product seems an impossibility. It has discouraged many a young man from entering the field of medicine or the field of law. But it can be done. Others have made it. Why not you?

Christ invites you to a high calling—a target worthy of your life. He offers you all the resources of His kingdom. He guarantees you personal help. *Only the choice must be yours.*

The eternal sorrow is this—*to accept yourself as a finality.* Heaven cannot remove the curse from any son of Adam who says: "I am what I am. Nothing can be done about it. I was born this way. I have to follow my own temperament."

Mister, there is something that can be done about it. Jesus Christ offers you a miracle of change and a program of development, so vast, that you will arrive "without spot or wrinkle."

Paul accepted that offer. He writes to the Romans about it. "I see another law in my members, warring against the law of my mind, and bringing me into captivity.... O wretched man that I am! who shall deliver me from the body of this death?" (Romans 7:23, 24). That was the groan—his sweat and condemnation. But mark you how it ends. "I thank God through Jesus Christ our Lord" (Romans 7:25). That is the answer for you, sir!

Read the biography of Peter in your New Testament! If ever a man had trouble with the raw material with which he began life, he did. *But he took sides.* He determined that he would not be dragged toward hell by a foul-mouthed, quick-tempered, murderous disposition. He found the same answer as Paul—"through Jesus Christ our Lord." He puts it this way in his letter to us—"Sanctify in your hearts Christ as Lord" (1 Peter 3:15, ASV). Let the Saviour do it for you! *Stop fighting yourself.*

One of Napoleon's veterans said: "Sir, give me a grasp of thy conquering hand, and I will dare the impossible." Friend, there is a nail-pierced hand stretched toward you. Grasp it, and then attempt the impossible!

A REVIVALTIME TESTIMONY

"I was saved three years ago, but Satan has really been strong in tempting me, especially here in Vietnam. So, I thank God that I am able to hear *Revivaltime.* It really strengthens me."

THE POWER AND THE PRESENCE

Text: "*We were not following cunningly devised fables, when we told you of the power and presence of our Lord Jesus Christ.*"

2 Peter 1:16, *Montgomery*

I CAN'T be anything without the *power* to become. It's silly to talk about being Christlike unless some *dynamic* is available.

The opposition is overwhelming without it. The downward pull is more than any human being can correct in himself. The New Testament recognizes this problem immediately. The word "power" seems to appear on every page.

"All power is given unto me in heaven and in earth" (Matthew 28:18). "The gospel of Christ: . . . is the power of God" (Romans 1:16). I "will . . . glory in my infirmities, that the power of Christ may rest upon me" (2 Corinthians 12:9).

The disciples experienced this thrust. They gladly acknowledged it. They testified that this holy religion consisted of "the *power* and the presence of our Lord Jesus Christ." They submitted that He had changed and possessed them. If they were different, that was the reason.

The sinner needs an immediate release from guilt. We have a past. Every uncleansed, unforgiven day adds to that drag. Every 24 hours the likelihood that I can still make some headway, in spite of it, becomes less and less. Who and what shall deliver me?

These are the barnacles of the soul. "What's the use?" and "It doesn't matter anyhow," and "It's too late to do anything about it now" can bring the soul to a *standstill. The sense of guilt is a fact.*

I'm not going to argue total depravity or environment and heredity limiting responsibility. I know there is something common to the human race. It is a sense of sin, and it hurts just the same in Africa as it does in America, just as a toothache hurts in Africa as it does in America. *And a human being knows when it quits, or when it is lifted.*

Calvary must start there. My freedom must begin there. The only answer is forgiveness. I cannot undo a single trespass. I cannot revoke one act of personal disobedience. I must turn somewhere. The fright in my soul must be dissipated. I must relate to something. I sense that same storm at Golgotha. I know that sin—my sin—has asked for a full reckoning. It will not be delayed. The account must be rendered in full or else!

"In due time Christ died for the ungodly" (Romans 5:6). Mister, I *relate* to that. I know the guilt is mine. I know the sentence is mine. I know the death is mine.

Suddenly I realize something even more eternal. I realize that God's love will not permit me to bear that sentence or die that death. God is determined to take my place. He is covering for me. He makes it possible for me to have a new beginning. It is impossible to be a Christian without it.

A new and plentiful line of credit is established for me. I have pled bankruptcy. I have no assets to meet my moral obligations. So I throw myself on the mercy of the court. That "power" must start here. It is the assurance that my guilt is a canceled thing.

Let me put this as simply as I can. In Jesus Christ we may start, not only *clear,* but *clean.* The drag consists not only of a *burden,* but an *impotence.* In and of and by myself, I can't do anything about it. Maybe it is lying. I don't want to lie, but I am a liar. Maybe it is greed. I don't want to grab, but I am a grabber. *There is a moral paralysis, just as there is a physical paralysis.*

> "O for a man to arise in me,
> That thc man I am may cease to be!"

Here is the deepest need: not to be cheered, but to be saved; not to be encouraged, but to be changed; not to be enlightened, but to be redeemed. I need something more than a backslapper. *I need a miracle.*

Jesus Christ offers this. "As many as received him, to them gave he the right to become children of God, even to them that believe on his name: who were born, not of blood, nor of the will of the flesh, nor of the will of man, *but of God*" (John 1:12, 13 ASV).

Listen to it! "Not of the will of man." It isn't reformation or self-improvement. It is *regeneration.* It is a new motivation. And it is an absolute gift. God *gives* it, mister.

I can ask as Nicodemus did, "How can these things be?" (John 3:9). God doesn't *explain* it, sir. God *gives* it. You *receive* it. You don't *analyze* it. It's like the air you breathe.

Jesus used the simile of the wind. I know that if I set my sail and allow it to fill my sail, the wind will propel me. The new birth is a propulsion. God provides it. I accept it.

There is something further. The power by which I start clear and clean is the power by which I *continue.* This grace sustains me. Note this in the text! "We told you of the power *and the presence* of our Lord Jesus Christ."

Don't forget His *presence.* "Lo, I am with you" (Matthew 28: 20). "I will never leave thee" (Hebrews 13:5). That is important. I can't make it without that fellowship. He isn't a remote Administrator who sends me memos. He is a Companion. He is my Yokefellow. *Nothing is to be attempted apart or aside from Him.*

Christ knew this was the mind of God. It is the divine provision. He made it plain to the disciples that Something, Someone, was coming after Him, whose power and work would mean more to them than He could ever be while He was among them in bodily presence. He, the Holy Son, was to be followed by the Holy Spirit. God had arranged an Eternal Presence, "even the Spirit of truth," "that he may abide with you for ever" (see John 14:16, 17).

They needed more than a memory. They needed more than an ideal. They needed His everyday presence. They needed His Spirit. It had to fill them and circulate in them. It is clear that Christ meant that the same Spirit who dwelt in Him should, when His bodily presence was no more with them, return and dwell in them.

A central fact underlines the gospels. What Jesus Christ was and did in the days of His flesh, are explicitly described as "through the Spirit of God."

Thus God had His *complete expression* in flesh. Again God's Spirit "moved upon the face of the waters" (Genesis 1:2). And when He put off that flesh, *what remained?*

Am I to believe that the personal life of the strong Son of God was blotted out on the Cross forever, and that there was nothing save impersonal influences, precious as these are?

He *remained.* His perfect unity with God the Father, and His perfect identity with the Spirit of God, had all along made the will, purpose, provision, and Spirit His very own. In the Spirit Jesus Christ is forever that which He was manifested in the flesh as being. "I will not leave you comfortless" (John 14:18).

You need never be without that Presence—not for a moment. He is always dispensing grace. He is always teaching and monitoring. He is always cleansing. He is always challenging. He is always perfecting His strength in our weakness.

"He shall *glorify* me" (John 16:14). That is the word Christ used about the gift of the Spirit. His conquering presence—His radiant beauty within the soul—so shames and expels my passion, my deceit, my temper, my covetousness, my prejudice *that I am being constantly saved.* His assurance and unwavering obedience triumph over my timidity.

Paul says the secret is this. "If any man be *in Christ,* he is a new creature" (2 Corinthians 5:17). It is that complete envelopment in another life—"in Christ."

We often use such a figure of speech. We say of someone, "He seems to be totally wrapped up *in her.*" Someone asks, "What does she see *in him?*" It is *mystical,* but it is not *magical.* Lives can be invested in each other. It happens all the time. So it is your salvation and mine, to be "in Christ"—*to invest ourselves in Him.* Jesus said, "Abide in me, and I in you" (John 15:4).

The total impact is in a *Person.* From the cradle to the cross to the crown I see my past, my present, and my future in Jesus Christ. There is transferred from Him to me a life principle.

Sinner, without His Presence in this world, nothing that the Christian testifies to could possibly happen! A *myth* could not produce it. "We did not follow cunningly devised fables." *Sin won't yield to paper talk.* Sin yields only to a superior force.

You can refuse. It's hard, but you can. You don't have to *breathe.* God knows all the pressures are there to make you do it. Still, you can refuse. Likewise, you can refuse the Spirit of God. It's difficult because God so loves this world, and it is the hardest thing you will ever accomplish to be able to withdraw from the love of God.

Far better to respond to God's Spirit. It is so easy and so vitalizing. There is an immediate transformation when you do. It is like a blood transfusion. You find strength. You find appetite. You find desire. You are *quickened.* That is what this divine relationship does for you. Say "yes" right now to Jesus Christ.

POSSESSION AND PROSPECT

Text: "*Beloved, now are we the sons of God, and it doth not yet appear what we shall be: but we know that, when he shall appear, we shall be like him; for we shall see him as he is. And every man that hath this hope in him purifieth himself, even as he is pure.*"

1 *John* 3:2, 3

JOHN is the apostle of love, but he is *bold*. Love is always an *adventure*. John never paddles in the shallows. He never strikes sail to a fear. He is always the *believer*. I read John for faith. There is never a question in John's mind that he and I and every believer are sons of God.

"Beloved, *now* (at this present moment) are we the sons of God." This has been accomplished by the love of God. It is a *divine gift*. I do not deserve it. I could never have earned it. "Behold, what manner of love the Father hath bestowed" (1 John 3:1). God *wanted* to do it.

Never forget it for a moment! Man is God's idea in the first place. "It is he that hath made us" (Psalm 100:3). You will find it in plain, newspaper language in your New Testament. "Enos, . . . was the son of Seth, . . . Seth was the son of Adam, . . . Adam was the son of God" (see Luke 3:38). The Holy Spirit would never have allowed it to be written if it were not true.

If it is not true, it is *blasphemy*. It is a *libel* against God. Humanity is a stream whose sources are in God. God did something that He loved more than anything else He created. "And God said, Let us make man in our image, after our likeness: . . . So God created man in his own image, in the image of God created he him" (Genesis 1:26, 27). Without that, there is no reason or explanation for the eternal yearning of God for reconciliation. *There is no reason for Calvary.*

But there is more to it, sir, than the universal Fatherhood of God. You can spread that doctrine thinner than grape jelly. You can make Hitler and Castro and Nasser and Stalin and every cutthroat and every thief on earth a son of God. Jesus has something to say about that. There is no doubt about it that God *wants* every person to be His child, and that He has provided the means by which every person *can* be His child.

Christ made that plain in the story of the prodigal. "And he arose, and came to his *father*" (Luke 15:20). And Jesus states, "His *father* saw him."

What hope would there be, sinner, should you come to a great Corporate Executive? What would be your chances against the great moral debt and default you have accumulated? Your relationship isn't that of a client with a banker or a deserter with a general court martial. You have something going for you, sinner. You have Someone who cares for you more than you will ever know.

God cares, but do you care, sinner? You are *no son,* or in the words of the prodigal, "I . . . am no more worthy to be called thy son" (Luke 15:21), when you swill around in the swine troughs of sin. If that is your happiness and intent, you cancel every obligation God has toward you. When you profane, when you fornicate, when you hate, when you lust and steal, when you mock everything that is holy—you strip two of the greatest words in our Christian vocabulary, and leave them dead and dry. You take the moral and spiritual content out of *fatherhood* and *sonship.*

John says so in plain language. "As many as received him (honored Him), *to them* gave he the right to become children of God, even to them that believe on his name: who were born, not of blood, nor of the will of the flesh, nor of the will of man, but of God" (John 1:12, 13, ASV).

There is a predicate, sir. It's an *inward change.* That change takes place when you head in the right direction, when everything within you says, "I have sinned." You'll feel it the moment you start; the moment you conclude that rebellion's payoff to you is famine, swine, and loneliness. You will anchor your soul in the fact that there is a better relationship available to you. It will lead you home.

There is an eternal difference between "husks" and a "fatted calf." There will never be a common denominator between "feeding swine" and wearing "the best robe." You can't have it both ways, lady. You must make a *choice.* The next move is yours. "I will arise and go to my father" (Luke 15:18). Christ makes that possible.

There can never be any question toward God's love for you. God has never entertained any other thought than that you should come back. When we "receive" that divine intention, when we accept as fact that God waits to erase the pain and guilt of transgression—"this my son was dead, and is alive again; he was lost, and is found" (Luke 15:24)—you and I experience a new birth.

It is an *emancipation.* Every claim of the pigpen is rejected. Every fetter of the old crowd that helped you "waste" and "spend all" and then scorned your bankruptcy, is broken. You become a *new creature.* You will know a *harmony* that you groped for all your life. Jesus describes such joy in terms of "music and dancing." You will feel *alive.*

The second thing is that the glad fact opens into a new possibility. "Now are we the sons of God, and it doth not yet appear what we shall be." The possibilities are *limitless.* When you find Father and home, you start an adventure that never quits.

That is a fact that hell hates to have exposed. What hell offers to the rebel is short-lived. You can move through it in an inning or two. "When he had spent *all,* there arose a mighty famine . . . and no man gave unto him . . . and I perish with hunger" (Luke 15:14, 16, 17). That doesn't sound enticing to me.

God's program for you is a long-range program. "And it doth not yet appear what we shall be." You move from "glory to glory."

I like that "commercial" which states: "You've got a lot to live, and we've got a lot to *give*." Once you have started and evil thoughts, adulteries, murders, thefts, covetousness, wickedness, deceit, luxuriousness, an evil eye, blasphemy, pride, foolishness have been evicted, your fellowship with the Evictor leads you into a fantastic world of spiritual miracle. *God has eternal designs for the material that is you.*

You ask, "What guarantee do I have that it is possible?" John answers in utter simplicity, "*Now* are we the sons of God." If God can make a sober, provident, devoted husband and loving father out of a drunkard—if God can make a trustworthy executive out of an embezzler—if God can make a truthful citizen out of a con-man—if God can make a noble lady out of a prostitute—He can make any member of the human race anything He cares to make that person. That is the argument.

You ask, "Will He do it?" *Yes.* It is His nature. He works for perfection in the flowers and plants on earth. Examine His handiwork on earth. Let the botanist preach you a sermon! He works for perfection in space. Let the scientist preach you a sermon! Will He do less for His greatest creation—man? If He does it for a flower that is beautiful for a day, how will He extend Himself for an eternal soul? I say this. The same God who has written perfection into matter—and the mighty atom is an example—must be the same God who determines perfection for the spiritual. Otherwise God would be mightier in the atom than He is in the human spirit.

No, sir, God is not finished with you. It is *exciting.* It's lots better than the hog wallow. "It doth not yet appear what we shall be."

Is it ethereal—an Aesop fable? No. "We shall be like him." He is the forerunner, the pattern. No goal could hold so much promise. Master of His material world; Conqueror of death; supreme in space; untouched by pain, poverty, and time—"we shall be like him."

There are lines I learned a long time ago which say:

"A fire-mist and a planet,
A crystal and a cell,
A jelly fish and a saurian,
And caves where cavemen dwell.
"Then a sense of law and beauty,
And a face turned from the clod;
Some call it Evolution,
And others call it God."

Who measures the distance onward? Plainly we are unfinished creatures. What man is capable of is yet to unfold. The greatest music, the greatest art, the greatest engineering, the greatest expression "doth not yet appear." Every present record will be broken. Every present achievement will be surpassed.

Born of the flesh, I achieve in part. Born of the Spirit, there is *no limit*. Paul sensed it. He said, "Your life is *hid*." It is impossible for you to conceive "the things which God hath prepared for them that love him" (1 Corinthians 2:9). Only God can reveal something of that future to you through His Spirit. "Your life is hid with Christ in God" (Colossians 3:3).

So, sir, what will it be? You have an option. One man said, "I have no room." This is what he died of—"no room." He said it about his warehouses but, in substance, he was describing himself. He let merchandise cage him in—*suffocate his soul.* He had reached the end so soon. "What will I do?" He had no room. His "barns" were his sky.

There is another way. Paul wasn't bothered with warehouses. Can you conceive Paul asking, "What will I do?" After Antioch, there was Ephesus; after Ephesus, Philippi; after Philippi there was Corinth; after Corinth, there was Rome; and after Rome, there was a "a crown of righteousness" laid up for him. The prospects were dazzling and eternal. Life to him was a constant sunrise. "I count not myself as one that has attained" (see Philippians 3:13).

The challenge becomes the motivation. "Everyone that hath this hope in him purifieth himself." It takes *plain morality*—a disciplined soul—to achieve it. There isn't any magic, mister. It takes character to head upward. You can't move in the stars with a ten-cent attitude. "Having . . . these promises, . . . let us cleanse ourselves from all filthiness of the flesh and spirit, perfecting holiness in the fear of God" (2 Corinthians 7:1). You can't orbit with the "swine" and in your "Father's house" at the same time.

When you anchor in God, mister, you can harness a stubborn temper. You can bridle an unruly tongue. *Possibility* becomes *performance.*

"Even as he is pure." *None of us need ever be discouraged.* "We shall be like him." His companionship is always helping us. He has eternally identified Himself with me. I will avail myself of that help, and with it, all of my possibilities will be realized. The New Testament describes it as "the powers of the world to come" (Hebrews 6:5). Through the Holy Spirit, I feel the full force of those "powers" moving upon my soul.

A REVIVALTIME TESTIMONY

"What a wonderful way to close the Lord's Day—by tuning in to *Revivaltime*. My wife and I are caught up in the inspiring music and wonderful, wonderful messages given from God, His Word, and from God's man, C. M. Ward. We encourage others to tune in to *Revivaltime*."

FIVE WRONG ANSWERS

Text: *"Casting all your care upon him; for he careth for you."*

1 *Peter* 5:7

EVERY preacher of the gospel has felt the lash of bitter and cynical souls who demand: "Where was your God when my son died in Vietnam?" or "Where was your God when my wife was snuffed out in an automobile accident?" You hear the catcalls and the bronx cheers. It isn't easy for a preacher to stand like an umpire behind homeplate and call them according to the Book.

I admit it at once. I cannot solve the age-old riddle of how a good God can allow evil in His universe. I suppose I should ask you how you put up with that unsaved, ungodly, heart-breaking, insolent college youth in your home Dad? How do you put up with that deadbeat husband of yours, wife? How does society put up with all the free-loaders, the dull, and the unproductive?

I admit I do not know any direct answer to this age-old riddle of how a good God can allow evil in His universe. But there are several wrong answers I believe we can discount.

God wills it is one wrong answer often used to shrug away every catastrophe. That answer blames a God of love and goodness with some things that can never be expressions of love or goodness.

God wills no man to either be lost or go to hell. I have His word for that. Here it is. "The Lord is not . . . willing that any should perish, but that all should come to repentance" (2 Peter 3:9).

God told the preacher, Ezekiel, "Say unto them, As I live, saith the Lord God, I have no pleasure in the death of the wicked; but that the wicked turn from his way and live" (Ezekiel 33:11). And there's certainly a verse you can quote. "For God so loved the world, that he gave his only begotten Son, that whosoever believeth in him *should not perish,* but have everlasting life" (John 3:16).

No, sir, you can never say God *wants* any man to go to hell. You can't say that! We know why the penitentiary of the universe was created. It was "prepared for the devil and his angels" (Matthew 25:41).

A good God and a loving God doesn't *want* you to go there, but He will *permit* any man to do so. A good and a loving God respects your choice, as a responsible adult, sir, even though He knows you are making the wrong choice.

The early brethren recognized this in the case of Judas that in the final analysis he made his *choice,* that he went "to his own place."

The same people who choose hell on earth choose hell for eternity. No, sir, you can't blame God for every catastrophe. Paul recognized it in a brother he loved. "Demas hath forsaken me, having loved this present world, and is *departed*" (2 Timothy 4:10).

God will never force a preacher to preach. He will never usurp a teacher to teach a Sunday school class. He will never commandeer a parent to conduct a family altar. The preacher, the teacher, the parent can "depart" at any time. God will struggle with your soul, mister. He will tug you toward the right direction with every grace and providence at His command, but He will never overpower you. The decision must be *yours.*

Sin caused it is a second glib solution. This frame of mind sees every pain, every "tummy ache," as a punishment for some wrong committed. Wrongdoing, secret mischief, are easy whipping boys for wrenched shoulders, fallen arches, damaged budgets, student dropouts, poor sermons, bad marriages—the list is endless.

This was the solution assumed around Job. He lost his fortune, his family, and his health. It was all attributed to sin in Job's life. His friends refused to accept any other reason.

It's such a handy bit of theology! If you are a real goody-goody, you work your way into favor and become God's pet. As a result you must make money, live in a four-bedroom house with two and one-half baths, complete with a two-car garage, cook, and gardener. If you are bad, you are a financial failure. Even the plants die on you. You are always under medical care. You are haunted with losses. It simply proves beyond reasonable doubt your guilt. If you were *innocent,* the bank balances, the health chart, the furniture would show it.

What are the facts? Try this one on for size! "For whom the Lord *loveth* he chasteneth, and scourgeth every son whom he receiveth" (Hebrews 12:6). Mrs. Job didn't believe that, and most of the congregation agreed with her.

Ponder this! "Who are kept by the power of God through faith unto salvation ready to be revealed in the last time. Wherein ye greatly rejoice, though now for a season, if need be, ye are in heaviness through manifold temptations: *that the trial of your faith,* being much more precious than of gold that perisheth, . . . might be found unto praise and honor and glory at the appearing of Jesus Christ" (1 Peter 1:5-7). That is quite a different view.

It's all for the best is a third wrong answer to the question. This answer does a disservice to the very text that it usually claims for support. For "we know that all things work together for good to them that . . . are the called according to his purpose" (Romans 8:28).

Granted! God can and does overrule even bad things in His purpose so that good comes from it. That much the verse declares. But that is certainly not the same as saying, "It's all for the best." The end cannot justify the means. Benevolent despotism is despotism just the same.

It is still wrong to drop out of school and abort your education. God is never on the side of ignorance. It is still wrong to force marriage and defy convention. It is still wrong to sit around in wet clothes and trifle with a handsomely made body.

This great promise of Romans 8:28 in your New Testament is limited to God's elect. It is not a blanket policy. Only God's children, going God's way, can claim this miracle, "All things work together for good."

Furthermore, there is a big difference between a "bad happening" being labeled good, and a "bad happening" fitting into a pattern *for ultimate good.* A tragedy can finally drive a man to God, but a tragedy is always a tragedy. It may take your son's death, sir, to open your eyes. That will be *the ultimate good.* But it will never be *good* that your son died—never!

The devil did it is a fourth slick solution. If you like what happened, you credit God; if you don't like it, you can blame the devil. But this answer does not relieve God really. It only removes the cause one step. *Then you must ask why God let the devil do his dirty work.*

You really can't go around assigning blame and blessing. None of us can qualify as umpires. If preachers ran the weather, for instance, we would produce a national crisis in one year. I would never have it rain on a service night, or at Sunday school, or during an evangelistic campaign, or during the Sunday school picnic, or the night the church is celebrating my birthday with a surprise party. The fact is, I schedule so many meetings in a year that I might not have it rain at all.

So God sends some things upon the just and the unjust. Let me read that to you from the Bible! "For he maketh his sun to rise on the evil and on the good, and sendeth rain on the just and on the unjust" (Matthew 5:45).

Not long ago a church burned. Some said, "This is the work of Satan." Others said, "God is trying to tell us something." Could both be right?

Another popular answer is *God is dead.* It's a contemporary way of saying what faithless men for centuries have chosen to affirm—*blind fate rules.*

But who and where and what is fate? What better off are you to believe in fate, than you were to believe in God? You must still exercise faith; and that is what you are trying to avoid, isn't it?

There are too many signs pointing to a Creator's care and thoughtfulness toward the creature to rule out a personal God. There is that thermostatic temperature control in your own body—set at 98.6 degrees. It regulates the heating and cooling of the physical house in which you dwell. It adjusts automatically to change of clothing, to seasonal change, to change of environment, age, exercise, and so many other factors. It says to you, "Somebody loves you."

As I read the Bible, I am encouraged to reject all of these man-made solutions and rest on God. "Trust in the Lord with all thine heart; and lean not unto thine own understanding" (Proverbs 3:5).

Where was God when your son died? Where was God when your wife was taken? *He was right where He was when His own Son died—caring for you.* Or have you forgotten that in your grief and bitterness and rebellion?

God saw His Son mauled, dishonored, and nailed to timber. They cut Him and disfigured Him even in death. Where was God then? He was in Christ reconciling you and me to Himself. *That is how much God cares.*

You need God, my friend. Turn now and sob it out on His eternal bosom.

GO UP!

Text: *"Go to my brethren, and say unto them, I ascend unto my Father, and your Father; and to my God, and your God."*
John 20:17

I HAVE been terribly negligent with this truth during the years of my ministry. I have preached the Gethsemane, the Golgotha, and the Garden story, and neglected the *Ascension.* I apologize both to myself and to you.

"Go to my brothers, and say I go up." That was the message which Christ entrusted to a prostitute to spread throughout the world.

It has always intrigued me. "He was taken *up;* and a cloud received him out of their sight" (Acts 1:9). He went *off* the earth. Why? Why did He disappear into a cloud?

Space is infinite. Heaven is where God is, and God is everywhere. Then, why did Jesus visibly go *up* off the earth? That seems to me a proper question to ask.

Jesus never did a thing that wasn't meaningful. The lesson was for His disciples. "While they beheld, he was taken up" (Acts 1:9). What spiritual thing did Jesus want His disciples to learn by a visible act? That is my message to you in this service.

Christ always acted out spiritual things by outward and visible forms. It wasn't *necessary,* when He healed a leper, that He should stretch forth His hand and *touch* the man. He could have healed him by an effort of the will, as He often did heal over great distances. But the touch of His hand was *a visible act* that He was invisibly healing the man.

It wasn't necessary that the *stone* of the Easter sepulcher should be rolled away. Christ's Resurrection Body, which no longer conformed to the laws of this world and was able to come through closed doors, could have left the sealed sepulcher. But the stone was rolled away *because God always gives us the outward and visible sign.*

From the moment God committed Himself to the Incarnation, He committed Himself to expressing spiritual things in outward, visible, tangible, and audible forms. I'm so glad He did. It accommodates my faith.

It's as if the Eternal Spirit said: "You dear people, I understand how impossible it is for you to grasp My infinite and incomprehensible Self. And My heaven, too, belongs to a world of which you have no experience, and, therefore, no terms to express. I must translate these things into easy terms for you." So the Eternal Spirit set about to accomplish this, the greatest of all missions—to successfully reveal Himself to mankind.

How can a deaf man understand a Beethoven symphony, unless it is translated into some medium which he can experience? God had to find terms by which He could be understood by man. The plan the Eternal Spirit put into operation was Christ. *He wrapped Himself in Christ.*

Christ is God the spiritual, encased in an outward form. Accept Christ, and you are accepting God. Trust in Christ, and you are trusting in the invisible God. Learn the character of Christ, and you learn the character of the invisible God. Where Christ is merciful, God is merciful. Where Christ is stern, God is stern. Where mercy outweighs wrath in Christ, it outweighs wrath in God. The *answers* are all there for you to see, mister. They are in Jesus. That is why the Eternal Spirit "hath committed all judgment unto the Son" (John 5:22).

That is the way God does things. God left *pictures* for us. Water baptism is a picture. A baptismal tank cannot take lies and thefts and greed and lust and profanity out of a man. If it could, we would have the water running day and night. But we do need to *wash!* A man becomes dirty inside. An appropriation of Calvary does that, when a sinner truly believes, "That blood was shed for me."

God doesn't need an outward form, *but I do.* So He allows me a perfect picture outwardly for what He has already done for me inwardly. It's something a child can understand. It simply says without argument, *Cleansing is necessary.* It says' "You need a complete bath—every part of you." How could I possibly express salvation better?

He left another picture for us. If God wants to come right inside our beings to nourish and strengthen them, it is not necessary to come into our bodies through bread and wine. God can enter us without any *outward form.*

But in His eternal understanding and mercy, He gives me a picture of what He is doing—of *how* He is literally becoming a part of me every day. He incorporates Himself in my life—becoming strength and mind and initiative and talent and will and sensitivity—just as bread and wine become mysteriously muscle and color and step and reach and knowledge. Again, the simplest child can understand this, and, yet, the deepest philosopher can appreciate it.

I, myself, am put together this way. I am conscious of being a thinking creature. *I think.* But thought is an impalpable, spiritual thing. I can't take a thought and visibly or audibly examine it.

All life is thought. When conscious thought stops, conscious life stops. So, you see, the *real me* is invisible. I find expression in a body, a material, earthly body. It is related to the soil. It provides a temporary liaison with this physical planet. My thoughts can find expression through my eyes. They can also find expression through words. Hands and feet are instruments. These are tangible media. They make the invisible me known to other earth-dwellers.

You may be *intensely amused.* How would anyone know if you were an unclothed spirit? Your amusement is an invisible thing. It must find an avenue of expression in order to communicate. So the Eternal Spirit has provided me with a visible, alteration in the face, and a strange noise called *laughter.*

You may be *sad.* That is an inward condition, an invisible thing. How can you express it and share it? The Eternal Spirit has provided something called *a tear duct.* A tear is a beautiful thing. It communicates.

You may be *enthusiastic.* You feel something inside when the United States Marines are marching by, or your football team is winning, or you are present at a crowded, pulsating Sunday night service. It's away down inside, invisible and unuttered. No one would ever know unless some medium had been provided. The roar of the crowd, the handclapping of the audience, tell me that there is a stir and a response.

You may be in *love.* There are surges and urges within that are very real. They command and seek expression. But they are invisible and inaudible unless the unseen inner man can find help and understanding and interpretation through the outer, visible man. So, then, there is the kiss, the grip of the hand, the embrace. God has so beautifully arranged it all. He has provided speech and communication.

His greatest triumph was in Jesus Christ—the God-Man—His perfect medium of expression. "God, who at sundry times and in divers manners spake in time past unto the fathers by the prophets, hath in these last days spoken unto us *by his Son*" (Hebrews 1:1, 2).

So everything Christ did was a *message*—an exact message to mankind.

How could He express the very difficult idea *that He had finished His mission*—that He must now change His conformity with Earth and conform again with a world we do not yet understand, but shall understand some day?

Our Big Brother did something, so simple, and so easily understood by all us "little brothers." It said better than any actor has ever said it by leaving the stage—"It's done! Every necessary scene has been thoroughly acted. The story is evident. It has turned out the way the Eternal Playwright planned it. The good has overcome the evil. *It is a happy ending.*"

"Go to my brothers, and say unto them, I *ascend.*" This is the first time Christ calls them "brothers." He now identifies Himself with them as *Brother.* He says: "*I ascend*—I am the Winner—the villain is deposed. Nothing could keep Me down—nothing! The direction, My brothers, is *always up.* That is My message to you."

He went, not as God returning where He has been before, *but as Man arriving for the first time.* Adam, created on this tiny planet out of tiny planet materials, has made it all the way—*I ascend.*

"That is how big *lift* is. That is how strong what I have accomplished at Calvary has proven to be. I ascend unto my Father, and your Father; and to my God, and your God—*and nothing can stop Me.* Where Man has once been, other men can go. As your Brother, I ascend. What the state is that I am entering you cannot understand. *I can only express it by ascending like this.* You will follow. You will conquer death, as your Brother has done, and you will ascend. Nothing can keep you back."

It's a marvelous moment in the history of this planet. That was the message that Christ entrusted to a prostitute for conveyance to ten renegades. He sent them word that they would rise higher. Already He had brought them a long way. But He wasn't through. *He was their Brother.*

Are you unhappy about your failures and dismal record? Christ has one message for you, "Ascend!" Climb *up* with Him. Take courage!

I bid you take courage. Christ sent this message by a repentant sinner to worrying sinners: "Go to my brethren, and say unto them, I ascend unto my Father, and your Father; and to my God, and your God."

That is the message. Is there any other way for you, sinner, but *up?* Believe it, and head in that direction! Turn that heart, those eyes, that head *upward* now, and begin to feel in your own soul *the ascension.*

A REVIVALTIME TESTIMONY

"A Thai man who speaks English well walked into the Christian Servicemen's Center and said, 'I have heard *Revivaltime* broadcasts on the FM station in Bangkok and have come to become a Christian. After prayer, he went on his way rejoicing and plans to attend church regularly. I have met many people recently who have been blessed by the broadcast."

YOU WERE MEANT TO BE A PRIEST

Text: "*And he brought the other ram, the ram of consecration: and Aaron and his sons laid their hands upon the head of the ram. And he slew it; and Moses took of the blood of it, and put it upon the tip of Aaron's right ear, and upon the thumb of his right hand, and upon the great toe of his right foot . . . and Moses sprinkled the blood upon the altar round about.*"

Leviticus 8:22-24

ANYTHING else you may be is *incidental,* just grocery money —expenses. You and I came to this planet to be *priests.* You will never be fulfilled or really challenged until you know yoursef to be a priest.

First, *you relate to the sacrifice Jesus Christ made for sins.* The Blood spilled at Calvary is the greatest eloquence in the universe. It is speaking "better things than that of Abel" (Hebrews 12:24).

The possibilities and grandeur for mankind are unlimited. "Eye hath not seen, nor ear heard, neither have entered into the heart of man, the things which God hath prepared for them that love him. But God hath revealed them unto us by his Spirit" (1 Corinthians 2:9, 10).

I do not become a priest by my own will. Neither do I become a priest because another man consecrates me. This would simply further the religious business. God, Himself, must act upon me. He does so because the Blood was shed for me.

There is no other ground of commitment. It isn't because I'm musical or aspire to art. It isn't because I am suitable for the clergy and a number of preachers have been in my background. God calls me through Calvary, and Calvary alone. The blood of that sacrifice must touch you.

I stood in the Georgetown, Guyana, South America, Airport recently, ready to fly to Trinidad, and later into Venezuela. Among others bidding me God's blessing, was Brother Ally, a Guyanan East Indian—out of a Muslim home, whose mother had died when he was very young; who is one of five sons; and whose father, after the wife's death, turned to serious sin and left the family lonely and bankrupt.

Today, Brother Ally is a power for God, a *priest* in the New Testament sense, whose ministries are healing the sick and converting the unregenerate. When the blood of the sacrifice touched him it took a stammerer, who could not make himself understood, and gave him a message that holds his audience spellbound.

Here is what a mighty God says to us: "For ye are bought with a price: therefore glorify God in your body, and in your spirit, *which are God's*" (1 Corinthians 6:20). Bought and paid for—never forget that! The rest becomes the most simple deduction on earth—*the total purpose of your life and my life on earth is to glorify God. . . .*

That precious blood is not only a saving, cleansing blood, *it is also a possessing blood.* It places a claim on your life, sir, that supersedes every other claim. Believe it! *What it touches it claims.* I repeat it. You are no longer your own. You belong to the One who "bought" you—all of you, "body" and "spirit."

The blood was put upon three points of the body—the tip of the right ear, the thumb of the right hand, the great toe of the right foot. There must be a meaning in that for us. God never does anything for the sake of ritual.

The ear was touched to say, "Your ear no longer belongs to you, but to God." That is what happened to young Samuel.

"Speak, Lord; . . . thy servant heareth" (1 Samuel 3:9). Mister, the important thing to hear is what God says.

Christ had His ear open for His Father's voice. In Psalm 40:6 we read: "Sacrifice and offering thou didst not desire; mine ears hast thou opened." This passage is quoted in the Book of Hebrews. However a portion of it reads differently. "Sacrifice and offering thou wouldest not, but a body hast thou prepared me" (Hebrews 10:5). That is significant. *If God has your ear, He has your whole body.*

Another translation says, "Mine ears hast thou *pierced.*" It was an old-time ceremony in Israel. If someone was placed into servitude, and the one in servitude grew to love his master because the master was kind and considerate to him, he might say: "If I go free (bringing this relationship to a close), I leave a master whom I love, a service that I love, a family that I love. That is too big a price to pay for independence. I am going to stay right here with my master."

Then he would say to his master: "Master, I do not want to go free. I want to be your servant *forever.*" The master would then put a mark on him to indicate that he was his servant forever. That mark was on the *ear.* The servant was taken to the doorpost, and his ear lobe was put against the doorpost and pierced. That marked him as a willing servant forever.

That is the picture brought forward to define our Saviour-Servant, Jesus Christ. He became the willing servant of the Father. "Let this mind be in you, which was also in Christ Jesus: who, being in the form of God, thought it not robbery to be equal with God: but made himself of no reputation, *and took upon him the form of a servant,* . . . he humbled himself, and became obedient unto death, even the death of the cross" (Philippians 2:5-8).

I have always been blessed by a passage in Isaiah which says: "The Lord God hath given me the tongue of the learned, that I should know how to speak a word in season to him that is weary: he wakeneth morning by morning, *he wakeneth mine ear to hear as the learned.* The Lord God hath opened mine ear, and I was not rebellious, neither turned away back" (Isaiah 50:4, 5).

It works that way. "The Lord God hath given me the tongue of the learned, that I should know how to speak a word in season to him that is weary." *That is persuasiveness.* God will give you the know-how if you will give yourself to Him. The person who has the quickened ear is the person with the tongue of the learned.

The world will never weary of *anointed utterance.* It thirsts for it as mankind yearns for gold. Billy Sunday, the baseball player, became one of God's priests. A conversation has been captured of two Iowa farmers, talking at a crossroads blacksmith shop, about the meetings:

"See here, Jones; there never was any preachin' done jes' like that baseball man does it. I tell you, John, he's got more life in him than any two-year-old colt you ever saw. I would never 'a' believed it if I hadn't seen it, that anybody could ever be so much in airnest at jes' preachin'. He's got a platform to stand on more'n as big as two wagon boxes, and he kivers every inch of it in every sermon he preaches. Why, in the meetin' last Sunday *he got so fired up that he tore off both his vest and coat,* jerked off his collar an' kervat, an' then rolled up his sleeves as if he was agoin' to help thrash. . . . Why, John, he pounds his p'ints clear through you, and makes 'em stick out on the other side. I thought I'd been a-hearin' ruther strong preachin' all my life, *but I never heard none that took hold of me like his'n does.*"

That was Billy Sunday. There were criticisms. But the best ever said of him was that he reached millions—the outcasts, the strays, and deserted—whom the church could never have reached. Those who heard him never forgot him—or his blazing, bare-handed evangelism. *He gave the message, and audiences listened.*

Jesus said: "The words that I speak unto you I speak not of myself" (John 14:10). "For all things that I have heard of my Father I have made known unto you" (John 15:15).

The Holy Spirit is the same wonderful Listener and Communicator. "He shall not speak of himself; but whatsoever he shall hear, that shall he speak" (John 16:13).

If, within the Godhead, there is this consecration of ear on the part of the blessed Son and the Holy Ghost, how much more there must be the consecration of the ear in you and me, if we are to do the will of God!

Martha tried to consecrate her hands without consecrating her ears. It didn't work. She became irritable and impatient with the Lord Himself. She wanted things to go her way instead of going His way. That will always lead to unhappiness and failure. She asked our Lord: "Why do You allow that lazy, good-for-nothing Mary to sit at Your feet, when she ought to be helping me?"

Unless your ear is "pierced," your life will be a selfish life. It will never count. When a line is drawn and the years added, the answer will always read: "Thou art weighed in the balances, and art found wanting" (Daniel 5:27).

The blood was next placed on the right thumb. The hand must render service. The blood-touched hand means that we carry to mankind something better than our own resources.

I have a feeling so many times that all of us in the kingdom are busier than we ought to be. We are inclined to get our hands into everything—committees, profit organizations, educational pursuits, politics, social services, and civil rights. Most of the time we are frustrated and worn. We accumulate mileage and expense, and see so little accomplished—lots of gross effort and very little net reward. Why? The answer is right here. *We need hands filled with His inventory.*

The hands of men bear the marks of their toil. You can tell

a farmer by his hands. You can tell an oil worker by his hands. What kind of a man am I? Are my hands marked by sacrifice? Can you see the compulsion of Calvary there? Are my hands grasping, greedy hands—excusing my love and demand for this "present evil world" by sometimes carrying a Bible and placing on the Sunday morning collection plate a "tip" for God? Oh, God, dare I show Thee my hands and my feet?

Then the blood was placed on the great toe of the right foot. The feet signify movement. I can only go as my feet carry me. But, where will I *walk?* After what will I *run?* The blood will make the *difference.* It will bring me into the way of holiness. I must never, never carry that precious mark elsewhere.

This world needs to see folk on another street, moving in a different direction—headed for heaven instead of hell, interested in righteousness instead of sin, fearing God instead of loving the devil. But "you hath he quickened, who were dead in trespasses and sins; wherein in time past ye walked according to the course of this world, according to the prince of the power of the air, the spirit that now worketh in the children of disobedience" (Ephesians 2:1, 2). *Thank God for the priestly walk!*

The New Testament makes it clear to me how I should walk. I must walk in *newness of life* (see Romans 6:4). I must walk *honestly* (see Romans 13:13). I must walk *in the Spirit* (see Galatians 5:16). I must walk *worthy of the vocation* (see Ephesians 4:1). I must walk in *love* (see Ephesians 5:2). I must walk as *a child of light* (see Ephesians 5:8). I must walk *circumspectly* (see Ephesians 5:15). I must walk *worthy of the Lord* (see Colossians 1:10). I must walk in *wisdom* (see Colossians 4:5). I must walk *pleasing to God* (see 1 Thessalonians 4:1). I must walk *as He walked* (see 1 John 2:6). That doesn't leave room for questions.

Isaiah knew the joy of carrying the message. "How beautiful upon the mountains are the feet of him that bringeth good tidings, that publisheth peace; that bringeth good tidings of good, that publisheth salvation; that saith unto Zion, Thy God reigneth!" (Isaiah 52:7). So when men trace my life, I want them to say above all else, "He was a gospel preacher. He was a witness."

Pheidippides was present at the great battle of Marathon, when the Greeks smashed the power of the Persians. When the battle was done, he threw down his spear and shield and said: "I want to take the good news to Athens." He ran and ran until he burst into the council chambers in Athens and shouted, "We have conquered! We have beaten the enemy!"

Pheidippides was an eager runner. He was also a sacrificial runner. He had given the last ounce of strength to carry the news. And he fell dead. He gave his life to publish the news.

Our Lord gave His life to create the news. He is reaching toward you now—to mark your ear, your hand, your foot for His imperial service. That is your life!

A REVIVALTIME TESTIMONY

"I try to listen to *Revivaltime* every Sunday morning. I deeply appreciate this presentation of the gospel. My heart continues to say 'amen' as C. M. Ward preaches. I am an evangelical in a movement that is basically liberal at the top, but I shall continue to bear my witness as a pastor within this context as long as possible."

SAMUEL—A MAN WHO PRAYED THE PRAYER OF FAITH

Texts: *"And Samuel . . ."* *Hebrews* 11:32

"And Samuel said, Gather all Israel to Mizpeh, and I will pray for you unto the Lord . . . and Samuel cried unto the Lord for Israel; and the Lord heard him."
1 *Samuel* 7:5, 9

A VERY important portion of the Bible bears this man's name. His name is included among the worthies in Hebrews, the 11th chapter. Thus *the principle of faith* operated in this man and his ministry. We are thankful for a full and extensive record from which to search.

Samuel approached God for others. No child of God can render a greater service. But it is more than saying words. It is more than a beautiful religious form. *It requires faith.* "Jesus . . . saith . . . Have faith in God . . . whosoever shall say unto this mountain, Be thou removed, and be thou cast into the sea; and shall not doubt in his heart, but shall believe that *those things which he saith* shall come to pass; he shall have whatsoever he saith. Therefore I say unto you, What things soever ye desire, when ye pray, believe that ye receive them, and ye shall have them" (Mark 11:22-24). Samuel qualified.

Samuel faced a "mountain." Israel was floundering in a *spiritual declension.* Twenty years passed, and the ark of the Lord was stored in the house of Abinadab in Kirjath-jearim. The nation lacked spiritual vitality. The Philistines threatened momentarily. Israel sickened of the false gods and the false habits they had copied from the world about them. They needed help, and they came to Samuel. He told them: "Prepare your hearts unto the Lord, and serve him only: and he will deliver you . . . and I will pray for you" (1 Samuel 7:3, 5). That prayer was wonderfully answered. I want you to see what it involved.

First, *it was accompanied by penitence, confession of sin, and amendment of life.* We needn't be in the dark about what constitutes "a prayer of faith." The Bible says: "If I regard iniquity in my heart, the Lord will not hear me" (Psalm 66:18).

Isaiah gives us a plain word, "Behold, the Lord's hand is not shortened, that it cannot save; neither his ear heavy, that it cannot hear: but your iniquities have separated between you and your God, and your sins have hid his face from you, that he will not hear" (Isaiah 59:1, 2).

The first thing Samuel did was to tackle the *hindrances.* The record bears witness. "They gathered together to Mizpeh, and drew water, and poured it out before the Lord, and fasted on that day, and said there, We have sinned against the Lord" (1 Samuel 7:6).

You can't pray over disobedience. And you can't pray for people who are not willing to go God's way. Samuel uses strong words to Israel, "return . . . put away . . . prepare . . . serve Him only" (1 Samuel 7:3).

No man can serve two masters, and a house divided against itself cannot stand. Faith, first of all, must *close ranks.*

The second thing Samuel did was to *meet the challenge of doubts and fears, and persist in spite of every discouragement.* The Philistines will mobilize every time. They threatened Israel. "And the children of Israel said to Samuel, Cease not to cry unto the Lord our God for us, that he will save us out of the hand of the Philistines" (1 Samuel 7:8).

Fear will overwhelm you as you look at your difficulties. The remedy is to turn your eyes toward God. Peter did, and the trip back to the boat was sheer pleasure. All of us get that sinking feeling at times.

Doubt will attack you. I am sure Noah was harassed by it. But he looked steadfastly toward God. "Thus did Noah according to all that God commanded him, so did he" (Genesis 6:22).

Abraham must have trembled. "Now the Lord had said unto Abram, Get thee out of thy country, and from thy kindred, and from thy father's house, unto a land that I will show thee" (Genesis 12:1). It wasn't an easy decision.

I am sure that Joshua was tested before Jericho. But he and the congregation *shouted* in front of walls that resisted them. Faith faces problems and renames them opportunities.

The third thing Samuel did was to *make his prayer specific, and direct it to the Lord.* He didn't engage in a general form and send out a mimeographed appeal. He "cried unto the Lord." The only prayer that is effective is a prayer between *friends.* "And the Lord spake unto Moses face to face, as a man speaketh unto his friend" (Exodus 33:11). Jesus said a lovely word about Lazarus to the twelve: "Our friend Lazarus sleepeth; but I go, that I may awake him out of sleep" (John 11:11). James says of Abraham, "He was called the Friend of God" (James 2:23).

You don't need ceremony among friends. Samuel prayed as Hannah, his mother, had prayed before him—specifically and directly. "Wilt give unto thine handmaid *a man child*" (1 Samuel 1:11). That was her prayer. You receive what you *ask.*

David did this. "My soul, wait thou *only* upon God; for my expectation is from him" (Psalm 62:5). That is the trouble with unspoken requests—they are simply *unspoken.* God says: "Call upon me in the day of trouble: I will deliver thee, and thou shalt glorify me" (Psalm 50:15).

Fourth, *the prayer of faith must be offered on the grounds of a blood sacrifice.* Someone must pay for the provision. "Samuel took a suckling lamb, and offered it for a burnt offering wholly unto the Lord: and Samuel cried unto the Lord for Israel; and the Lord heard him" (1 Samuel 7:9). Any other attempt at access will fail. None can bring any merit of his own.

Cain's way failed, but Abel's succeeded. The difference was the blood. Cain presented the beautiful work of his own hands. He came with his own harvest. He asked God to receive, admire, and bless what he had grown. "But unto Cain and to his offering he had not respect" (Genesis 4:5). God has designated one way —"a new and living way" (Hebrews 10:20).

The Pharisee's way failed, but the publican's way succeeded.

Let me read you the rule! "Having therefore, brethren, boldness to enter into the holiest by the blood of Jesus, By a new and living way, which he hath consecrated for us, through the veil, that is to say, his flesh; and having a high priest over the house of God; let us draw near with a true heart in full assurance of faith, having our hearts sprinkled from an evil conscience, and our bodies washed with pure water" (Hebrews 10:19-22).

Five, *Samuel was challenged by the powers of darkness.* While Samuel was offering up the burnt offering the enemies drew near. "And as Samuel was offering up the burnt offering, the Philistines drew near to battle against Israel: but the Lord thundered with a great thunder on that day upon the Philistines, and discomfited them; and they were smitten before Israel" (1 Samuel 7:10).

We "wrestle" against "principalities, against powers, against the rulers of the darkness of this world, against spiritual wickedness in high places" (Ephesians 6:12).

Daniel did. He had a revelation of what it took. "For from the first day that thou didst set thine heart to understand, and to chasten thyself before thy God, *thy words were heard,*... But the prince of the kingdom of Persia withstood me one and twenty days: but, lo, Michael, one of the chief princes, *came to help me*" (Daniel 10:12, 13).

Hold on! God will send you all the help you need. Hell won't give in easily. Satan will challenge every intercessor. Count on it.

Sixth, *the prayer of faith is a prayer that is aways answered.* "So the Philistines were subdued, and they came no more into the coast of Israel: and the hand of the Lord was against the Philistines all the days of Samuel. And the cities which the Philistines had taken from Israel were restored to Israel, from Ekron even unto Gath; . . . And there was peace" (1 Samuel 7:13, 14).

Samuel got through. There is no doubt of that. God promises: "Call unto me, and I will answer thee, and show thee great and mighty things, which thou knowest not" (Jeremiah 33:3).

Every prayer that is offered in faith, in the Name of Jesus and for the glory of God, is always answered abundantly. "And whatsoever ye shall ask in my name, that will I do, that the Father may be glorified in the Son. If ye shall ask any thing in my name, I will do it" (John 14:13, 14). That is a wonderful credit card to carry. Samuel used his.

Finally, *Samuel gave God all the glory.* That is so important.

> Here I raise mine Ebenezer;
> Hither, by Thy help, I'm come;
> And I hope, by Thy good pleasure,
> Safely to arrive at home.

"Then Samuel took a stone, and set it between Mizpeh and Shen, and called the name of it Ebenezer, saying, Hitherto hath the Lord helped us" (1 Samuel 7:12). It means something to say it, and then do it, "I'll give the glory to Jesus." Is very easy to vaunt and publicize and credit to self success after the victory. Give God the glory! It belongs to Him.

It is always well and pleasing to say with the Psalmist,

"The Lord hath done great things for us; whereof we are glad" (Psalm 126:3).

Samuel knew how to touch God. There are those among us who have attended the same school of faith and have learned these same lessons. This altar is for *you.* You will find the help you need as you come. "The effectual fervent prayer of a righteous man (or woman) availeth much" (James 5:16). God bless you as you kneel beside such a person.

A REVIVALTIME TESTIMONY

"I wish to express my appreciation for the spiritual enlightenment that *Revivaltime* offers. I am 17 years old and a senior in high school. Some young people may think that a gospel radio broadcast isn't 'where it's at,' but as far as I'm concerned, the *Revivaltime* broadcasts are relevant and show that God through Jesus Christ His Son makes life worth living."

THERE IS A GENERATION

Text: "*There is a generation that curseth their father, and doth not bless their mother. There is a generation that are pure in their own eyes, and yet is not washed from their filthiness. There is a generation, O how lofty are their eyes! And their eyelids are lifted up. There is a generation, whose teeth are as swords, and their jaw teeth as knives, to devour the poor from off the earth, and the needy from among men.*"
Proverbs 30:11-14

THERE have been *marked generations* before. Roman history will always mark the generation of Julius Caesar, Cicero, Anthony, Cassius, Pompey, and Brutus. Churchill described such moments as "the hinge of fate."

The antediluvian past will always mark the generation of Enoch, Lamech, Methuselah, and Noah. It is a pivotal time in history.

The United States will always mark the generation of Washington, Jefferson, Franklin, Adams, Mason, Hancock, Hamilton, and Monroe. It changed the direction of Earth.

Russia will always mark the generation of Lenin, Trotsky, Kerenski, Stalin, and Molotov. Nothing has ever been the same since.

France will always mark the generation of Danton, Robespierre, Marat, Louis, Marie Antoinette, and Napoleon, the Corsican. It left an imprint on Europe that has never been erased. *There is a generation*—and we have come to one again!

What causes it? It would be as foolish to assign blame or praise to immediate predecessors as it would be to indict the mother of Judas Iscariot. This planet has a ponderable called fulfillment. So here we are again!

Suddenly there is something amazingly different among us. No one really knows from whence it came, or why. It has made the scene and created a vortex. Everything from politics to religion is being relentlessly sucked toward it. "There is a generation . . ."

The senior adult is stunned. That adult doesn't know where his world disappeared. It seems all out of date, illusionary, and irrelevant.

What is this current thrust toward openness in human relationships—the new life styles, the "mod," that people discuss? What are these radical experiments in political and social action that are changing values overnight? The young are an inexhaustible fountain of dissent. No force has been able to cap the eruption. It is *wild* and *weird.*

The mainstream consists basically of at least four characteristics: the use of drugs, principally marijuana; radical political action; sexual freedom and experimentation; and the expanded family and the commune. It crosses all lines. It isn't the spew or the drainage of the ghetto or the gutter. The beat is never silenced. It reverberates like the sound of doomsday. *Permissive* and *punitive*—the Far Left and the Far Right—seem set on a collision course.

The *youthquake rumblings* are felt in every home. No island of refuge remains. The campuses are caldrons. Why bother with the great scientists, thinkers, and artists of the various traditional schools when you can sit at the feet of the new apostles of culture, the avant-garde of today, and hear them argue that the battle for sexual freedom is not yet won?

It's a strange system—living without earning regular wages—an integral part of the dropout economy—scrounging and utilizing welfare and unemployment checks with subsidization from stunned and indulgent parents. "There is a generation. . . ."

These *marked generations* have signaled cataclysmic changes in history and in the social structure of mankind. The shock-power of the current generation portends the greatest change of all time. *Some event of immense dimension is in the wings.*

The fulfillment is exact and on schedule. First, "that curseth their father, and doth not bless their mother." The law of the home and family discipline are lost virtues. Paul designated it prophetically—"disobedient to parents." Authority has broken down here. Father is blamed for the legacy of war, the draft, selfish corporate profit, phony respect for pseudo ideals that serve the privileged and rape the impoverished.

This marked generation "*curseth* their father." There can be no dialogue between with at a generation defines to be the establishment, the vested rights a society has acquired and seeks to protect, and the protestor. The invective is vile. It tumbles out in four-letter words of obscenity. It isn't an argument of reason. It is a Niagara of unmitigated filth. The "curse" has become the language of the young militant.

This marked generation "doth not bless their mother." The *daughter* has freed herself from shame, all the way from open dormitories on the campus to uninhibitive and provocative dress on the streets. Mother's first line of refuge has become the Pill. Fifteen-year-olds ask for, and get freedom, that a generation ago belonged only to grandparents. The moderating influcnce of mother is rapidly becoming confined to the sentimental gush of a single calendar date, nominated Mother's Day.

One is almost afraid to ask, "What is the standard of womanhood?" Mother has surrendered her God-iven prerogatives to the professional baby-sitter, the school psychologist, and the county social worker. The daughter feels like a combination tax deduction and a status symbol, a piece of property.

This nation eats at franchises—hamburgers and Cokes during the week, and a steak and baked potato on Sundays. The electric dishwasher, garbage disposal, wall-to-wall carpeting, wash-o-matics, miracle detergents, and magic cleaners confine the girl to one semester in high school in home arts where she learns to make muffins and hemstitch. She comes to marriage prepared as much as a Plymouth Rock chicken is prepared to make a nonstop flight from Boston to Kansas City. "Doth not bless their mother." That's what your Bible says.

Second, "that are *pure* in their own eyes, and yet is not washed from their *filthiness.*" This marked generation wallows in pornography and pot (or narcotic stimulation). The peddlers and the pushers have taken the places of the bootlegger and rumrunner of the roaring twenties. And their victims get younger and younger, and state institutions are crammed with their victims.

This marked generation take their trips into the far, far fantasy land of psychedelic unreality. They "are *pure* in their own eyes." They recognize no rules except the rules of their own tribal councils.

It's a turned-on generation! According to the Bureau of Narcotics and dangerous drugs, a farmer in Turkey legally sells 10 kilograms (22 pounds) of raw opium for $165—but it can be black marketed for $350. Those 10 kilos produce one kilo of morphine base (or 100 percent heroin) in France, where the price is about $4,000. Smuggled into the United States this kilo of heroin brings $25,000 from a wholesaler. He adulterates it to produce four kilos of 25 percent heroin, which he sells to pushers for about $75,000. Pushers further adulterate this heroin until it is only six percent, and they sell it on the street for $5 per five-grain packet. They get more than 45,000 packets and a total take of $225,000 out of that original 10 kilos of opium that was black marketed for a mere $350 in Turkey.

The profits are astronomical. And the victims are this marked generation. They "are pure in their own eyes, and yet are not washed from their filthiness."

Add to it the "filth" of the stage and the screen in the name of art and uncensored creativity and the slime and debauchery of the current novel, and these words ring in your ears, "and yet is not washed from their *filthiness.*"

Third, "O how *lofty* are their eyes! And their eyelids are lifted up." Who will tell them anything? University presidents have been made prisoners in their own offices—held hostage on campus while a list of demands preempt what will be taught, who will teach, and what will constitute administration. Quiet university communities have become the scenes of riot and carnage.

No one seems willing to listen to reason. The word is nihilism, anarchy, revolution, pull down the existing order—all on the base of superior intelligence gathered by their sophomore or junior years in college.

Paul put his fingers on it when he wrote prophetically: "proud and arrogant and contemptuous boasters. They will be abusive . . . relentless—admitting of no truce or appeasement . . . trouble makers; intemperate and loose in morals and conduct, uncontrolled and fierce, haters of good. They will be . . . rash and inflated with self-conceit" (2 Timothy 3:2, 3, Amplified).

Yes, mister troubled academic professor, it is all written! You may have scorned your Bible for years. Now look at it! This amazing prophetic passage I am using in this service, *There is a generation,* was written centuries ago. You will find it in the 30th Chapter of Proverbs. The God you so easily dismissed from your life and classroom predicted your dilemma.

Finally the passage reads—"There is a generation, whose teeth are as swords, and their jaw teeth as knives." They are going to bring in the new world, *the new order.* "To devour the poor from off the earth, and the needy from among men." Everybody is going to be a king in the heaven they intend to build on earth.

The fact is this. A wave of 58 million youths aged five through nineteen—nearly one third of the population of the United States—was poised, in 1966, to sweep over our institutions in the seventies.

They cannot and will not be silenced—"whose teeth are as swords, and their jaw teeth as knives." They have *repudiated* a national philosophy that has cost this nation $182 billion in foreign aid since World War II—supposedly an investment in world peace and security, while during the same period the defense of this nation has cost about 1.5 trillion dollars. *They say something is wrong.*

Soon the *dissent* will become *disaster.* The language will become "swords" and "knives." The diagram is easy to sketch —confrontation, martyrdom, and world charges that this nation is plunging into fascism. So in scores of cells, explosives are being readied. We will soon face the language of the dynamiter, the sniper, and the saboteur—"Whose teeth are as swords, and their jaw teeth as knives."

Yes, we have come to a *marked generation.* Heaven is writing a big, big sign. It means the greatest change in history is coming. That is what it means. *That change cannot take place without involving Jesus Christ.* The last change of enormity came with His first appearance. It changed every calendar on earth from "B.C." to "A.D." *This mighty rumbling on earth warns that His Second Coming draweth nigh.*

It is like your own life, mister! Hell seeks to tear you apart as the Son of God moves toward you. Christ moved toward a man with a thousand devils. They raged in that man until he could not be bound nor tamed—until he shrieked in torment and sought to take his own life. But they respected and feared the Son of God. *Jesus Christ of Nazareth was more than equal to their revolt.*

So, as this Man has already, and will again, make the biggest changes in history, He is mighty and prepared to make the biggest change in you.

That is what all this rage and hell and evil are saying right now—"(Please, oh, please)—don't send us away!" God's Truth and Majesty are coming to cleanse this planet of devils. You can be as sure of that, sir, as you are that before the year A.D. 33, He "came over unto the other side of the sea, into the country of the Gadarenes. And . . . there met him out of the tombs a man with an unclean spirit" (Mark 5:1, 2).

"There is *a generation* . . ." Take a good look at it; and then say, "Come quickly, Lord Jesus!"

A REVIVALTIME TESTIMONY

"I am a pastor and am amazed at the good reception by every denomination of the *Revivaltime* broadcast. This makes it easier to tell men and women about Jesus. I know that *Revivaltime* is truly a blessing in this area. The church in which I pastor has a man who was saved through the broadcast."

ROMANCE

Text: *"She became his."* *Genesis* 24:67

MY mother loved the story of Rebekah. Through her lifetime she drew sustenance from it. The pages were better marked here than elsewhere in her Bible.

Life must incorporate romance, as it must incorporate learning and travel. Salvation, as I understand it and experience it, is *romantic.* Somebody loves me and seeks a meaningful relationship with me.

This Old Testament story has an overlay that is apparent to any reader. We have the planning love of the father seeking a bride for his son. We have the persevering search of the servant. We have the patient waiting of the son. That tells it all—the participation of the Holy Trinity—Father, Spirit, and Son.

That should remove all the fear that accumulates to frighten you from God. I find members of this audience who quake at the thought of God, who suffer tremors of anxiety at what God may ask them to do, who face the future with tension. The entire action of God is for your welfare. Believe that! I do.

First, *the Father, the most interested party, moves toward the prospect with wealth.* When the servant set out to seek a bride he did not go out with empty hands, but he went out with a caravan of gifts.

That is how God approaches you, sir. There is nothing cheap about God. There is about the devil. He has a cheap hell and cheap company. He'll treat you mean from the start. He'll rob you as quickly as he can of health, home, and happiness. He'll beggar you and strip you and abandon you. No one can ever say that about God.

"God so loved the world, that he *gave* . . ." (John 3:16). He approaches you with an open bank account. He invites you to register and open an account on the house. He stands back of you with unlimited credit.

Love's great desire is to give, not to take. That is the eternal difference between heaven and hell in your life, lady. God's approach to you is this: "I am come that they might have life, and that they might have it more abundantly" (John 10:10). *That is an invitation to gracious living.*

There is a lie that the devil tells that I hate worse than any other lie—*that Jesus is a thief*—that He wants to rob you of every good time, and hustle you as early and as cheaply as possible to the grave—that He wants to strip you of fun and advantage, and stand you in a corner until you promise to be real good.

Listen! In this story that my mother loved and taught me, "the servant took ten camels . . . and departed; for all the goods of his master were in his hand: . . . And the servant brought forth jewels of silver, and jewels of gold, and raiment, and gave them to Rebekah" (Genesis 24:10, 53). *That is how the Spirit approaches every one of God's intended.*

Salvation is an invitation to wealth. The Prodigal thought so. He exchanged rags for a robe; famine for a feast; loneliness for love. Jesus called it the sound of music. God's ministry toward you is *grace.* "By grace are ye saved" (Ephesians 2:8). The servant can't bring it all. He simply loads "ten camels" of samples. The rapture you feel in God's approach toward you is only a fraction of what awaits.

I have never been able to swallow this penury bit, the poor-mouth approach to religion. It isn't the relationship between God and man described in my Bible.

I'll say this in personal testimony. God has always been better toward me than I deserved. I'll vouch for it that "no good thing will he withhold from them that walk uprightly" (Psalm 84:11).

Second, *the Servant asks for your word.* God's reward is your response. The purpose behind the long journey that Abraham's servant took—the quest behind the display of Abraham's wealth—was very simple—*a response.*

That is the heart of romance. People ask me again and again, "How will I know? How can I be sure?" Don't make it difficult. Is it closing in on you? Can you think of nothing else? Does it affect your appetite and your sleep? Does it leave you in a permanent sense of excitement?

Laban and Bethuel felt something eternal was happening. They said, "The thing proceedeth from the Lord" (Genesis 24:50). They knew it wasn't blind chance. The circumstances weren't coincidental. They sensed God was in it.

That is the heart of a great gospel meeting, preacher. I have been in a thousand of them. The service doesn't stumble along. It isn't haphazard entertainment. There's a grip. You know Someone is looking for someone. You can feel it, whether you are in the choir or you are an usher. There is authority. "The thing proceedeth from the Lord" (Genesis 24:50).

No one is ever redeemed by luck. If God doesn't really want you, mister, there isn't a chance. The moment of your salvation has been planned. The circumstances have been appointed. Mine were for a certain Friday night long ago.

And when the invitation is extended it is for the *now,* the immediate. There were voices that suggested delay. "Her brother and her mother said, Let the damsel abide with us a few days, at the least ten; after that she shall go" (Genesis 24:55).

That is never good enough for a lover. But the servant said unto them: "Hinder me not, seeing the Lord hath prospered my way; send me away that I may go to my master" (Genesis 24:56).

So many plausible, good reservations attack your soul. "Just wait; take time to think it over a bit more deeply; wait till you get home." I've watched that metamorphosis 10-thousand times in the past 40 years as I have given altar calls. The servant says, "Hinder me not."

The Spirit has come to you for one purpose. He wants to lead you without delay into the Father's will. God's choice for you, sir, is so important that there isn't any time to lose. Abraham's servant arrived in the evening, and he left in the morning. That was quick work. What God offers you isn't to be taken under advisement or placed before your relatives for a group decision. It is simply "yes," or "no."

"They called Rebekah, and said unto her, Wilt thou go with this man? And she said, I will go" (Genesis 24:58). It raises the hair of my flesh as I read it. It was an act of faith. Everything had to be new and different. It required trust. She headed toward a lover and master that the servant could only describe. She placed herself into his care, and confided herself to his provision for her. The New Testament describes it this way. "Whom haven't seen . . . yet love!" (see 1 Peter 1:8).

I have placed this question before many women at the marriage altar. "Wilt thou have this man to be thy wedded husband, to have and to hold from this day forward, for better, for worse, for richer, for poorer, in sickness and in health. . . ?" I have anxiously waited to hear the reply.

There is a greater altar. It is the altar of life. God's Servant, the Spirit, awaits your answer. He has pressed upon you the claims of God the Father for His Son. "Wilt thou go with this Man—the Man who heals the sick, the Man who loves little children, the Man who bore indignities in Pilate's court, the Man who gave us Easter Sunday—*will you go with this Man?*"

I want to hear in this service the answer the servant heard, "I will go."

Third, *there is fulfillment.* "And Isaac . . . lifted up his eyes, and saw, and, behold, the camels were coming. And Rebekah lifted up her eyes, and when she saw Isaac, she lighted off the camel. For she had said unto the servant, What man is this that walketh in the field to meet us? And the servant had said, It is my master: . . . And Isaac . . . took Rebekah, and she became his wife" (Genesis 24:63-65, 67). I have seen my mother weep for joy as she came to those lines.

I'll tell you this. *Isaac is expecting you.* Isaac went out to pray in the field at the eventide. Who was he praying for? He was looking for someone.

I know this, sir. Jesus Christ is expecting me. I've been on the road a long time. Thank God, I've headed in one direction. The Faithful Servant is leading me toward my Intended. Jesus has been praying for me ever since I started the trip on that Friday night. Not a day has passed since then that He has not watched for my arrival. "He ever liveth to make intercession" for us (Hebrews 7:25). I feel it especially as Earth's eventide sets in.

I have this confidence. I shall know Him. And I'll love Him more fully than in the pilgrimage years when I have relied upon the Faithful Servant to describe Him to me. Jesus said: "He that loveth me . . . I will love him, and will manifest myself to him" (John 14:21).

Yes, mister, I am really looking forward to it. My whole manner of living is geared to it. "She became his." That is what I want. There is nothing else of eternal value. I want to belong to Jesus Christ—all there is of me.

Salvation to me is a complete marriage. There isn't room for a third party, or an outside interest. My mother lived like that, and I have been living the same way.

THE WELLS OF SALVATION

Text: *"Behold, God is my salvation; I will trust, and not be afraid: for the Lord Jehovah is my strength and my song; he also is become my salvation.*
"Therefore with joy shall ye draw water out of the wells of salvation. . . . Cry out and shout, thou inhabitant of Zion: for great is the Holy One of Israel in the midst of thee."
Isaiah 12:2, 3, 6

THIS is one of Isaiah's finest passages. What will strike you immediately, as you read, is the plural, "*wells* of salvation."

You cannot *localize* like the Well of Beer-sheba, the Well of Shechem, the Well of Bethlehem. *Salvation isn't packaged that way.*

Even our speech idioms suggest a *wideness.* We say: "You know, her salvation is in her children"; or we say, "His salvation is in his work"; or we say, "In all probability, he will find his salvation in his writing."

Morrison found a well in China. Judson found a well in Burma. Livingstone found a well in Africa. Isaiah calls them "wells of salvation." They are everywhere. Until you find yours, sir, your life will be parched, tormented, and wasted. *Without it you will die.*

I'll tell you this, lady, when you discover God's will for your life, you'll prove one thing, personally. It is this. "Therefore *with joy* shall ye draw water out of the wells of salvation." The *happy moment* for you is the moment you start in God's direction for your life. That is the moment when you start "drawing"—receiving benefits, thrilling to a sense of reward and accomplishment.

These are the happy people of earth. They are the Dr. Albert Schweitzer of Africa, the David Wilkerson of Teen Challenge, the William Booth of the Salvation Army, the Clara Barton of the Red Cross.

This text in Isaiah is a little verse of promise set in the midst of two songs. One song praises God for what He has wrought in salvation. The other song sets forth the joy there is in the proclamation of this salvation to the ends of the earth. Salvation is the biggest theme on earth, whether you are willing to agree or not.

More people, by far, mister, want *a happy ending*. Salvation is a happy ending. It's the story that says right triumphs and the investment is saved. Remove that and you have reduced this planet, and all life on it, to unmitigated hell.

Isaiah chose a fitting simile. The layers of the crust of earth provide one vast storehouse of water. Some granites in their ordinary state contain a pint and a half of moisture in every cubic foot. Ordinary sandstone holds nearly a gallon to a cubic foot. Common loose sea sand holds two gallons to a cubic foot. Water is stored everywhere. The rains replenish the great reservoirs. No amount of usage can totally exhaust them. Salvation is like that. *There is enough for everybody.* And you can "draw" upon it for any amount of time. And it will sustain you wherever you may be challenged.

Salvation isn't limited to the United States. It is in Ghana, West Africa. It is there in El Salvador, Central America. It is there in the Philippines. It is there in Vietnam. *You can find the same answer where you are that I find where I am.*

Salvation is more than deliverance from death. It's more than remaining sober. It's more than keeping your temper. It's more than remaining a virgin. It's more than saving your money. It's more than being truthful. *Salvation is inspiration.* It's finding a being. It's fulfillment. It is the best possible adventure.

Let's settle something right now. There's nothing without

God. Without God you draw a blank. There has got to be a force, an intelligence, a will, a love you feel with which you can *identify*. That "trip" you launch by the force of drugs, sex, beat, alcohol—will take you out into space. *It's the reentry that is the problem.* It's how to get back! There are built-in elements of destruction. So, I ask you, "Escape to where? Escape from what? Escape, how long?"

It's different when you make God your propulsion. "All my springs are in thee" (Psalm 87:7). Nature does its best, sir; but nature itself must rely upon the *supernatural.* So you need something more than the weed, the grape, and human form. *You need to tie in with the Source.*

And don't mistake the bucket for the water. A lot of folk make that mistake. Prayer is a magnificent bucket. Praise is another. So are the ordinances of baptism and communion. But they are not the well. Remember that!

You can have dry prayers. Your worship can become a vague echo. Your baptism can do less for you than the weekly luncheon with the local Rotarians. You need something infinitely deeper. "How canst thou draw for the well is *deep*?" (see John 4:11). Yes, sir! Get to the Source. Find God!

You say, "How can I?" You say, "How do I start?" The answer is in and through and by Jesus Christ. God has totally revealed Himself in the Man of Nazareth. Ask yourself: "Do I like what I see in Jesus Christ? Do I want to become what I behold in this Carpenter? Will I affirm that here is the answer to my struggle, my agony, my confrontation with myself, to become what I want to measure for eternity?" That is when you will begin drawing water out of the wells of salvation. I promise you.

I'll tell you this. You won't find a beginning anywhere else. Jonah argued. He was the celebrated *dissident* of his day. He objected. He believed there was another route just as good, if not easier and better. No God was going to tell him what to do. He had his own ideas.

I'll tell you this. He got all the "hippie" he wanted. Unshaven, filthy, reeking of stale juices, he has left this testimony for other hippies, "Salvation is of the Lord" (Jonah 2:9).

Peter thought for a few dark moments and sentences that violence, the knife, profanity, subversion, betrayal of ideals and friends would give him answers. He has left this testimony: "Neither is there salvation in any other: for there is none other name under heaven given among men, whereby we must be saved" (Acts 4:12).

I only cite these facts, sir, to let you know there have been others before you who have raised the same questions—who have demonstrated the same objections—who have rebelled. What do you hope to find that they couldn't find, if your goal is peace of mind, a sense of fulfillment, and a right relationship?

I made this discovery early. Let me share it with you. This *marvelous stream* flows ceaselessly through the Word. I have been drawing satisfaction out of the Bible for 45 years. And its flow is as deep and as full as when I first began to draw. I draw every day.

You can't stop it. I know. You may be one of those who despise the Bible. You felt relieved when they took it out of our public schools. But, there it is on the editorial page of your newspaper! There it is in a full-page ad in your favorite magazine! There it is all over the place every Christmas season.

You might as well try to shut off Niagara Falls with a shingle, mister. The well is too powerful for your puny effort to stop. And God will make your infidel soul witness the time when the knowledge of the Lord shall cover the earth as the waters the channel of the deep.

The Bible has blessed every nation it has touched. Let the record speak. The dark, unprogressive countries of earth have been the countries without the Bible. The standard of living has risen where the Bible has lifted man where God intended him, into His own image, and given the soul freedom and dignity. Yes, sir! Take your history book and you can trace where this well of salvation has touched.

Goethe, the great German poet, testified: "It is belief in the Bible, the fruits of deep meditation, which has served me as the guide of my moral and literary life. I have found it a capital safely invested, and richly productive in interest."

It may seem like a dull weight between black covers to you, there in the university—something to put in a hotel room. Do a little investigating! Read law, and you will trace it back to the Bible. Read social science, and you will trace it back to the Bible. You are enjoying the modern fruits. Don't forget for one moment there couldn't be any sweet-tasting fruits of present-day achievement without, first, the old roots of truth which have borne these delicious advantages of the seventies.

Girl, I find it all in the Bible! There is something there for every mood. Its message has never failed me. Where can you find a better solution than, "Come unto me, all ye that are weary and heavy laden, and I will give you rest?" (see Matthew 11:28). It's an offer that Earth's literature cannot match.

Isaiah appreciates something else. "Cry out and shout, thou inhabitant of Zion: for great is the Holy One of Israel in the midst of thee." There is always something to be said for the *Church.* Christ loved it and gave Himself for it. No greater credential is needed.

The life-giving stream has flowed through it. Salvation is not in the height of the steeple or the thickness of the carpet. It isn't in the value of the organ or the scholastic achievement of the preacher. The wealth that makes you a child of God isn't the treasure of the strained-glass window. The power that breaks the fetter of trespass on your soul isn't the denominational tag that makes this valuable piece of real estate the holding of some corporate body.

These ornate hinges are meaningless unless "the Holy One of Israel" is in the midst. It's His Church. Unless His presence is there, mister, it's only a Methodist church or a Baptist church, or a Nazarene church, or an Assemblies of God church, or a Lutheran church.

A magnificent building isn't a *church.* A church is "where two or three are gathered together in my name" (Matthew 18:20) —*where His presence presides.* That is where you find "a well of salvation—*not in some fancy game room, or ornate choir loft,* or paneled set of offices. It takes the power of the Risen Christ to satisfy your thirst for freedom.

The Son of God is moving toward you, friend! Respond at once. *That experience will be your salvation.* I promise you joy. Christ's program for your life—His plan for your talent and person—are an ever-expanding miracle. He says, and none can refute, "I am the way, the truth, and the life" (John 14:6). Start drawing on that possibility now.

A REVIVALTIME TESTIMONY

"Brother Ward, I am very thankful to God for you. I want to help you because you are reaching people who won't go to church, but who will listen to the radio. My son just returned from Vietnam and said you were the only preacher he ever heard on the radio over there."

HOW MUCH DO YOU WANT IT?

Text: "*And Caleb said, He that smiteth Kirjath-sepher, and taketh it, to him will I give Achsah . . . to wife. And Othniel the son of Kenaz, . . . took it: and he gave him Achsah his daughter to wife. . . . Caleb said unto her, What wilt thou? And she said unto him, Give me a blessing: for thou hast given me a south land; give me also springs of water. And Caleb gave her the upper springs and the nether springs.*"
Judges 1:12-15

CALEB is a strong name in the history of Israel. He was a stouthearted warrior. He knew how to get the best out of a man. When you think of Hebron, you think of Caleb.

South of Hebron was a community called Debir, or as the Canaanites knew it, Kirjath-sepher. Caleb had a strong desire to take that town. Desire had to be translated into action, and a way found. What is yours on the drawing boards, mister, can only become yours by a winning effort. Every Christian has to learn this lesson. The earth belongs to the saints; it is theirs by inheritance; it awaits conquest.

Caleb offered his daughter as incentive. More than once a beautiful, gracious woman has brought out the ultimate in courage and drive in some man. Othniel fought and won the hand of the fair lady.

Caleb's daughter is a resourceful woman. She is one of the great women of the Bible. She recognizes that she has found in Othniel a brave and virtuous man, but she also recognizes that her hero is a very poor man. She set about at once to change that state of affairs.

Caleb is already a wealthy land baron. His rich, fertile, well-watered fields stretch out from Hebron. Achsah has come to

Othniel with no further dowry than the town he has just won in battle. He is content to possess a marvelous wife. She is all the heaven he feels he needs.

She has different ideas. She is a practical woman, as well as a spiritual woman. So, if he won't ask, she makes up her mind that she will. She is not going to live a threadbare existence of some frontierswoman, living on pride, when better things are available and can be had for the asking. It is stirring to see this woman swing into action. She is every inch and every pound Caleb's daughter.

She moves so quickly that Caleb asks, "What is the matter with thee?" She replies: "Thou gavest me away in a dry land; give me also springs of water. Thou gavest me to a poor husband; give me something for his enrichment." I'll tell you this right now. *You get what you ask for.*

It doesn't take Caleb long. He recognizes the worth of manhood in his new son-in-law, and decides to make an investment in him commensurate with the character he sees in him. He hands over to Othniel the water rights of the recently acquired territory. The dry land, acres of it, was meaningless without that water.

What lesson is there in this Old Testament story for us? The lesson is the lesson of *desire*. Nothing will happen without desire. Desire is built-in incentive. The kingdom of God cannot exist without it.

The great desires of the soul must be cherished and nourished. Every preacher must learn this. Every parent must recognize it. Every leader in government must discern it.

Of course, lusting against these noble incentives are the "desires of the flesh" (Ephesians 2:3). They are merchandised daily in every possible way. *They lead to the vast wasteland.*

Preacher, parent, politician, *there is something better.* Yes, sir, there are wells of desire that can be acquired and used by the educator, the home, and the nation.

I believe this. An emotion or a passion which drives the soul forward to the attainment of a possession which is a real benefit to oneself or another, should not only be nourished, *but stimulated.* Feed it, parent! Preach it, congressman!

I don't think we are accentuating the positive enough. We yield to the dissident and the detractor. *Achsah pushed for what she knew would benefit everybody.*

There are better desires resident in human beings, mister, that should be fed, than the desire for money or the desire for sex. *Stimulate the worthier desires.* That is the answer to a host of today's problems.

I've heard it said since I was a child, "If wishes were horses, beggars would ride." Wishes—strong desires are horses. Beggars do ride. That has been the story of this nation and of the Pentecostal Movement around the world. Small, lowly beginnings, a few people in obscurity, have seen wishes fulfilled in a half century—and beyond their fondest dreams. *Desire is the unquenchable drive of the soul.* Without it, nothing can happen in your church, mister, or for that matter, in your own life. *Neither God nor man can do a thing with a person who doesn't want to be.*

In this story, Caleb had a desire. He wanted to strengthen and enlarge the borders of Israel. Debir was a book city. It was a Palestinian Hermopolis—a seat for literature. It was a rallying place for intellectuals. The libraries of the Egyptians, the Phoenicians, the Babylonians were on deposit. *It was a competitor to the law of God sheltered in the ark.*

Caleb, the old warrior, wanted to control that city for God. And he set out to accomplish it. He fanned desire in young Israeli idealists to a hot flame. "He that smiteth Debir, and taketh it, to him will I give Achsah my daughter to wife." That did it! *It produced an Othniel.*

That is the basis of evangelism. *It's a sense of worthwhile accomplishment.* A believer has to get involved. You have to believe literally what Jesus said, "*Occupy* till I come." *We are to move in.* I believe that.

I have a right to that family for Christ. I have a right to that property for Christ. I have a right to the media for Christ. I have a right to a favorable church bank loan for Christ. I have a right to government concessions for Christ. Caleb said: "I want Debir, and I want it badly enough for the God I serve, that I'll give my beautiful daughter to get it." *You can't stop a dedication like that.*

Caleb gave his *best* to the effort. He said, "I'll give my daughter." And that is what it always takes to win. It will take your *best.*

It *paid.* He got a son-in-law that could grace any family line. Othniel is a young man of sterling character. His name means "lion of God." And he was lionhearted. He became the first Judge or President of Israel in a long list of famous names that includes Ehud, Gideon, Samson, and Samuel. He delivered the nation from her enemies after the nation had fallen away after the death of Joshua. *Othniel was the strong man that rallied the nation.*

Desire sped Othniel. He was a penniless youth by birth—brave, modest, willing, but without social or material advantage. That can be changed, mister. Lots of us have proven that. All the laws in Washington won't accomplish it for you unless you have some "git-up-and-go" in you.

He decided to fight and compete for a better place in life. When Caleb offered his daughter, he said, "Why not me?"

I'll say this, in passing, one of the best things any of us can do on earth is to *marry right.* That is a personal decision. You can take your time. You can set your sight high. Othniel did.

Jacob never let up until he got Rachel. I'll always belive it was the making of Jacob. He gathered forces there that helped him persevere when most men would have quit.

Yes, a right marriage can provide a leap forward. A great woman—a woman that will fight for her husband's advantage—can motivate a man to the heights.

Achsah was that kind of woman. I doubt whether or not the poor farm boy, Othniel, would have ever made it to the Presidency of Israel without that marriage. Get yourself a Christian home, and that home will become a spiritual nuclear reactor, furnishing unlimited energy for your success in life.

Othniel's bride has desires of her own. She wasn't about to settle for a dry piece of land. "Give me a *blessing*: for thou hast given me a south land; give me also springs of water. And Caleb gave her the upper springs and the nether springs." She felt that life was worthier than a struggle to make ends meet. So do I.

We have a right to ask our Heavenly Father for a blessing on top of a conquest. Any member of His family who is willing to fight for it, and believe for it, has a right to ask for the better things of life. Don't settle for a piece of dry land! Your Father has resources to bestow.

There's no law that says that God's people must be poor people—good, pious, dependable, but scrounging out a living. The very nature of God is enlargement. He giveth and giveth and giveth again.

I signed a contract with the Lord many years ago. "Seek ye first the kingdom of God, and his righteousness; and *all* these things shall be added unto you" (Matthew 6:33). I have kept my word with the Lord, and He has kept His word with me. He promised "*all* these things shall be added unto you" (Matthew 6:33). That is exactly what I expect.

I thank God for the story of Caleb's daughter. She has given me an insight into a life of grace and a story of success that provides guidelines for me today.

This is the life that satisfies. It's the choice and contest of good things. They are worth fighting for. They are worth demanding. They never come easily. You have to *want* them enough to go after them and place a personal claim. This is that moment for you.

A REVIVALTIME TESTIMONY

"Certainly *Revivaltime* is rendering a wonderful service to needy humanity. The members of the Harlem All-Denominations Youth Center in New York City tune in to the *Revivaltime* services each Sunday.

"It is not possible to tell you how much strength, faith, and courage your prayers have given me."

IS IT LUCK OR LOVE?

Text: *"The Lord shall preserve thy going out and thy coming in."*

Psalm 121:8

THAT *is a lot to believe.* "The Lord is my shepherd" is as important to me as the Lord is my Saviour. Have I a right to base on fact this assurance of *divine vigilance,* or is it only poetic imagery?

When David Livingstone bade farewell to his home, it was with this Psalm as his parting words, as his sister has written: "We got up at five o'clock. Mother made coffee. David read the Psalm and prayed. 'The Lord is thy keeper: . . . The sun shall not smite thee by day, nor the moon by night' (Psalm 121: 5, 6). Then he walked to Glasgow to catch the Liverpool steamer. He never saw his father again."

Thus Greatheart goes, without much speech but with great sureness, to the opening of the dark continent to the light. Is it ever right to question such a confidence?

When Bishop Hannington took his last journey, knowing well that it was almost certainly the end, it was with this Psalm as the hidden music of his march. Every morning of the march he greeted the sunrise with what he called his "Traveling Psalm" —"The Lord shall preserve thee from all evil: he shall preserve thy soul" (Psalm 121:7). *Can I really claim this preservation?*

Martin Luther believed it *and rested his case on it.* A cardinal legate sent from Rome discusses with Luther at Augsburg: "What do you think the Pope cares for the opinion of a German boor? The Pope's little finger is stronger than all Germany. Do you expect your princes to take up arms to defend you—you, a wretched worm like you? I tell you No! And where will you be then? Where will you be then?" And Luther makes answer: "Where I am now, in the hands of Almighty God."

That is magnificent. It affords *rest.* But, is it a hypothetical security? What *substance* is there to it?

There is Cromwell at the threshold of his career, saying: "Verily I do think the Lord is with me. I undertake strange things, yet do I go through them. I do feel myself lifted up by a strange force. I cannot tell why. By day and night I am urged forward in the great work."

There is Cromwell's biographer also, Thomas Carlyle, who was a "doubting Thomas" all his life, and had moments of fierce disquiet and of infidelity. Yet he had other moments too, and here is the record of one of them: "One night late I rode through the village where I was born. The old kirk-yard tree, a huge gnarled ash, was nestling itself softly against the great twilight in the north. A star or two looked out—and the old graves were all there—and my father and my sister—*and God was above us all.*"

I have felt that so many times—"and God was above us all." *That is faith.* Why is it there? Why does it keep appearing in humanity? *Why do you find it in unusual places and in unusual people?* You have to ask such questions. There must be cause for such effect.

Christ reaffirmed it in His earthly ministry. "Are not two sparrows sold for a farthing? and one of them shall not fall on the ground without your Father. But the very hairs of your head are all numbered. Fear ye not therefore, ye are of more value than many sparrows" (Matthew 10:29-31). That is *assurance* beyond what the Old Testament suggests.

What does the modern man think of all this—deeply involved in his expensive insurance programs? Does he find such religion credible, or even workable in his crowded and accident-prone world?

I think there is less *trust* today—less belief in Providence. The idea today is to go out bravely *and make things happen.* God, more and more, is being reduced to a sort of Sunday morning "tip-of-the-hat"—a vague recognition.

We are modern men and women. The formulas we have put together in our laboratories seem to explain away the simplicity of those romantic days when God's visible hand was everywhere, in the rainbow and the comet, in the thunder and the wind. We know so much more about the physical universe, and the more we know, the more it comes upon us that in nature there is no sign of overruling care. What does nature care for the individual life? Does the blizzard take thought of the sparrow? Education asks you to come to grips with reality.

Does the earthquake separate the believer from the unbeliever? Does the enemy's bullet ask whether or not the target is a child of God? Does the rampaging flood consider whether it should inundate a Christian's property?

Man has become conscientious, and is dismayed when he cannot find a conscience behind the universe. He is apt in his bewilderment to say with the messenger in the *Antigone,* that it is "*chance* that raiseth up and chance that bringeth low, and none foretells a man's appointed lot," and to believe with William Watson that man, for all his boasted power and dignity, is the:

> "Child of a thousand chances 'neath
> The indifferent sky."

Present-day philosophy reduces it, therefore, pretty much to this—*life is a gamble.*

There is also a highly developed *social conscience* today. We are more aware than ever of the tragedy and tears of life. It's not easy to accept a text that indicates that a Supreme, all-powerful Being really cares and interposes Himself. So what, if any, are the answers?

I'll start point-blank. *What are you prepared to substitute for God?* Are you better to discard faith?

There is a strange item in history that will interest you. The great Lisbon earthquake made many people atheists. Suddenly a call to faith was issued. By whom? *By Voltaire.* He wrote a poem counseling silent and trustful resignation in the face of an inscrutable providence. Out of the deeps, this man—full of questions himself—felt that folk could only cry unto God. *To whom else can you speak, mister—to a voiceless nature?*

"It is a fearful thing to fall into the hands of the living God" (Hebrews 10:31). *But to fall out of them is a far more fearful experience.* Remember that! Fall out of them into what? Name your options—caprice—accidentalism—luck—unconscious energy—impersonal omnipotence at large in the universe. Is that what you substitute?

If you have nothing better to offer, mister, I prefer faith in God. It seems to me that the difficulties of unbelief are greater than those of faith. You send me out into an unknown wilderness without chart or compass.

Sir, the very heart of Christ's gospel is here—that God, the Father, *cares.* And it is all total mockery to me to say He cares, and at the same time exercises no *obligation* toward me. Religion, to be worth anything to me must render service. I need something more than sentiment. I need *direction.* I need *provision.*

Christ appeared to establish this faith—to get man's relationship with the Divine out of ornate buildings and hairsplitting debates—back to a simplicity of a child and parent. He said, "When ye pray, say, Our Father which art in heaven" (Luke 11:2).

Life demands commerce—"going out and coming in." I cannot remove myself from traffic. This is my everyday pattern. Thus this text tells me that God is concerned about me.

If I were reduced to endless repetition, to an assembly line, to routine boredom, and felt there were no overtones; that the patterns were meaningless, I could not exist. All of us would be in prison. But it is not drab. It is not meaningless. *Someone watches.* Someone is putting it all together.

I become conscious of this glory. I am preserved for a purpose. It ceases to be drudgery. It ceases to be routine—"going out and coming in." I am conscious of His presence, and if it means something to Him, it must be all right with me.

The housewife, with her repetition of cleaning, cooking, and children, is sustained likewise by the knowledge that a husband loves her and thinks that what she is doing counts for everything. Without that faith, mister, regardless of the job you are doing, you can't face endlessly the routine, the boredom, the unmitigating pattern of "going out and coming in." I'm not built for *unrelieved monotony.*

Solomon touched it in Ecclesiastes: "The thing that hath been, it is that which shall be; and that which is done is that which shall be done: *and there is no new thing under the sun*" (Ecclesiastes 1:9). Everything soon becomes a job.

What keeps you going beyond sheer economic necessity? The secret is in this text—that what you are doing matters, and that the job you are doing is known to the great Keeper.

Without the upward look the weariness of the ordinary, the repetitious, would smother us. *When life becomes a trust, it is different.* Heaven is over us and God is for us. That is what redeems my existence as a traveling evangelist—packing and unpacking—living in a room with a number on it—eating from unrelenting menus—obeying schedules and meeting deadlines. I do it for one reason. I believe it is what God wants me to do. When you believe, you no longer chafe or resent. You live with a sense of spiritual dignity.

I'll tell you this. Nothing is common unless we are common.

What you are doing is important if God thinks it is important. *Life imposes a discipline.* The "going out" is regulated by the necessity of its "coming in."

You feel tied down and harassed. It isn't only teen-agers who want to run away. Adults are so often overwhelmed by the same impulse. You fret because of the short rope. You don't want to "come in" when every desire would have you "going out." You inwardly fume at the circumstances that control your life. But you will shatter your life unless you submit to your Keeper—"The Lord shall preserve thy going out and thy coming in." No, sir, you are not burying yourself in the trivial! God has no intensions of wasting your life.

In the Name of Jesus, keep "going out" and keep "coming in." When you ally yourself to Him, your job is never tame nor dull nor unrewarding. I believe every day is meaningful. I believe I will find a deeper interpretation to what I am doing, as I work today, than I knew as I worked yesterday. So, there is new wonder and excitement, even though physically, I am doing the same thing that I have been doing over and over again for years. God's presence with me on the job assigned, transfigures the commonplace and gives it overtones of the eternal.

This is the lesson that sustained Jacob. He came to rest on *a hard place*—his pillow a stone. God's watch-care changed that. "Surely the Lord is in this place; and I knew it not" (Genesis 28:16).

Wife—buried there in the kitchen—you will make the same discovery. Missionary—alone and recoiling from disease and ignorance around you—you will make the same discovery. Soldier—asking yourself, "Why am I here? How can this possibly matter?"—you will make the same discovery.

Look up! Then confess with Jacob in your hard place, "Surely the Lord is in this place; and I knew it not" (Genesis 28:16). Now, you know it, and things are *different*.

"AND BE NOT CONFORMED TO THIS WORLD"

Text: *"Wherefore Jesus also, that he might sanctify the people with his own blood, suffered without the gate. Let us go forth therefore unto him without the camp, bearing his reproach."*

Hebrews 13:12, 13

THE other day I stood at Calvary again in the city of Jerusalem. The surge of modern-day motor traffic forces 1970 upon you. Just below the brow, a bus terminal tries its best to turn your mind *forward* instead of *backward.* You force your gaze from the diesel-driven buses and look above a few feet and remember that the most important death in all history took place above those diesel-driven buses. Most of the brow is an unkempt cemetery today. Not many tourists scramble through the weeds, rocks, and grass. It has never been a thing of beauty.

Jesus Christ died there. The practices of His day are not difficult to trace. As an act of atonement, a beast was slaughtered before the altar. The sins of the people were loaded on the sacrificial animal. It was always the story of *substitution.* Some living thing had to die instead, so that the guilty might be absolved.

Then the *carcass* was taken outside the camp, or beyond the city's wall and burnt.

That is the picture the mind recalls that superimposes itself upon the movement of buses and 1970 equipment as you stand and gaze at a place called Calvary.

One day, hundreds of years ago, there was a substitutionary

offering for me. Jesus, like a criminal, was taken outside the walls of Jerusalem and destroyed. It's an unforgettable picture. No amount of tire squeal and exhaust-pipe roar and horn blowing in 1970 can erase the eternal meaning. It got to me again and again. "Wherefore Jesus also, that he might sanctify the people with his own blood, suffered without the gate."

Beyond what walls do the message and ministry of Jesus Christ reach? You can name many more than I am prepared to name in this service.

First, *Jesus Christ reaches beyond the wall of society.* The Nazarene was led outside because He dared to challenge the sophisticated standards of His generation.

He detonated established practices. He healed on the Sabbath. He dined with sinners. He treated women of shady and questionable backgrounds with respect and tenderness. He touched lepers. He uncovered religious hypocrisy. He interpreted Moses and the Law. He introduced new styles of evangelism.

It was disconcerting to the establishment. They excommunicated the blind man whom Jesus healed, and his parents, from the synagogue. They sought to destroy Lazarus. They spied and plotted to entangle Jesus in His words. Again and again He was incorrectly reported.

He challenged the worship of possessions. He never owned a boat or chariot. He never built a bank account or acquired property. *Jesus was different.* When He would not conform, society ostracized Him. He "suffered without the gate."

There is no suffering quite like the suffering of being *shut out.* I knew it for years when unmentionable tags describing the Pentecostal religion of my family were shouted across the school yards where I attended classes. There wasn't room in the ball game for me. I was never named to a school committee. My clothes and my language identified me. There was no room for a lad who wouldn't attend shows, cuss when angry, dance at parties, or drag on cigarettes. *I knew the sting of rejection.*

No wonder the thirst that has almost become a rage, has been *accreditation.* We want to be *accepted.* To do so we have changed our styles and our habits and moderated our beliefs. The popular preacher among us would never turn to this text: "Let us go forth therefore unto him without the camp, bearing his reproach." The emphasis has been to stay *within* the camp.

A minister of our time has underlined the fact that at Calvary there were three crosses. On two of them were men dying who had fallen below the accepted standards of society. *On the central cross was Jesus who had risen above the moral level of His time.* The reward of society for both was exactly the same—a cross.

I am as sure of one thing today as I was at the beginning of my religious experience. *To be a real Christian requires you to be different.* The message of Jesus Christ must challenge the dictates of a world system.

Most of us want to be *comfortable Christians.* We seek a paragon of personal attainment in being able to get along with everybody. So, what do you do with directives like these: "Having a form of godliness, but denying the power thereof: from such turn away?" (2 Timothy 3:5), or "Wherefore come out from among them, and be ye separate, saith the Lord, and touch not the unclean thing; and I will receive you?" (2 Corinthians 6:17), or "Love not the world, neither the things that are in the world?" (1 John 2:15).

Are these New Testament passages rhetoric, or are they *commands?* Make up your mind! A comfortable Christ could never have saved you. That is what I thought as I gazed at Calvary a few days ago.

Second, *Jesus Christ reaches beyond the wall of established holiness.* Religion repudiated Him even more strongly than the society of His day.

His *birth* was unacceptable. No synagogue wanted to include His birth record with the official minutes. To the orderly clerical mind everything from the stable to the virginity of Joseph was a sordid story too nasty to place beside the tenets of faith. *He knew what it was to be rejected by the Church.*

The Son of God was never advertised to be the convention speaker by the denominations of His day. They thought His country-style preaching unpolished. So His pulpits were *outside* —the side of a mountain or the shoreline.

Good people crucified Him. They gave Him "his grave with the wicked" (Isaiah 53:9). No fund was started for a memorial stained-glass window in the downtown church of His hometown of Nazareth.

His gospel is still *inclusive*. It seats a Jairus, a religious executive, with the Gadarene, out of whom He chased a thousand devils. There are never any *preferred* seats in His service.

Gradually, we all build our churches so *grand,* with lavish expenditure from air conditioning to marked, paved parking lots; that the needy of earth feel too frightened and too unwanted to come in. *We become our own prisoners.* We wrap and label our own "shibboleth," and the Woman-at-the-Well-of-Samaria and Zacchaeus are forever unwanted. We spend our time making rules about how to get to heaven.

Jesus Christ reached out and gathered me to heaven. He was neither Presbyterian nor Methodist, Lutheran nor Assemblies of God. He said: "For whosoever shall do the will of God, the same is my brother, and my sister, and mother" (Mark 3:35).

Third, *Jesus Christ reaches beyond the wall of time.* He would not allow His life to be circumscribed. He wanted His Name inscribed on something more eternal than massive piles of stone. Each city in this nation has its tower of memory. There is the Chrysler Building in New York City. There is the Fisher

Building in Detroit. But, look where you may on earth, and you will never find the Jesus Christ Building!

He believed it and practiced it. "Here we have no permanent home, we are seekers after the city which is to come" (see Hebrews 13:14).

Always Jesus was conscious that He came from God, and would return to God. In a very true sense, the world had no hold on Him. *It could not fence Him in.* His citizenship was above. He moved beyond the restricted area.

Mister, it's the biggest trap of all to be brainwashed and imagine this planet is our permanent home. *Do you know of any who have stayed?* Every day the shocking news arrives that another dear friend or some well-known celebrity has left. We strive so hard. We squirrel away so much. We build our walls higher and higher—*but never quite high enough to shut out death.*

The executive, managing surgeon of Parkland Hospital, Dallas, Texas, personally conducted me to the trauma room where President Kennedy made his hurried exit beyond the walls of fame, wealth, youth, and privilege. You may not leave from the same station—*but you and I will leave.*

We are *transients.* No advertising, no philosophy, no educational major can change that. Let me repeat words that you have sung, and pray that they may fall upon your ears with new and deeper meaning in the service:

Lord, I care not for riches, neither silver nor gold,
I would make sure of Heaven, I would enter the fold;
In the Book of Thy Kingdom with its pages so fair,
Tell me, Jesus, my Saviour, is my name written there?
Is my name written there, on the page white and fair?
Tell me, Jesus, my Saviour, is my name written there?

Lady, you will leave it all behind! Take a look at your

jewelry! Take a look at your party gowns and furs! Take a look at your needlepoint and tapestry! Take a look at your period furniture and modern appliances! You must part company.

Sir, there is an eternity out there! Take a look at your golf clubs! Take a look at your credit cards! Take a look at the new-model automobile parked in your driveway! Take a look at your factory! There is a farewell ahead. This Man "without the gate" left wearing only a loin cloth. The rest of His blood-stained clothes had become gamblers' items. *His inheritance was on the other side.*

I felt it again as I looked at Calvary—*He is there to receive us.* We will never find the peace we are searching, nor the contentment that makes a human life regal within the walls. "Let us go forth therefore unto him."

In the prize-winning play, *Death of a Salesman,* Willy Loman, in his sixties, loses his job. He is overwhelmed by despondency and despair. One night his son takes him out for the evening. As they leave, the wife of Willy Loman speaks quietly to her son: "Be kind to your father, son. *He is only a little boat looking for a harbor.*"

That is a great line. I thought of it as I looked toward the brow of Golgotha—"only a little boat looking for a harbor." That center Cross is earth's Harbor. Prostitutes, alcoholics, compulsive gamblers, rebels, drug addicts, the cynical are those "little boats looking for a harbor."

And Jesus Christ is looking for them! He is everyone's Saviour. So come!

A REVIVALTIME TESTIMONY

"I read the *Revivaltime* sermons I received last month over and over, and have decided to give my heart to Jesus. *Revivaltime* is an inspiration to me."

WHERE IS THY GOD?

Text: *"My tears have been my meat day and night, while they continually say unto me, Where is thy God?"*

Psalm 42:3

PEOPLE want more than church. They want authority. They want refuge. They want redemption. They want peace.

How can I justify my religious conviction today in the face of riot, ribald manners, and global ravage? How can I answer the sneer that says to me: "You go to church, you say prayers, you profess. But where is your God? What is He doing? Let's see the evidence if you expect us to believe!"

When I point to beauty, the unbeliever points to ugliness. When I point to answered prayers, the unbeliever points to prayers that have not been answered. *There's a counterargument for every argument we advance.*

I like what Jeremy Taylor said: "It is possible to be *sure* of a thing though not sure of the argument." The deep things can't be explained.

You can't explain, in a laboratory sense, why you love your wife. You can't explain why you prefer the music of Mozart against the music of Wagner. You can't explain why you feel differently toward the painting of Raphael than you do toward the painting of Rembrandt. In this sense, sir, a Christian can be quite sure of God, but hard pressed to find argument to tell you why he is sure.

Again! I am neither ignorant nor avoiding your question and indulging in generality, when I say, "God is *everywhere.*" He etches His presence everywhere.

I am always refreshed when I visit beautiful Cypress Gardens in our state of Florida. I love the words of welcome:

"If you'd have a mind at peace
A heart that cannot harden,
Go find a door that opens wide
Upon a lovely garden."

When you visit the gardens at Winter Haven, Florida, stop, as I always do, at *the Traveler's Tree.* It is an import. Read the inscription message.

"In its native habitat, the leaves normally fan out in an EAST-WEST direction. In addition to serving as a *compass,* it also stores a *quart of fresh water* in a cavity at the base of the leaves and when pierced, offers a refreshing drink to thirsty travellers."

That is the handiwork of an intelligent, loving, and volitional Personality. Someone *planned* it. Someone *cared enough.* Someone brought it into existence. There can be no other explanation. It isn't the product of happenstance.

The doubter wants God *pinpointed.* He wants more than the bees and the flowers and the Traveler's Tree. Where can he find God in this mixed-up world?

Mister, you will get a face-to-face answer by turning to the 30th chapter of the Book of Deuteronomy in the Old Testament. You aren't the first man to ask. Your doubts aren't anything new. Others before you have asked.

"For this commandment which I command thee this day, *it is not hidden from thee, neither is it far off.* It is not in heaven, that thou shouldest say, Who shall go up for us to heaven, and bring it unto us, that we may hear it, and do it? Neither is it beyond the sea, that thou shouldest say, Who shall go over the sea for us, and bring it unto us, that we may hear it, and do it? *But the word is very nigh unto thee, in thy mouth, and in thy heart, that thou mayest do it"* (Deuteronomy 30:11-14). That passage is in your Bible, sir.

God is not "up there," or "out there." He is "*in* there." God is not *extraneous.* He is *integral.* In Him, every moment of our lives, we live, we move, we have our being.

You may deny it, but you cannot prove it that life has no *depth.* Life is never *shallow.* It may be misspent, wasted, but never shallow. Grief is deep. Disillusionment is deep. Sin is painful. Loneliness is real. Yearning lingers. No! Life is more than just a bowl of cherries. If it were not—if you could deny loneliness, desertion, guilt, passion, memory, remorse, you could be an atheist. The fact is this. *You are only trying to be an atheist.* It is a discouraging effort.

No student of English literature can long escape *Conrad.* His stories of the sea are classic. In his great story, *Lord Jim,* the man who, to save his own life, deserts a sinking ship and leaves the Indian seamen to their fate, is saved *but he is never at peace again.* He lives night and day with his overwhelming sense of guilt and shame. It is like a built-in volcano that erupts. It is devastating. He cannot *escape.*

That is where you will find God—*inside.* "The word is very nigh unto thee, in thy mouth, and in thy heart, that thou mayest do it" (Deuteronomy 30:14).

Shakespeare knew it when he wrote *Macbeth.* After Macbeth murders Duncan, he groans:

What hands are here? Ha! they pluck out mine eyes!
Will all great Neptune's ocean wash this blood
Clean from my hand? No; this my hand will rather
The multitudinous seas incarnadine,
Making the green one red.

Like Pontius Pilate, Macbeth could not wash away the blood of murder. He had to live with his crime. The ceaseless monitor was within. That was the warning to Cain: "If thou doest not well, sin lieth at the door" (Genesis 4:7).

You can't change the rules, mister. "Be sure your sin will find you out" (Numbers 32:23). You are never secure. Sin makes you a fugitive. You ask me, "Where is thy God?" I answer, *Within.* "The word is very nigh unto thee, in thy mouth, and in thy heart, that thou mayest do it" (Deuteronomy 30:14). You ask for specifics. That is a *specific.*

Let's look at the other side of the coin! Paul knew it when he cried, "O the *depth* of the riches both of the wisdom and knowledge of God! how unsearchable are his judgments, and his ways past finding out!" (Romans 11:33).

Each of us has similar great moments of reflection. They are there when I am deeply moved by music or drama. They are there when I stand by the dying. They are there when I take a sweet babe and dedicate the child to God's care and service. Oh, yes! Suddenly I am aware of something more than groceries and automobile fumes and clothes to be cleaned and pressed and classes in the morning. I sense a Presence—*the Eternal.* Again and again I experience it—"deep calling unto deep"—the eternal dialogue. God knows how to get hold of us, fellow! *He lets you know that He is there.*

Not long ago this group of Singing Evangelists, who work with me, were ministering to you the words of an old Wesleyan song: "I need no other argument. I need no other plea—than Jesus died, and that he died for me." And as I sat on this platform, waiting to step to the microphone, I felt once more as I had felt as a young man in my home city of Toronto, Canada.

I could hear again the call of the trumpets, cornets, and French horns of that city's great Salvation Army bands—and then the muffled drums as the songsters' brigade of Salvation Army lassies sang it out along the street, and their skirts swayed in perfect cadence with the beat: "I need no other argument. I need no other plea—than Jesus died, and that He died for me."

I stood as a young man on the curb, spellbound. It was more than spritely tune and splash of uniform that raised goosepimples on my flesh. The Spirit of God was speaking to me. It had deep, deep significance. "The word is very nigh unto thee, in thy mouth, and in thy heart, that thou mayest do it" (Deuteronomy 30:14).

Then, sir, *I can discover Him in those men and women who have dedicated their lives to His great purposes.*

Read Ernest Gordon's book, *Miracle on the River Kwai.* That infamous Japanese prison camp, during World War II, deep in the heart of the jungle, was an excellent place in which to ask the question, "Where is thy God?" But God came to Ernest Gordon in two Christian corporals, Miller and Moore, who so patiently nursed him back to health.

I'll never forget the testimony of one of our great Olympic runners, who served in the Marines, and who was taken prisoner by the Japanese. Emaciated and nauseated by confinement, and at the point of collapse, one day a giant Japanese guard said to him in broken English, "You be a Christian?" And when the American nodded assent, the guard smiled, "I be a Christian too!", and smuggled extra rations to his prisoner at the risk of being discovered and instantly shot. *God was in that Japanese guard.*

There is a striking marginal translation of a verse in the Book of Judges. It says, "The Spirit of the Lord clothed himself with Gideon." Remember that! *God clothes Himself again and again.* He clothed Himself in former times with Amos and Jeremiah and Paul. He clothed Himself with Jerome and Augustine and Luther and Wesley. And, mister, God hasn't gone out of business.

Alfred Noyes, the poet, once wrote: "If ever I had any doubts about the fundamental realities of religion, they could always be dispelled by one memory, the light upon my father's face as he came back from early Communion." I say that about my parents. There was no other answer. *God lived in them.*

I have a very dear friend, whom I have known for at least 45 years, a Jewish news-vendor in Toronto, Canada. He, like myself, is in his senior years. Educationally, Isadore Kayfitz never got as far as junior high school. He has stood in front of the city's fortresses of high finance in the heat of the summer and the chill of the winter. But I'll tell you this about Isadore. Not only do many of the giants of Canada's trade and commerce depend upon Isadore for their news journals, but they depend upon him, year after year, *for a witness.* They see in him, and his personal, happy greeting to them, what they expect when they ask, "Where is thy God?"

I want you to remember something I am going to tell you, because it is true. *The biggest argument for God is a life that needs God to explain it.* There are people in your presence, sir, that could not live as they do unless God were living through them.

The supreme answer is in Jesus Christ. "God was *in* Christ, reconciling the world unto himself" (2 Corinthians 5:19). There is no other answer to this Man's appearance across the pages of history. "The Word was made flesh, and dwelt among us" (John 1:14).

Yes, sir, you'll find God! Look again—then *believe.*

A REVIVALTIME TESTIMONY

"This morning, as I sat and listened to *Revivaltime,* I began to think. Right there I decided that I would take Christ as my personal Saviour. I am 16."

A RADIO INVITATION

Great victories are being won at this long, long altar that stretches thousands of miles along the Revivaltime network. So, find a place to kneel.

The quickest way to know God's presence is to enter with thanksgiving and praise. Begin to thank God for everything that is good. You are fortunate in so many, many ways! I have my sight, my speech, my food, my friends—and, best of all, *my salvation.* Oh, yes! I have my problems and my needs—but these would threaten to be catastrophies without my blessings. So, I am here with you, confident that God will help me find a way to be victorious.

Let our Heavenly Father strengthen you! In a moment or two you will feel *able.* That is what such communion accomplishes. You realize that you are not alone. There is unlimited help. Now, pray as I pray:

"Heavenly Father, we come in, and through, and by Thy Son, Jesus Christ. We become 'more than conquerors' through Him.

"Let this be our week of victory. *And each victory will be credited to Thee.* Strengthen our testimonies for Thee.

"Cleanse us from all unrighteousness. Make us evangelists to this generation of confused souls. Fill us to overflowing with blessed assurance.

"Do a new thing among us in healing the sick. I pray Thee, extend life and health along this altar. *Destroy disease that is destroying us.*

"I ask these favors in the Name that is above all names. Amen."

There is revival in our souls. I feel it. I know this week will be a week of *exciting adventure* for this congregation. People are going to be saved. Sick bodies will be healed. And the gifts of the Spirit will be poured out. So, praise God with me!

You and I are in blessed hands! The Comforter is directing Calvary's victory through us—for "it is not by might, nor by power, but by My Spirit, saith the Lord."

THUNDER

Text: *"I answered you in the secret place of thunder."*
Psalm 81:7, *Goodspeed*

IN Missouri, especially in the Ozarks, we are acquainted with thunder. It cannonades here until I have been lifted from the mattress. I have never grown fond of thunder. Every element, *unleashed,* can *humble* me in a hurry.

Today we can explain this phenomenon of nature. Our radar screens can, and do, forewarn us of its approach. But science hasn't made me any more fond of it. I am still intimidated. Given a choice, I wouldn't select thunder as entertainment. There is something primitive about it.

Away back in the centuries of the Old Testament, God was associated with thunder. It "thundered" at Sinai when the Law was given. Old Testament preachers connected awe and majesty with thunder when they used it for a simile. But there is more!

The entire text reads: "In *trouble* you called and I rescued you; I answered you in the secret place of thunder" (Psalm 81:7, Goodspeed). The roar and booming power, the roll and the crescendo of what I hear, the Psalmist says, is likened to the arrival of God Himself, when I call upon Him.

That swift fighter plane that streaks across the atmosphere, out of sight, but ominous, because its boom breaks the sound barrier, is minuscule compared to the "thunder" of *God's chariot* as He charges to my defense. "I answered you in the secret place of thunder."

That "thundercloud" was there in the Wilderness to escort

Israel and preserve her from the devourings of ambitious enemies.

I'll tell you this, sir! *God can reach me in a hurry.* There is no speed on record like God's help. "God is . . . a very *present help* in trouble" (Psalm 46:1). He is *instant.* "Before they call, I will answer; and while they are yet speaking, I will hear" (Isaiah 65:24). The air force of every nation would like to achieve such an alert and response.

David prayed: "O God, be not far from me: O my God, *make haste* for my help" (Psalm 71:12). There are times when you can't wait for a committee.

Elijah got help on Mount Carmel in less than 15 seconds. He couldn't have waited a half hour. The demonstrators were in an ugly mood. Violence was in the air. It was provocative. So God's man prayed: "Hear me, O Lord, hear me, that this people may know that thou art the Lord God, and that thou hast turned their heart back again. Then the fire of the Lord fell . . ." (1 Kings 18:37, 38).

No power of hell can compete. "I answered you in the secret place of thunder." No wonder Luke describes it "as of a rushing mighty wind" (Acts 2:2). God has all the force necessary to be at our side before the aggressor can violate our safety. I believe that. I have experienced it.

I stood to speak one time in a great summer convention before several thousands. I had gone to the platform in the Name of Jesus. That week I had had considerable dental surgery. My bite and means of shaping my words had to be rearranged. Moments before I was announced to speak, I could not make myself understood to those who sat with me on the platform. I scribbled a note to the chairman telling him what had happened to me. Suddenly I was announced to speak. *I needed help in a hurry.* As I opened my Bible and my mouth to read God's Word, I discovered that I could speak as clearly and as distinctly as you have ever heard me speak.

Count on it, friend of God! "I answered you in the secret place of thunder." God's help is always on the *alert,* and He breaks the sound barrier crashing to your deliverance. God will meet your need, lady, where you *are* from where He *is.* He bridges the distance before you can count.

I'll tell you another thing. *There is enough power available.* Job speaks about "the thunder of his power" (Job 26:14). In the Book of the Revelation, thunderings are said to proceed out of the throne of God's sovereignty.

There is a supreme headquarters to this universe. Decisions are rendered. It isn't all vague and murky. I think we are busier *debunking* on our campuses than we are *searching.* It has become smart to spoof at God and ridicule those who believe in Supreme Authority and Intelligence.

It isn't that easy, student! Go back to your classroom and your microscope. It is inconceivable that the intricate mechanisms basic to survival of small creatures could have developed without the influence of a higher Power.

This is the season in which to take a good look at the *mosquito.* You will discover several organs there that could not conceivably have been developed through evolution. The mosquito has two double-edged swords for piercing the skin, and two rotary drills for boring. It uses an anesthetic so you won't feel the stabbing, and it dilutes the blood so it won't clog up the two "soda straws" it uses to drink the blood. It uses one of the straws to pump saliva in, and the other to draw the blood out. Try and duplicate that action—using two straws simultaneously—one going in, or *inhaling* and the other going out, or *exhaling!* That ability in the mosquito isn't there by accident.

I'll tell you another fact about that little pest. The wingbeat of that insect is 35,220 a minute. That rate produces the perfect tone to stimulate the growth of corn. Scientists have discovered that corn planted in an environment where that *tone* is *constant,* grows twice the normal rate. Scientists are inclined to believe that there is an *insect wingbeat* geared to each plant. Bananas are now grown with a certain tone played constantly in the plantation to stimulate their growth.

God's power makes a believer out of you. God's claim, sir, is authoritative and incontestable.

Personally, I am glad for that *greatness.* I rejoice in the thunder of His majesty. No one can escape the evidence of this Authority. You may *rebel,* but you cannot *escape.* Like "thunder," there is an *ultimatum.*

A God that is not *all-powerful* is not a God at all. Jesus Christ, God in the Flesh, demonstrated authority over every situation. "What manner of man is this, that even the winds and the sea obey him!" (Matthew 8:27). Demons were as subject. "For he said . . . Come out of the man, thou unclean spirit" (Mark 5:8). No disease was an unsolved puzzle. "And when he had called unto him his twelve disciples, he gave them power . . . to heal *all manner* of sickness and *all manner* of disease" (Matthew 10:1).

Yes, the Name of Jesus comes up "like thunder" against every enemy of mankind. God is the El-Shaddai—the *all-sufficient* One. You can't exhaust Him with your problem.

A further truth contained in this text suggests the *endless discovery* that fascinates us about God. *There is always more to know about God.* The text says, "I answered you in the *secret* place of thunder."

Take a long look at that word "secret," preacher! It's like the song says: "*Deeper,* deeper in the love of Jesus . . . *higher,* higher in the school of wisdom . . ." There's no end to it.

God's designs are always marked "top secret." Slowly they are unfolded to His intimates. "The secret of the Lord is with them that fear him" (Psalm 25:14).

Paul discovered and shared with mankind so many *mysteries.* He says of himself: "And lest I should be exalted above measure *through the abundance of the revelations,* there was given to me a thorn in the flesh, the messenger . . . lest I should be exalted above measure" (2 Corinthians 12:7).

Paul's penetration and explanation of God's final intent toward the believer was a far greater breakthrough than Einstein's discovery and reduction to formula of the law of relativity. "Behold, I show you a mystery; We shall not all sleep, but we shall all be changed, in a moment, in the twinkling of an eye, at the last trump: for the trumpet shall sound, and the dead shall be raised incorruptible, and we shall be changed. For this corruptible must put on incorruption, and this mortal must put on immortality" (1 Corinthians 15:51-53). *Something thundered again and again in Paul's soul.*

That same privilege is for the believer today. "Let a man so account of us, as of the ministers of Christ, and *stewards* of the mysteries of God" (1 Corinthians 4:1). I want something—some precious eternal truth—to "thunder" in my soul as I stand at the pulpit. I believe this with all my soul, preacher, that God is anxious to unfold revelation and spiritual intent toward mankind and His disposition toward the Church to those of us who will become present-day "*stewards* of the mysteries of God" (1 Corinthians 4:1). That position immediately rebukes the irreverence, the lewdness, the profanity of this hour.

God is not a joke, Mr. Comedian! He is still that *Mystery* that fascinates a young scientist-soldier like Moses, beholding the bush aflame: "I will now turn aside, and see this great sight, *why* . . ." (Exodus 3:3).

That is the attitude and respect of every great scientist who has added to this planet's archives. God doesn't yield to your flippancy, entertainer! He is bigger than your cheap vulgarity.

Charles Lamb recorded how the poet Wordsworth, in an unusually egotistical moment, was caught remarking that he did not "see much difficulty in writing like Shakespeare, if he had a mind to try it." Charles Lamb added acidly, "that *nothing is wanting but the mind.*"

Don't make mockery of God, sinner! We have just scratched the surface. There is endless discovery. The next generation will know more of God's secrets than we have known—as much a difference between grandfather's discovery of the automobile and our discovery of supersonic jet plane.

Job expresses the awe of a real scientist. "Lo, these are but the outskirts of his ways; and how small a whisper do we hear of him! But the thunder of his power who can understand?" (Job 26:14, ASV). Ah, yes! There's enough *mystery* left over for this generation to explore.

Let me say one more thing to you out of this text. *That thunderclap seems right next to you.* Let me talk to you for a moment about *God's nearness.* God has never, never been *remote* from mankind. You are always conscious of His Presence. It isn't a distant, fading echo. It is a fullness that filleth all things. God has interjected Himself into the affairs of mankind. *God didn't ask permission for Calvary.* He always comes seeking. God lets you know He is there.

There is a Father to this whole affair. "God was in Christ, reconciling the world unto himself" (2 Corinthians 5:19). God *answers.* That means God is *concerned.* "I answered you in the secret place of thunder." That is your assurance. God *answers.*

God's mercy is louder than Satan's mismanagement of your life, mister. An old Welsh preacher, referring to the burying of Moses, explained: "In that burial not only was the body buried, but also the grave and the graveyard. 'No man knoweth of his sepulchre unto this day.' " That is the way God buries your sin —*without a trace.*

That "thunder" won't *hurt* you, lady. It never will. Its message is presence. You can't ignore it. God *reminds* you again and again of His thoughts and acts toward you. We should not have to be prompted and sharply brought to attention. But negligence is the virus of human nature. So God *reminds* us.

Think now, sir, how indebted you are for the "answers" you have experienced in the past. Then humbly recognize God's claims. Do it now.

A REVIVALTIME TESTIMONY

"When listening to your broadcast, it is truly 'revival time.' In the hearts of 'born-again Christians,' your program brings to life the newness of God's grace. It is like a 'well of water springing up to eternal life.' It revives the entire life."

WHAT TO PREACH WHEN THERE IS NO ONE THERE BUT CHRISTIANS!

Text: *"I am eager to preach the gospel to you in Rome also."*
Romans 1:15, *Weymouth*

SO many evangelists face this situation. They are gospel preachers, *but there are no sinners in the audience.* What shall they preach? The answer is *the gospel.* But does the congregation need it? Do they want it? Paul thought so.

The readers of his letter belonged to Christ. They were saints by vocation. They were Roman believers. *Why should Paul preach the gospel to them?*

I think it is this situation, multiplied again and again, that makes our evangelists want to go overseas and face audiences on mission fields where there are large percentages of unconverted. The evangelist doesn't know what to preach at home. Here is Paul's answer! *Preach the gospel.*

A fear abides that the reaction on a Monday or Tuesday night church service may be: "We have heard all this before. We do not need it. We do not want it. Show us some pictures. Entertain us with music. Cut the service short." *And the evangelists grow fewer in number.*

You also face a certain amount of pride. "To whom is he talking? Does he think we are sinners?" *And little by little that church is without gospel preaching.*

Paul admits he is going to preach the gospel to Christians. *Why?* What could be his purpose?

If some church member objects, I should ask that church member: "Do you object to the communion service being observed repeatedly?" In that service I proclaim the gospel. I set forth His death and resurrection.

Why repeat this service? What *value* is there? Paul says that a gospel testimony meeting is an asset. I will read you Ephesians 4:29: "Let no corrupt communication proceed out of your mouth, but that which is good to the use of edifying, *that it may minister grace unto the hearers.*"

I'll tell you, sir, what I feel when I preach the gospel to believers. I feel that the words of the preacher can cease to be mere words. They can become, under Holy Ghost anointing and direction, *the linguistic bread and wine for the believer.* "That it may minister grace unto the hearers" (Ephesians 4:29).

First, *every time I preach the gospel my faith is strengthened and the faith of the audience is strengthened.* Salvation is an experience that enriches again and again each time memory is quickened. It is a love story that never loses its thrill.

I remember when I was without citizenship. I was a foreigner to God. I was without privilege and sanctuary. *A gospel preacher helps me relive the miracle of acceptance.*

I sat one evening with Mrs. Ward in the beautiful, outdoor forum, edged by gardens and air-conditioned by the breezes of a Hawaiian beach, and listened, under the stars, to the Honolulu Symphony Orchestra. Frequently I glanced at other faces. Each was deep in his own memories. That seemed to be the purpose of the music and the skillful artists. The magic of their talent carried us *back*, and perhaps *forward* a little as well.

The evangelist performs the same service. Suddenly the hearer is reliving the magic, the miracle, the experience of salvation. It is a gracious and enjoyable warmth. So, "Tell me the old, old story!" It's like that classic the artist presents at every concert. He knows the effect upon the listener. I am not ashamed of that tear that comes again. I am not embarrassed by that lump in my throat that I experience again. It is good for me. *When I stop feeling like that in church, I am in jeopardy.*

I am not mortified, even as a preacher, to tell you that gospel music, sung in the power of the Spirit, gets to me. I feel *alive* with it. I want to *go* with it. It finds chords within me that start to vibrate. It does the same thing to me that the martial music of Sousa's "Stars and Stripes Forever" does to a veteran. Each battle comes back with force. Each marching comrade keeps step. Each test of strength is recalled.

So often I pray in my heart: "Choir, I want to hear that melody. Sing my salvation loud and clear. Let me live it again with all the force I knew when I was born again."

No sir, my gospel soloist—you are not an *intruder.* You are welcome. "I Will Sing of My Redeemer." Please help me to do it. I want that from you, Mister Musician, more than I want anything else. Sing to *me!* And while you do, I will reaffirm my pledge and my loyalty to Jesus Christ.

They play the national anthem at every ball game. Why? Why does the crowd arise? Why are thousands of pairs of eyes turned toward the flag? Why don't audiences react, and say: "We don't want it. We don't need it. What do you take us for—aliens?"

No! It reminds us of our privileges. It tells me that *I belong.* I become aware that I have a personal stake in the nation. Suddenly I know what home, security, freedom, and opportunity are worth. So I stand at attention. I remove my hat. I have done it all a thousand times before, but the first bar of the national anthem brings me to my feet. The gospel is like that, preacher.

Paul didn't argue. His position was this. "Woe is unto me, if I preach not the gospel!" (1 Corinthians 9:16). It is the *power* of God. Introduce it into any kind of service, and there will be a *stir*. Other sagas and properties stale. Their length of viewing on television is short-lived. A handful survive a dozen years of ratings. The gospel is different. *It is eternal life*. It grows sweeter as the years roll by. You are in trouble when you substitute.

Second, the gospel is *taught* as well as preached. There is a difference. "I still have much to tell you," said Jesus (see John 16:12). The gospel has a thousand splendors to it. It is a message of such dazzling beauty that an audience is entranced.

There are the *shadows* and *types* of the Old Testament. There are the *close-ups* given by Matthew, Mark, Luke, and John. There are the *applications to human tangles* given in the Epistles. There are the *mysteries* unfolded by Paul and John. It is set forth in *ballad* in the Psalms. We have the "more sure word of prophecy" (2 Peter 1:19). The great and beloved physician, Luke, documents case histories and substantiates *healing* in the gospel. There is a new vignette for every service.

You don't realize what a contract you have until some anointed gospel preacher explains the provisions to you. I have been studying the doctrine of salvation every day of my ministry, and I feel that I have only scratched the surface. I long to be able to tell you intelligently and forthrightly how much there is in Christ.

The more gospel you know, the better Christian you will be.

I remember when an evangelist brought me *security*. I loved Jesus, but my trust in Him hadn't taken root nor matured. I was miserably fearful. Suddenly I faced the source and strength of my salvation. Beyond my feelings and strivings there was this *anchor*. "He that heareth my word (I had done that), and believeth on him that sent me (I needed to do that), hath everlasting life" (John 5:24).

I needed to realize that I was saved because *God wanted* me saved. God sent Christ. Calvary is God's idea. My redemption was designed before the foundation of the world. God is my *Friend*. I believe that. I lean on that. It erases the ups and downs in my life. Paul says: "If God be for us, who can be against us?" (Romans 8:31). I needed to be *taught* that.

Then I could read and appreciate: "I . . . will be a Father unto you, and ye shall be my sons and daughters, saith the Lord Almighty" (2 Corinthians 6:17, 18).

"My sons and daughters you shall be
  Through the atoning blood;
And you shall claim and find in Me
  A Father and a God."

Yes, mister evangelist, you *teach* the gospel! "I commend you to God," said Paul, "and to the word of his grace, which is able to *build* . . ." (Acts 20:32). It builds spirituality. An older minister put it this way to student ministers: "In the evening service I said, 'Come to Jesus,' and in the morning service I said, 'Come *nearer* to Jesus.'" Preach the gospel, and you will build character.

Third, the gospel must be *applied.* The gospel is a claim on a man or woman's obedience. Hearing is not enough. Paul exhorted the Philippian believers to live in a manner that would be *worthy* of the gospel.

That is the question that is always before me. "How can I be an effective advertisement for the gospel?"

Do I keep my cool under provocative circumstances? Am I quick and generous to forgive? Am I compassionate? Am I an instrument, or am I a sponge? Does the public see Jesus in me? What about my own family, or my employees? What impression have I made?

Paul said that he was "set" for the defense of the gospel. The attack is bold. The church could be the next target, subject to the same assault as our campuses. *Are you at your post of duty?* There are attacks that must be repelled. Will you allow the gospel to be eliminated from your community by *default?* Are you "set" for the defense of the gospel? Are you going to allow the soldiers of hell to sweep it out of our school system? Are you going to protest the dance and the cocktail and the card party in the church?

The believer needs answers to the questions professional agitators raise. *Give that believer those gospel answers when you preach, evangelist!* Provide the ammunition.

Fourth, *experience* the gospel before the eyes of your congregation. Something happens *in* you, and *to* you, preacher, as you declare the gospel. It will charm and intoxicate your audiences.

Every preacher should have G. H. Morrison in his library. The Scot was a great pulpiteer. He had a style that was deceptively simple. Sincerity oozed out of him. Great numbers of professional men heard him. All week they had been immersed in the world—lawyers, merchants, professors. They saw the seamy side of life. They saw the squalor of the human mind. They moved amid sin and sordidness. And then they came to hear Morrison. They came to listen, and to watch a man who knew Jesus, a man who spoke of the Saviour and loved Him with all his heart. Then they could go back into the world *refreshed* and with a new vision.

Every congregation needs a lot of the same. They need to witness the gospel consuming a man. They need to be *convinced* again and again. When a preacher quits preaching the gospel, the congregation begins to ask questions.

I want to satisfy something in you when I preach—quench a thirst—answer a hunger. At no time do I ever wish to dominate your faith. That is not my goal. I want to be a helper of your joy. When you leave this service, my prayer is that you may say, "He *helped me.*" I know this. The gospel must sweep over *my* soul before it can saturate *yours.*

Oh, yes! I have been preaching the gospel for a long time. Rarely does a day pass that I am not in the pulpit. Yet as I stand before this network of microphones, this text reflects that inner urge, "I am eager to preach the gospel to you . . . also." It's something that I want to tell to you, and tell it to you as often as I can. And when you believe, I have all the reward I'll ever crave.

A REVIVALTIME TESTIMONY

"The *Revivaltime* broadcast is certainly a great boost to thousands around the world. There are people I know who regularly listen, even though they are not saved. The anointing grips them in a way no other power could."

SEVEN SNEEZES

Text: *"Then he returned, and walked in the house to and fro; and went up, and stretched himself upon him: and the child sneezed seven times, and the child opened his eyes."*

2 *Kings* 4:35

NOT long ago I was the pulpit guest at the First Assembly of God at Dyersburg, Tennessee. Pastor Jerald Ogg drew my attention to this passage and shared with me his interest in this Old Testament account. It is *provocative and dramatic.*

Elisha must be reckoned as one of the greatest evangelists of all times. What he accomplished through the Spirit of God was always headline copy. Under him, General Naaman of the Syrian armies lost his leprosy. Under him, sentence against Jezebel was executed. This passage describes his confrontation with death which lay upon a youth, *for whom God had intended better things.*

Perhaps Webster, of dictionary fame, can give us a clue to finding a truth, or truths, involved in this narrative. He says to sneeze is *to drive out, or get rid of.*

May the impact of godly initiative arouse the youth of this globe, and quicken them out of a deadly stupor which lays upon them! I long to see a powerful and complete expulsion of this seven-headed monster.

First, the *malaise of unbelief must be expelled.* It is a killer. Paul found the key. "If thou . . . shalt believe in thine *heart*" (Romans 10:9). That is where defeat or victory lodges. Lip service to ideals is only a charade, an act, unless it is made meaningful by inside decision.

Unbelief is the cancer of the soul. Elisha faced it in public officials on occasion. One, highly placed, sneered at his declaration of faith, and said: "Behold, *if the Lord would* make windows in heaven, might this thing be?" (2 Kings 7:2).

Unbelief is deadly. It can initiate panic. It can create economic disaster. It can fold battle lines and start retreat. It can empty churches. It can shatter marriages. It can cripple bodies.

The stock market reflects it instantaneously. The song service is either vibrant or monotonous. The parting kiss is either a promise or a perfunctory gesture. The ball game lags or sparkles. The doctor looks for either fight or failure in his patient. *Medicines won't help a person who doesn't want to make it.* Belief says, "I can."

Faith gives you David's victory over Goliath. Unbelief gives you the disaster in the Garden of Eden. Faith gives you Daniel. Unbelief gives you King Saul. Faith writes a Book of Acts. Unbelief burns libraries and wrecks campuses.

A strawberry can teach you, young man! Inherent in that berry is a vigor that says: "The sun, the rain, the earth are my portion. I will be a strawberry, not a cucumber, an onion, or a green pea. I will have my own shade of red, and not that of a radish or an apple. I will produce the flavor and the response I was created to produce. There aren't enough devils in hell to make me different to what God intended me to be." That is what that strawberry affirms. There is that same potential in you, young man. Let God have it and use it to His glory!

Second, *the virus of pride must be extracted.* Pride heads the list of seven things which are an abomination to God. "A proud look, a lying tongue, and hands that shed innocent blood, a heart that deviseth wicked imaginations, feet that be swift in running to mischief, a false witness that speaketh lies, and he that soweth discord among brethren" (Proverbs 6:17-19).

And pride heads the list of things most of us dislike in the other person. It's a hairy cliche, but still true. If some folk could buy themselves for what they are really worth and sell themselves for what they think they are worth, they would be self-made millionaires. *Pride is another killer.* "Pride goeth before destruction, and a haughty spirit before a fall" (Proverbs 16:18).

Here is the rule! "And whosoever shall exalt himself shall be abased; and he that shall humble himself shall be exalted" (Matthew 23:12). *The way to strength is through service.* Every great corporation on earth has proven it. The genuine desire to help creates wealth. One of the frightening signs is the dearth of service. Where can you get a painter, or plumber, or gardener, or doctor?

Not long ago I ministered in an East Central Illinois community. They are without a dentist. The community has raised $15,000, as a bonus, attempting to attract some young dentist to the community. The committee has sent several hundred inquiries to prospective dental graduates of our universities. They received only one reply.

Sometimes you wonder whether or not anyone wants to *work.* The Son of God said: "My Father worketh hitherto, *and I work*" (John 5:17). Yes, sir, preacher! He *worked.* He worked in that carpenter shop and He worked long, long hours in His evangelism. He never felt it beneath Him, or too dusty a task, to go the extra mile.

Third, *greed has got to go.* Nothing will take the life out of you so quickly as greed. It did the man, who said, "I shall build me yet *greater barns*" (see Luke 12:18). He strangled his own soul.

I'll tell you this, young man! You let greed get hold of you, *and you will experience the bottomless pit.* "Let your conversation be without covetousness; and be content with such things as ye have: for he hath said, I will never leave thee, nor forsake thee" (Hebrews 13:5).

So, choose your company! You can mortgage your soul and try

to keep step with the financially overextended, bragging set of social climbers, or you can move steadily toward heaven in the fellowship of Jesus Christ.

One contact with Jesus Christ renovated Zaccheus. He said: "Lord, the half of my goods I give to the poor; and if I have taken any thing from any man by false accusation, I restore him fourfold. And Jesus said, . . . This day is salvation come to this house" (Luke 19:8, 9).

You are in slime up to your chin, mister, when you become so greedy that you even stoop to blackmail. Zaccheus' sneeze was one of the greatest sneezes in history. *He got rid of greed right now.*

Fourth, *the deadly insert of discouragement must be dislodged.* Self-pity and depression can paralyze you. Suddenly you collapse under an avalanche of bad news. It's easy to surrender, to say: "What's the use? Everybody is serving Baal. No one cares any longer. I, only I, am left." *That is exactly what the discourager, the devil, wants you to think.*

Satan is the greatest "con-artist" in the universe. He will convince you that wrong is right if you listen long enough. He will persuade you that you are fighting a phony battle; that the ideas of God and Christian character are hangovers from an unenlightened past, and that man is *smarter* today. He leans on himself.

David often fought his way out of that swamp. He said: "O my God, my soul is cast down within me: therefore will I remember thee" (Psalm 42:6). Think back, sir, and you will recall the direction and provision of God for you. "The Lord is the portion of mine inheritance and of my cup: *thou maintainest my lot*" (Psalm 16:5). God isn't through with history.

Fifth, *hate will keep you down longer than anything I know.* It is poison. Love is the only known vaccine. Hate carries insanity. It blinds a person to consequences. It is a tiger in the system. It spreads jealousy and revenge and anarchy through the soul. "If any man say, I love God, and hateth his brother, he is a liar: for he that loveth not his brother whom he hath seen, how can he love God whom he hath not seen?" (1 John 4:20). Mister, try that on for size!

That thing in you will explode and tear you to pieces. Get rid of it!

Calvary can stop that in you, lady. You got a raw deal. Someone let you down. You took the rap while others vanished. I know how those things can *fester.* It isn't easy to utter that word "forgive"—*but you start living again.*

Sixth, *tension must be relieved.* There are stress and strain. Anxiety tightens neck and stomach muscles.

Guilt pounds at you until headaches develop that no prescription can stop. Sleepless nights multiply. And the torment and weariness increase.

You have tried the bottle. You have tried the needle. You have tried the wild party. You have tried the gambling casino. But you need more than fantasy. You need *peace.*

I am glad to tell you that the invitation still stands. "Come unto me, all ye that labor and are heavy laden, and I will give you *rest*" (Matthew 11:28). That is what you want more than anything in this world—rest. You can *confide* in Him. I have. I have told the Son of God things I wouldn't breathe to a soul on earth. I accept His promise to me. "Ye shall find rest unto your souls" (Matthew 11:29). The burden is lifted.

Seven, *selfishness must be erased.* There is a law of life which says: "For whosoever will save his life shall lose it: and whosoever will lose his life for my sake shall find it" (Matthew 16:25). You lie in a state of spiritual death until you give your life away to God. Paul stated his case again and again. He appraised his life as, "Paul, a *servant* of Jesus Christ" (Romans 1:1).

It is not enough fulfillment to be a member of some fine denomination or to attend some Bible class regularly. Are you a *servant* of Jesus Christ? Are you instantly at His beck and call?

Selfishness will destroy you. One man learned that lesson too late. He cried out in the only unselfish moment of his existence: "I have five brethren (warn them); . . . lest they also come into this place of torment" (Luke 16:28).

That hell starts, mister, with *unconcern.* You wrap yourself in a wardrobe of fine clothes and "fare sumptuously every day" while others lie at your gate "full of sores," and I'll guarantee you'll wake up on the wrong side.

These are the things that can kill a generation. Every generation is a miracle of God. There is a verse in this passage that says: "And when the child was grown, it fell on a day, that he went out to his father to the reapers" (2 Kings 4:18).

That moment of opportunity and responsibility comes to every generation. Can the boy and the girl meet the challenge? Will he and she leave behind a vaccine for polio, color television, speed faster than sound, interplanetary travel, finer food and meat, refrigeration, a conquest of illiteracy with schools for everyone, missionary passion and evangelism—or will your generation leave a shambles of moral and material and social wreckage?

Elisha "went up, and lay upon the (youth), and put his mouth upon his mouth, and his eyes upon his eyes, and his hands upon his hands: and he stretched himself upon the (youth); and the flesh of the (youth) waxed warm" (2 Kings 4:34).

That is what it takes to revive a generation that has caved in under the pressures of the day. That is how to close the so-called generation gap. It will take a personal interest. Heat is the answer to cold. God's Spirit within can quicken the casualties and disappointments that crush our souls. "And the (youth) opened his eyes" (2 Kings 4:35). *I believe in that kind of revival.*

It is that person-to-person resuscitation that will get a stricken generation back on its feet. There is still power in and through and by the man of God to drive out these agents of death. I believe it will come again. Suddenly there will be signs of life.

A REVIVALTIME TESTIMONY

"After listening to *Revivaltime* for more than 16 months, I followed your suggestion and found my way to an Assemblies of God church of which I am now an active and happy member."

IS A PERSON WHO HAS NEVER HEARD THE GOSPEL REJECTED?

Text: *"Go ye into all the world, and preach the gospel to every creature."*

Mark 16:15

THE gospel is preached *more* than it has ever been preached. There are more facilities and more preachers and more insistence. Yet multiple millions have passed without hearing, and great pockets of humanity today have not heard. *What is their position?*

The *easy* thing to say is this. As long as a person is living up to the light he or she may have, God cannot reject such a person. Everyone follows some code, some standard. Shouldn't that person be judged by his effort to achieve excellence under that code or standard?

Do not professing Christians fail again and again to meet the requirements of the spiritual light they receive? God forgives. Isn't it axiomatic that the same God would forgive the man or woman, who has never heard the gospel, but who *tries* the best he or she can to excel?

It's a favorite argument. It has been evangelized in many circles. What is the truth?

There are many enviable things to be discovered on this planet. You can discover reverence, sincerity, faith, and zeal. *Are these saving qualities*?

Every code, every standard, every religious effort prove one thing. *A human being is not an animal.* There is something called a soul. A sense of responsibility and accountability does exist. It is universal. Instinctively, a human being knows that he is related to a Higher Power. Thus there is an effort to effect appeasement or reconciliation. There is a compulsion, an inner motivation, that can be found wherever the explorer has been. The method chosen may be wrong, but it is there.

All manner of examining science agree on this point. All mankind, in whatever stage of culture, *has sought pardon,* many by blood sacrifice. We may judge them *wrong,* but we cannot doubt their *sincerity.*

Is sincerity enough?

Again I must have *God's Word* for it. It is not what I may, or may not think, which will excuse or condemn. The subject is not left to a hypothesis.

The resurrected Christ was most insistent that His gospel be preached to "*all* the world" and to "*every* creature." The four evangelists understood this. There is no doubt in their minds. The Pentecostal directive is "unto the uttermost part of the earth" (Acts 1:8).

Webster defines "uttermost" as *extreme* or *utmost.* The Word of God provides for no sanctuaries of private or communal self-effort. The gospel is as important in the "uttermost part," as it is in "Jerusalem."

Wishful thinking is predicated on the surmise that should a person not hear the gospel, but achieves to his standard the best he can, and such a person is accepted, then it is far better that such a person should not hear the gospel.

But, please, sir, explain this urgent command of the Saviour! Would not He have been the first to recognize your reasoning? Would He not know the mind of God? Why did He insist on such evangelism at such a cost in human life and human resources?

I have to face an additional problem. If a person is living up to the light he may have, and cannot be condemned, why give that person additional light, which, if misunderstood or rejected, will only damn that person?

In the light of codes and standards and customs, a lot of people do achieve excellence. Local history and testimony report it and confirm it. People, in all levels of humanity, are admired and approved by their contemporaries.

How much *light* has God given? What *standard* will He accept? Is the gospel the only light God has given? Certainly, it is the most important revelation ever granted. *But is it the only one?*

Paul tackles this question, facing a world in his day that he felt he had to evangelize. "I am debtor both to the Greeks, and to the Barbarians; both to the wise, and to the unwise. So, as much as in me is, I am ready to preach the gospel . . ." (Romans 1:14, 15). His conclusion is reported in the New Testament and therefore approved by the Holy Spirit for guidance.

Paul concludes that God has spoken to every creature. Disobedience to such revelation merits punishment. This is how he puts it. "For the wrath of God is revealed from heaven against all ungodliness and unrighteousness of men, *who hold the truth* in unrighteousness" (Romans 1:18). Those are very important words, "who hold the truth." They could not "*hold* the truth" unless they had first *received* the truth.

There you have it! God declares He has given every man "the *truth*." Therefore it becomes a prime matter of acceptance or rejection.

Paul tells us what has happened. He describes "men, who hold the truth in *unrighteousness*" (Romans 1:18). That means a person smothers what he knows to be right. To every person has been given a God-awareness, or a God-consciousness, that is given to monitor sinful desires and battle their invitation to hell.

You may agree or disagree that this is so or not, but it has been posted in the Divine Record, and I have read it to you.

Paul amplifies this conclusion. "Because that, when *they knew God,* they glorified him not as God, neither were thankful; but became vain in their imaginations, and their foolish heart was *darkened*" (Romans 1:21). This is how abysmal pagan *darkness* has developed. "When they *knew* God, they glorified him not as God" (Romans 1:21). There was that turning point in history. *They turned the light off.*

The testimony is this. They were not even "thankful" that God had made Himself known to them. They deliberately turned from the light.

The consequences of that terrible decision are a matter of record. "Professing themselves to be wise, they became fools, and changed the glory of the uncorruptible God into an image made like to corruptible man, and to birds, and four-footed beasts, and creeping things" (Romans 1:22, 23).

A person may not have a copy of the Bible. God, however, provides *conscience.* The conscience functions just as the stomach functions. Both approve or disapprove. Both register pleasure or pain. Paul makes a note of this. "Which show the work of the law written in their hearts, *their conscience also bearing witness,* and their thoughts the mean while accusing or else excusing" (Romans 2:15).

The worship of fear can never please God. Salvation is by grace "through faith." Genuine seeking for God is not mere appeasement. It involves a heart concern to know and love God. A person may perform many acts of worship, involving time and expense, and yet never experience *peace.* In fact, that is the basis of all forms of idolatry.

And there is something that should never be forgotten. Mankind lives in God's "house"—*both in outer environment and in his own body.* No one can spend resident years in both without asking questions.

God has furnished the *prodder.* "Because that which may be known to God is manifest in them; for *God hath showed it unto them.* For the invisible things of him from the creation of the world are clearly seen, being understood by the things that are made, even his eternal power and Godhead; so that they are without excuse" (Romans 1:19, 20). Those are powerful words, "God hath showed it unto them."

Although a person abandons God, still God does not abandon that person. Without there is *creation,* and within, there is *conscience.* That is powerful light.

And this says something to you, sir! You have heard the gospel. You know about Jesus. So, what chance will you have to escape? "Of how much sorer punishment, suppose ye, shall he be thought worthy, who hath trodden under foot the Son of God . . . ?" (Hebrews 10:29). You had better equate that with your own case.

Christ makes it absolutely clear. "*No* man cometh unto the Father, *but by me*" (John 14:6). He made no allowance for Confucius, Buddha, Muhammad, or any other wayshower. Whatever their rank—prophet, holy man, patriot, scholar—*none can save.* None can qualify as *mediator.* "For there is *one* . . . mediator between God and men, the *man* Christ Jesus" (1 Timothy 2:5).

The cure is in Christ. That places an awesome responsibility upon me as a saved man or woman. I live under such evangelism. It is spelled out to you in your Bible. "When I say unto the wicked, Thou shalt surely die; and thou givest him not warning, nor speakest to warn the wicked from his wicked way, to save his life; *the same wicked man shall die in his iniquity;* but his blood will I require at thine hand" (Ezekiel 3:18). That sanction has never been rescinded from your Bible, sir. You and I had better read it again.

No, it takes more than religion, more than sincerity, more than excellence to save. First, there must be *divine revelation.* The light must come from above. Second, there must be *a remedy provided for the guilt of sin.* Only the gospel of Jesus Christ provides both.

There are natural religions. Many of them are *beautiful.* They appeal to the ascetic. They offer programs of self-improvement. But the source of these religions is man, himself. It is an attempt of man to be his own savior. These religions neither provide divine revelation nor divine remedy. "For by grace are ye saved through faith; and that not of yourselves; it is the gift of God" (Ephesians 2:8).

However, I will say this much in defense of the heathen. I would rather, far rather, face the judgment of God as a pagan, born and raised with no chance to hear the gospel, than I would to face judgment as a member of a privileged nation, where I have had numerous opportunities to accept the gospel and rejected it. *In either case I perish, but the judgment in the second case will be far greater than in the first.*

This is what the Book says: "For as many as have sinned without law shall also *perish without law*; and as many as have sinned in the law shall be judged by the law" (Romans 2:12). Read it, mister, then be prepared to take your chances!

A REVIVALTIME TESTIMONY

"My family listens to *Revivaltime* every Sunday and has missed only a couple of broadcasts since 1965. We have turned to God through *Revivaltime.* Thank you for preaching the gospel as the Holy Bible records it."

IS THERE A CONSCIOUSNESS BEYOND THE GRAVE?

Text: *"I pray thee therefore, father, that thou wouldest send him to my father's house: for I have five brethren; that he may testify unto them, lest they also come into this place of torment."*

Luke 16:27, 28

JESUS made this a *big* subject. What comes after the grave was a major concern of our Lord. He never swept it under the carpet. He was forthright about it.

You will find an argument. Both sides reach toward the Scripture. Those who believe consciousness stops with the grave will quote: "For the living know that they shall die: but the dead know not any thing, neither have they any more a reward; for the memory of them is forgotten" (Ecclesiastes 9:5).

This side will also say that consciousness depends on the breath being united with the body, therefore it follows that when this union is broken and the breath separated from the body, consciousness is destroyed. That can possibly be the medical position.

There are theologians who explain what Christ meant when He said, "Lazarus sleepeth," and afterward interpreted it to be, "Lazarus is dead"; to mean *sleep* expresses the unclothed state, and that Christ wanted to make sure that He would not *mislead* us and so used the word *dead*.

I am sure that everyone who holds this position, and promotes it, is very honest and convinced in his conviction. *There is no attempt to defraud.*

But before you reach a personal verdict, please look at the total evidence! It is considerable.

Why did Jesus refer to the death of Lazarus, His friend, as *sleep?* It certainly has provoked discussion since. The *body* sleeps or awakens. I am considering the *soul* of man beyond the grave. I raise no questions about the body. I have buried many of them. I have seen bodies exhumed. I have witnessed autopsies. There have been no evidences of consciousness. *Physical death* is the only possible verdict.

Ecclesiastes 12:7 presents a distinction between body and soul. "Then shall the *dust* return to the earth as it was: and the *spirit* shall return unto God who gave it."

Psalm 146:4 furnishes incentive to both sides who investigate consciousness beyond the grave. "His breath goeth forth, he returneth to his earth; *in that very day his thoughts perish.*"

Young translates this last phrase, "in that very day his thoughts perish," this way: "In that very day his *schemes,* or purpose perish." Moffatt translates it: "Rely not upon great men—mere mortals who can give no help; when their breath goes, they return to the dust, *and on that very day their projects perish.*"

Yes, something quits! What is it? Schemes, plans, projects come to a sudden halt. Death is an *interrupter.* That is a fact beyond debate.

Also when I read the passage: "For the living know that they shall die: But the dead know not any thing," I should read the context for interest. Here it is: "Also their love, and their hatred, and their envy, is now perished; neither have they any more a portion for ever in any thing that is done *under the sun*" (Ecclesiastes 9:5, 6). The last three words, "under the sun," are key words. They suggest a perimeter—*this side of the grave.*

Death is a deadline. That is a serious thought. What you are going to do, must be done this side of the grave. There are no *second chances.*

This message deals particularly with *consciousness*. It implies sight, recognition, speech, hearing, reason, memory, feeling. Do these continue beyond the grave?

No Bible edition has yet deleted the record of *Samuel*. He is selected to be in that distinguished group who are met again beyond the grave.

Could Samuel *see*? Yes. "And Samuel said to Saul" (1 Samuel 28:15). This required *sight* and *recognition*. Could Samuel *speak*? Yes. Could Samuel *hear*? Yes. "And Saul answered" (1 Samuel 28:15). Could Samuel *reason*? Yes. "Wherefore then dost thou ask of me?" (1 Samuel 28:16). Did Samuel *remember*? Yes. "The Lord hath done to him, as he spake by me" (1 Samuel 28: 17). Could Samuel *feel*? Yes. "Why hast thou disquieted me?" (1 Samuel 28:15).

You certainly have every test of consciousness. Samuel was *conscious* beyond the grave. King Saul was convinced, and he was a hard man to convince of anything.

No Bible edition has yet deleted the record of the rich man and Lazarus. God has allowed a member of the human race, on the far side of the altar, to be met again beyond the grave. *This is a witness from the rejecter.*

Could he *see*? Yes. "And in hell he lifted up his eyes, being in torments, and seeth Abraham afar off, and Lazarus in his bosom" (Luke 16:23). Could he *feel*? Yes. "Being in torments." Could he *speak*? Yes. "Father Abraham, have mercy on me" (Luke 16: 24). Could he *hear* and *remember*? Yes. "But Abraham said, Son, remember . . ." (Luke 16:25). Could he *reason*? Yes. "Nay, father Abraham: but if one went unto them from the dead, they will repent" (Luke 16:30).

Again, there is every test of consciousness. This man was as conscious in *hell* as Samuel was conscious in *heaven*.

It all adds up to this, mister. *You are more than body*. And that is where you are making your greatest mistake, sinner. You are only living an animal life. You are allowing the eternal in you to be dormant. You refuse to listen to your real self. But the time will come when it will be heard—when animal existence, physical satisfaction alone, will be interrupted. Then you will be *eternally conscious.* That is what the Hoy Spirit is trying to make you now.

Let me give you a third witness from the Word of God. The last book in the Bible sets forth *things to come.* It is called Revelation.

Chapter six describes *martyrs.* A martyr is one who is put to death for what he believes and refuses, under penalty of death, to cease believing.

John reports a scene in the world to come "They cried with a loud voice, saying, How long, O Lord, holy and true, dost thou not . . . avenge our blood on them that dwell on the earth? And white robes were given unto every one of them; and it was said unto them, that they should rest yet for a little season, until their fellow servants also and their brethren, that should be killed as they were, should be fulfilled" (Revelation 6:10, 11).

This certainly is an instance of consciousness in a world beyond the grave. Here we have an example of *group consciousness.*

Could they *remember?* Yes. "How long, . . . dost thou not . . . avenge our blood?" (Revelation 6:10). Could they *hear* and *feel?* Yes. "It was said unto them, that they should rest yet for a little season" (Revelation 6:11). Could they *speak?* Yes. "They cried with a loud voice" (Revelation 6:10). Could they *reason?* Yes. "Dost thou not judge and avenge our blood on them that dwell on the earth?" (Revelation 6:10).

Here are three authentic reports. "In the mouth of two or three witnesses every word may be established" (Matthew 18:16). God has given us these *three* detailed insights to consciousness beyond the grave. Paul uses this same Biblical rule. "In the mouth of two or three witnesses shall every word be established" (2 Corinthians 13:1). I believe you and I have a positive answer.

You face death, sir. It isn't an option. "It is appointed unto men once to die, but after this the judgment" (Hebrews 9:27). Therefore, my question to you is important: If death should come to you this week, would you enter into the conscious enjoyment of God's provision in Christ for His own? If not—are you willing to enter into torment? That choice must be made *now*—before the grave.

You can deny you have a *soul.* Clarence Darrow, the eminent American lawyer of yesteryear, did. He recorded:

"When I die, as I shall soon, my body will decay. My mind will decay and my intellect will be gone. My soul? There is no such thing. There is no evidence of supernatural power. The universe is simply a product of evolution. I have been seeking some definite proof of God, but my doubts are at rest now. I know that such fact does not exist. I am a materialist."

That sounds *familiar.* It seems to me that I have heard it all before. "If they hear not Moses and the prophets, neither will they be persuaded, though one rose from the dead" (Luke 16:31).

God's Word is clear. It does not leave you in doubt. The grave is the *division point.* It is where a temporal body and an eternal spirit separate. It is not the *grand terminal.* You have lots more experiences ahead of you. Will they bring you *pain* or *pleasure?*

A few months ago I visited Quincy, Massachusetts. In a historic, downtown church lie the bodies of both Adamses—father and son—who were Presidents of the United States. The body of Abigail Adams lies between her husband and her son. She was a remarkable woman—the wife of one President and the mother of another. It is a moving experience to view the simplicity of their burial. However, in the description that tells the story of John Quincy Adams' burial, there is a line that moves me most of all. It simply says: "Here lies *all that could possibly die* of John Quincy Adams."

Solomon was right. "Then shall the dust return to the earth as it was: and the spirit shall return unto God who gave it" (Ecclesiastes 12:7). *Are you ready for that return trip?*

A REVIVALTIME TESTIMONY

"*Revivaltime* is a morale booster for us missionaries. We can close our eyes and imagine that we are back in the auditorium at headquarters in Springfield, Missouri, for a Sunday night *Revivaltime* service."

YOUR BANKER

Text: "My transgression is sealed up in a bag, and thou *sewest up mine iniquity.*"

Job 14:17

JOB is an old, old book. This verse is a proof. The very ancient oriental bankers and merchants had their own way of conducting credit operations. They weighed or counted so much coin or precious metal, put it into a strong bag, sewed it, and sealed it with wax, with a personal imprint on the wax.

After that it was sacred in trade. The banker's honor went with the seal. It was known as a "purse," and might go from person to person, or land to land, bearing the amount upon its seal. It would not be opened by anyone until it came back to the banker to be recounted. Such was the forerunner of our check system today.

But it always came back! It might pass from hand to hand, and circulate for some time, and be accepted wherever the banker's credit was acknowledged—but in the end it came back to be ripped open and its contents investigated, to see that all the transactions made upon its honor were right, and that proper debt and credit might be kept.

The one big truth here is that *something must always come home again to pass scrutiny and be audited.*

Moses, in his farewell address, poses an interesting question. "Their wine is the poison of dragons, and the cruel venom of asps. *Is not this laid up in store with me, and sealed up among my treasures?*" (Deuteronomy 32:33, 34).

What do I have in life that is "laid up in store with me" and "sealed up among my treasures?"

There are deep and dark cells in every man's nature where the hidden contents of his life are all on inventory. Personal memory "seals" and "sews" what is committed to it. "My transgression is sealed up in a bag, and thou sewest up mine iniquity." *Memory is a banker.*

God has built those *secret vaults* in the depths of the soul into which all motives, designs, thoughts, and actions are deposited. *And those vaults are theft proof.*

Memory accounts for it all. It is the scribe of the soul. It places everything in its perfect place and under its true circumstances. *No one has ever accused memory of dishonesty.*

History tells us that Themistocles could tell the name of each of the 20,000 fellow-Athenian citizens. Cyrus is credited with the instant recall of the name of every soldier in his army. Those are amazing feats. But they are minor compared to the engineering miracle of your own soul, sir. Your soul can account for every thought, every wish, and every deed. *You carry around inside a personal banker.*

The contents may make a long journey, but they are "sealed" and "sewn" tightly *and are always sacred for the homecoming audit.*

During my residency here the body brings problems and other propositions to the soul, on which it passes judgment. It makes regnant choice on what is brought to it by the agencies of the eye, the ear, the mouth, the touch, and the nose. The soul inspects all merchandise and exerts its office to accept or reject.

What happens to these decisions? They must be made a matter of eternal record. There is a "banker" in every one of us.

That banker was called to testify to the Rich Man in hell. "Son, *remember* that thou in thy lifetime receivedst thy good things, and likewise Lazarus evil things: but now he is comforted, and thou art tormented" (Luke 16:25). Every scene in the old home was recalled. He saw it all—the "good things" —carpets, groceries, furnishings, vacations, broad acres, servants, clothes, and sports. The entire tableau of his life fell in place.

But the banker was *honest!* He faced the entire picture. There had been placed to account the "evil things" as well—the haggard face of the beggar, Lazarus, and dogs licking sores, when he, himself, had neither time nor made the effort to throw a crust of bread. And the banker wasn't through. There was something additional. There were five stalwart and reveling brothers, each with a copy of Moses and the prophets in his hands, all heading the same way. "Son, remember!" *You will.* You can count on that, lady.

Thank God! It can work the other way. John on Patmos recalls hearing those repeating in another world: "Unto him that hath loved us, and washed us from our sins in his own blood, and redeemed us out of all kindreds, and nations, and people, and tongues."

The banker, too, recalled what they had been—*sinners*—carried away with unspeakable idolatries, unwashed, filthy in their unregenerate practices. The file was complete. Everything on deposit was there—redemption—tears of repentance, renunciation of sin, and the joy of pardon. Not a detail escaped them—the color of the skin, the circumstances of birth and youth, their fears within and their fightings without—"out of *all* kindreds, and nations, and people, and tongues."

No sir, your personal banker does not lie down in the grave with your body. *That banker follows you all the way into another world.* How important it is to make the right investments on earth! It will be the difference between profit and loss. You can either feast or famish on memories.

Your life is a trust, mister. What you do with it is your personal business unless by an act of sovereign will you deed that trust to Jesus Christ. Into that trust are placed your mind, your abilities, your education, your privileges, your body, your emotions, your friendships, your travels, your appetites, your affections.

These require constant decisions. What will I love? What will I despise? What will I learn? What will I ignore? Whom will I cultivate? Whom will I avoid? Where will I go? When will I stay? And each decision is *banked.* Moses pondered: "Is not this laid up in store with me, and sealed up among my treasures?" (Deuteronomy 32:34).

You will meet them all one day—irregularity of appetite, daring disobedience, unruly affection. Hosea said, "The iniquity of Ephraim is bound up" (Hosea 13:12). It is wishful thinking to say, "Oh, forget about it! That doesn't count." It's like playing golf, mister. Every swing, every stroke counts.

That is why I need every safeguard available. I think of the car I must drive every day amid the teeming traffic of a modern city. All the horses under the hood of that car can threaten a runaway and disaster unless I exercise absolute control every second. *But that is nothing compared to the energies and the desires within me.*

Eve's tastes betrayed her, and she brought disaster to her sex and Adam's seed. Achan's eyes betrayed him, and he brought tragedy to his family and to the nation of Israel. David's touch betrayed him, and he ruined a man's marriage and unloosed an avalanche of pain upon his own household. It doesn't take long to get *a bag full.* "My transgression is sealed up in a bag."

So many of you in this audience are counting on chance—that only the good you do will be remembered. What kind of a banker would that be? That kind of a ledger would send such a keeper to prison for tampering with the books.

No, mister, every treachery, every profanity, every vulgarity, every hypocrisy, every base thing will be in that "bag." You have a *banker* that cannot be bribed, and that banker "sews up" your iniquity. The record is exact, meticulous. That record cannot be stolen or disfigured. It is never lost. It will withstand the passage of centuries.

Unforgiven sin will always haunt you. It is like your bank check. That bank check seems only a piece of paper, but it can cross oceans, and survive weather, and pass through scores of hands, *and come back and face you.* Every time you sin, you write a check. And payment is due.

David learned this. He said, "My sin is ever before me" (Psalm 51:3). Many a distressed soul in this audience has cried out with David: "Lord, remember not against me the sins of my youth" (see Psalm 25:7). Only God can handle your *accou*nt. "I will cast thy sin behind my back as a stone into the depths of the sea, to be remembered against thee no more forever" (see Micah 7:19). That is relief, sir! That is grace! That is having your credit established. That is the most unforgettable of all. No wonder we sing in our churches: "I *remember* when my burdens rolled away. I had carried them for years, night and day."

I have met men in my ministry who would give the world, if they could, to forget one particular sin. The banker is always there to remind that man of such and such a transaction. I'm not imagining things. I'm stating fact.

Your banker is the most exact and impartial person in your life, beyond anything your teacher, your physician, your congressman, your preacher may mean to you. He will tell you exactly as it is. He can trace each step. So your banker inside asks you: "What have you done with your parents' legacy of a family altar, with a godly father's council, with a mother's intercession, with Sunday school lessons, with convictions, with feelings—in what way have you *spent* them?"

How will you face that moment when the "bag" is opened, when the seal is broken, when the stitches are removed? Every act of dishonor will tumble out. Every lie will be revealed. Every harsh word will ask for judgment. Every unkindness will require payment in full.

I don't know how any man or woman will be able to survive the sight of his or her total life's sins. I think a person could face the electric chair easier, or the gallows. Sometimes you break out in a sweat when you dream about it. It will be more than a dream some day, sir! Everything is going into that "bag." Every stitch is an assurance that you must face a full audit.

I've made my *choice!* I don't want to spend eternity looking at my sins. There's no thrill in wrong answers. There is no pleasure in misspent opportunities. I don't want to wail, "I wish I had done differently." I don't want to grind my teeth, "I was a fool." I don't want to look at myself forever a wasted life. I want to say with the other crowd: "Unto him that hath loved us, and washed us from our sins in his own blood, and redeemed us out of all kindreds, and nations, and people, and tongues." I want my "*banker*" to recall for me pardon and cleansing and fellowship with folk who have been "washed" and "redeemed."

Oh, yes! The "bag" will be opened for me, too. Someone will remove the stitches from my personal record. It will all be there. But I mean to rejoice in the old hymns I have sung, in the prayer meetings I have attended, in the hours I have loved and searched God's Word, in the companionship of the Holy Spirit I have enjoyed.

You will see what I have stored up in my life, as I will see what you have stored up in your life. And I am glad that in that "bag" of mine will be a decision that says, "I remember my Creator in the days of my youth" (see Ecclesiastes 12:1).

Take a moment, now, and ask your personal banker how it is with you in this moment. *What lies to your account?*

CAKE

Text: *"Make me thereof a little cake first."*

1 *Kings* 17:13

THAT short line says it all. It's the kind of sentence I would want to find if I were sending a telegram—*not a wasted word.* The simplicity of it is overpowering. It contains a lesson in spiritual matters for all generations.

There was more than appeared on the surface in this request, but it was not disclosed until the plain request itself was heeded. A marvelous bonus came to the woman who heard and heeded. And there is a *bonus* to be won again and again.

Deep depression gripped the nation. The preacher, Elijah, had been provided with food by the birds of the air, and his thirst was satisfied by the cool waters of the brook. These sources of supply closed and God sent His servant to a widow.

It wasn't an easy journey for Elijah. The state had set a price upon his head. It might have been one of the gloomiest situations mentioned in the Bible. The widow had collected the last of her supplies. It was to be a farewell meal for herself and her son. Starvation was in the land. How could she possibly feed another mouth? This woman is trying to heroically face the inevitable. The demand seems unreasonable. A hungry man, weary from travel, would take all she had—all that seemingly belonged morally to her household.

She must have looked intently at the man who made the request. He appeared to be neither an angel from heaven nor wear any badge of royalty upon earth. What right did he have to make such a demand? She and her child needed the food even more than he.

Elijah extended no word of sympathy or sorrow. Instead, he says, "Make *me* thereof a little cake *first.*" It would appear that only a completely calloused man could look at a starving child and his widowed mother, and make such a demand. *It isn't human.* Yet, she faced a command that required *obedience!* Her obedience saved her life.

What lessons are there in this incident for us? I believe there are *three.*

First, he asked for a *cake.* He might have made many requests. He might have asked for venison. She could have replied: "I cannot supply it. I have no means to secure it." He might have asked for fish. She could have replied: "I have no fish, nor any means of securing fish." He might have asked for fruit. She could have pointed to the withered orchards and wasted vines.

He made no request for luxury or delicacy. *He asked for what she had.* Nothing was required except simple obedience. All that was exercised was a *priority.* She could not say honestly: "I cannot do it. I don't have the means. I don't know how." She could refuse and give her reason, but his request was within her ability to grant. She could wrestle with her fear. She could form her own opinion of the person who dared to ask. She could show shock at his request. She could comment on the conditions of the nation. She could lament her misfortune. These were her prerogatives. But she could not say that she did not have oil and meal. *She did have the means to grant his request.*

God asks you to do what is *possible.* Remember that! So many refuse the call of God on the grounds of *inability.* Jesus cited such a man. "I knew thee that thou art *a hard man,* reaping where thou hast not sown, and gathering where thou has not strewed: and I was *afraid*" (Matthew 25:24, 25).

That is a smear upon God, mister. God never asks a man to

suddenly teach a class Hebrew who hasn't had a lesson in that language himself.

Christ does not make an unreasonable claim upon you, sir. God asks for what you have. The decision is made in that arena alone.

God asks for your *love*. That is something you have. You are bestowing it every hour of the day. You love your television set. You love your job. You love your summer cottage. You love your hunting dog. You love your daughter. You love to fly. You love to fish. So, God asks for your *love*.

God asks for your *trust*. That is something you have. You trust the customer who stops at your service station. You fill his tank with gasoline before you ask for payment. You trust your clothes to the cleaners. You trust your body to the doctor. You trust your letters to the mailbox. You trust your health to the water department of your city. You trust your life to the pilot of some jet craft. So, God asks for your *trust*.

God asks for your *repentance*. That is something you have. You can say, "I'm sorry. I was wrong." You say it when you dial the wrong phone number. You say it when the Internal Revenue returns your tax estimate and one of you has forgotten to sign it. Young man, you say it when you and your girl friend have had a misunderstanding, and you want to make up. So, God asks you for *repentance*.

God knows what you can do and what you can't do, sir. *Judgment will be on that basis*. Before the Eternal ever makes a demand on you, He knows what you can do and what you cannot do. If God's messenger is there, it is evidence that there is enough left to make a cake which is all that is required.

Second, he asked for a *little* cake. God is never *greedy*. That is a lie that hell peddles with a great deal of success—*that heaven is greedy*. Elijah measured his request by the size of the widow's possessions.

Look at that dollar in your hand! How much does God ask? He asks for *ten percent*—the smallest part of it—"a little cake."

Look at that calendar on your wall! How much does God ask? He asks for just *one day out of every seven*—"a *little* cake."

God is *sympathetic*. That is a marvelous discovery. "These things shall be added unto you" (Matthew 6:33). There are no outrageous demands. "There hath no temptation taken you but such as is common to man: but God is faithful, who will not suffer you to be tempted above that ye are able; but will with the temptation also make a way to escape, that ye may be able to bear it" (1 Corinthians 10:13). There is always a solution.

I sometimes think we become *religious dissipaters*. We crowd in religious activities and programs that rob our families of our presence and companionship. So many preachers are guilty. Their own children hardly know them. We fill every possible evening with some committee or study. We are so busy that we can't notice the grandeur of this beautiful planet. There isn't time to garden. There isn't time to romance. There isn't time to converse and exchange company. We forget this lesson—"a *little* cake."

There is a corollary that I must not ignore. There had been a time when this woman's inventory was full. Time and ravage had dwindled her resources.

God knows what we have left, mister! Some in this audience haven't much to offer. *There were better days*. You are like the group to whom the master came "about the eleventh hour . . . (and to whom he saith) . . . Go ye *also* into the vineyard; and whatsoever is right, that shall he receive. . . . And when they came that were hired about the eleventh hour (they received full payment)" (Matthew 20:6, 7, 9).

It is never too late to start. Hell will discourage you, and tell you that you have so *little* left that it is foolish to offer it. That is a lie. That is water under the bridge. The only thing that matters is that God comes to you now. He knows what is left, and He asks only for "a little cake."

Third, he asked for the little cake *first*. The emphasis is here, *first*.

If the woman in the generosity of her spirit was rapidly making up her mind to reply: "Yes, we will supply your need so far as we are able, *after* we have satisfied our own wants; we will even *deny* ourselves that there may be more for you," she is stunned by the sound of the word *first*.

No religious preference on your part can change that requirement—"first." God's part comes *first*. No other arrangement is acceptable.

You ask, "I'm on social security—how can I give?" The answer is in this text: "Make me thereof a little cake *first*." You ask: "I work six days a week and Sunday is the only day I have for my family—why should I go to church?" The same answer applies. You ask: "The children's schedules are so tight, with school and music lessons and extra assignments—where can I find time for a regular family altar?" Put God *first!* There'll always be enough for other things—*always*.

The triumph of the gospel lies here. The victory is won when selfishness is vanquished. It is an exercise of trust; that God will never let you down, and that He is abundantly able to take care of you.

This woman faced a crucial decision. *Should she hand over her entire life?* Yes, hand it over. Place it in trust. *You have met One who wants to become involved with you.*

This woman, obscure and worried about her tiny, shrinking personal world, might have moved on, *unknown*. But she made the biggest decision of her life in handing over to Another, in an act of complete trust, what seemed absolutely necessary to keep her alive a little longer. That decision brought her fame.

Her experience has blessed millions. That is what God wants to do with your life and opportunity—use it.

There is only one way to secure divine favor. Place God first. Go His way. The rule is inflexible. Business is important, but God's claim is more important. Accumulation and investment are needful, but regard for God's demand is more needful. An argument will only destroy you. Balaam tried it and lost.

The widow obeyed and found security. There was always enough. She exchanged a life of worry for a life of praise—a life of scratching out a living for God's care and provision. God gave her far more than she had ever given to Him. You will find that it works that way.

A REVIVALTIME TESTIMONY

"Since I began hearing *Revivaltime* each Sunday evening, I have a little more in life to live for. I have memories of my childhood—a church was an altar and people kneeling and praying—these are happy memories."

YOU ARE AT LIBERTY TO CHOOSE YOUR EMPLOYER!

Text. *"Know ye not, that to whom ye yield yourselves servants to obey, his servants ye are to whom ye obey; whether of sin unto death, or of obedience unto righteousness?"*
Romans 6:16

THAT is the *only liberty* given to me—the liberty to choose my employer. I was created to *serve.*

Every man *obeys*—obeys something. It is not a question *whether* we will serve, but: "Choose you this day *whom* ye will serve" (Joshua 24:15).

Every thing is obedient. The sun and sand go when and where they are drawn and blown. The stars and planets have their fixed orbits, bound by invisible cords of gravity. The migratory bird at the migratory season is drawn to a more convenient climb by influences that pull at the bird with the same inexorable vigor with which the sun pulls at the earth, or the earth at a falling pebble. *That bird has to do what that bird has to do.* Instinct is only another name for gravitation.

Man finds himself a part of such a creation. It is an intelligent existence amid moral splendor. Man is never *apart* or beyond or above these fixed forces. *I have given to me one particular power.* I can move toward, or from, these centers of gravity. I am in the same position as our astronauts. *I can choose which force I want to propel me toward which destiny I desire.*

I commit myself. The force to which I commit myself does the rest. This is shocking but true. *I do not have to save myself any more than I have to damn myself.* Salvation is an act of commitment. Damnation is an act of commitment. "He that hath the Son hath life; and he that hath not the Son of God hath not life" (1 John 5:12).

John underlines this many times. "He that believeth on the Son hath everlasting life: and he that believeth not the Son shall not see life; but the wrath of God abideth on him" (John 3:36). *You either orbit around this Man, Jesus, or you do not orbit around Him.* It is one or the other.

God provides the wind for your sails and the current and tide for your boat. *We are limited to choice.*

Association with businessmen and politicians has been a part of my public life. Personally, I am involved in no other business than the ministry. And I am not a politician. I am, by the grace of God, one thing only—a preacher. But it is not unholy to run for office or a crime to be in business. Government is a blessing. Business provides jobs and a national economy. All this spells the word *achievement.*

Achievement, or success, is not difficult, sir. Find, as quickly as you can, the wind that blows in the direction in which you want to go. *Then get on the windward side!* Avail yourself of the total energy it provides. Harness yourself to that driving force. You'll go places. I promise you.

Jesus had this in mind when He told His disciples: "But ye shall receive power, after that the Holy Ghost is come upon you: and ye shall be witnesses unto me both in Jerusalem, and in all Judea, and in Samaria, and unto the uttermost part of the earth. . . . And suddenly there came a sound from heaven *as of a rushing mighty wind*" (Acts 1:8; 2:2). It is so simple, believer! That "mighty wind" will take you places.

Ask the scientist! He will tell you that not one mechanical contrivance of man has ever created one degree of new energy. We simply make discoveries. We discovered what steam could do. We discovered what electricity could do. Now we are discovering what the atom can do. The forces are there waiting to be employed.

It is as true in the believer's life. Go on, my brother! You'll discover greater and greater amounts of energy placed at your disposal. "Therefore leaving the principles of the doctrine of Christ, *let us go on unto perfection*" (Hebrews 6:1).

Scientists, because they research, because they dig, because they will not be denied, find answers and apply those answers to a catalog of new blessings. Why don't Christians use the same sense?

Paul never quit. He found out how to break out of jail. He discovered how to survive snakebite. He learned how to ride out a Mediterranean typhoon. He outsmarted dishonest officials. He infiltrated Caesar's palace guard. He cast out devils. He raised huge amounts of money. He survived boycotts. He saw the sick healed. He brought Baptists into a charismatic experience. He wrote best sellers. He influenced businessmen. He finished a "course" that is history.

He simply believed it was a "*mighty* wind" that was available to the believer. He adjusted his life to that force. It carried him all the way. It will do the same for us. "Know ye not, that to whom ye *yield* yourselves servants to obey, his servants ye are to whom ye obey; whether of sin unto death, or of obedience unto righteousness?"

The keynote of every letter Paul wrote is in that line, "Paul a *servant* of Jesus Christ" (Romans 1:1). The secret is in that word *yield*. Yield. to that "mighty wind," believer! Too many of us are yielding to committees and programs and traditions. You and I need a greater force.

A child's finger can push a button that can detonate explosives. It isn't your power, your giant intellect, your diplomacy that God needs, mister. It is "not by might, nor by power, *but by my Spirit,* saith the Lord" (Zechariah 4:6). You are given *choice*. About whom and what will you orbit?

Yield yourself to liquor, and liquor will do the rest. Yield yourself to drugs, and drugs will do the rest. In the same way, yield yourself to the Spirit of God, and the Spirit of God will accomplish an entire mission. *God has provided the energy.*

One of the silliest sights I see, and one of the most frustrating, is to watch church circles trying their religious best to create energy. That is like a scientist trying to create an atom or a piece of coal.

Yield, mister! That much you can do. While I do not take the train, the train takes me; but I do choose what train I take. It seems to me that my greatest choice is to choose *what I will let be done in me and through me.* I have never allowed tobacco to touch my life. I know from heaped-up testimony what it would do *in* me and *through* me if given a chance.

We say we have the power to move our arms. Yes, and no. The power that moves the arm is the physical energy that has been physically stored in the body as a result of nourishment and assimilation. The power is resident. *I simply exercise the signal.* It is like the little girl who pushes the button that detonates the blast. She doesn't crack the rocks to pieces. The dynamite does that. She simply passes the signal.

Jesus was blunt. He asked: "Which of you by taking thought can add one cubit unto his stature?" (Matthew 6:27). You can't design your own salvation, sir! It has been designed for you. You exercise one option—*take* it or *leave* it. When you talk about being fully competent to be your own savior, you are talking like an idiot. The fact is that you and I are absolutely dependent. We always will be.

You are not a power, and the only way you can be a power is to get on the working side of something that is a power. "To whom ye yield yourselves servants to obey, his servants ye are to whom ye obey; whether of sin unto death, or of obedience unto righteousness." *Decide our orbit!*

No one is left alone. It is "either—or!" Some force engages your life, either of evil or of good. No man is an island.

When a man tells me, "Preacher, I do not care to become a Christian because I do not want to lose my freedom," that is a joke. *You haven't any freedom to lose, sinner.* There is no liberty in the sense of exemption from allegiance to some master. Something is your boss. *You can choose your master, but you cannot choose to have no master.*

Fame is a master. Ambition is a master. Money is a master. Alcohol is a master. Gambling is a master. And these things can make you crawl. I'll tell you this, sinner! Jesus Christ will never ridicule you the way liquor means to belittle you until you stagger, your tongue is thick, your mind uncoordinated, your hands shaking, your clothes filthy, your breath a stench, your home a shambles, your job gone, your memories a torment.

I'll tell you what Christ offers. "Come unto me, all ye that labor and are heavy laden, and I will give you rest. Take my yoke upon you, . . . For my yoke is easy, and my burden is light" (Matthew 11:28-30). Compare that offer to any other!

You say, "Brother Ward, how can I make the switch?" First, let me tell you a story.

Saint Boniface was a brave and conquering missionary in the Middle Ages. He plunged fearlessly into the dark and tangled forests of Germany and conquered thousands of those unconverted for Christ. But near Geismar, in upper Hesse, there stood a vast and venerable oak, sacred for ages to Thor the god of thunder.

Saint Boniface tried in vain to win the Germans from the superstitious adoration of that tree. At last he seized an axe. The Germans stood about in breathless wonder and alarm. He sent stroke after stroke ringing on the gnarled trunk. The priest of Thor implored the deity to avenge himself, and the Germans thought that surely a lightning flash from heaven would cut down Saint Boniface. But no flash came.

However, Boniface was wise. He knew that if he did not erect a better worship in the idol's place, the old idolatry, cast out for the moment, would regain entrance. So Saint Boniface built out of the fragments of the fallen and splintered tree a chapel. He replaced the worship of the thunderer with the worship of the Crucified.

That is what you have to do. *Place yourself under a better Master.*

Self-repression is not salvation. The longer a hungry wolf is kept from his meat, the more terrific will be the rush when the barrier is removed. There is no man who will sin with such avidity as a man who has been doing nothing for a week but making a business of being good. No man will drink like a reformed drunkard.

You will not acquire the art of purity by any battle you may wage with your interior tendencies to lust and uncleanness. You can't reduce your fever for money by attempting to bridle the pulse beats of your mercenary greed. *Mutilated depravity is not holiness. Starved worldliness is not Christianity.*

You have tried *good resolutions.* Try unconditional surrender. A resolution is a kind of *moral spasm* which disappears with the momentary causes that induced it. It is like a snow fort which vanishes when the snow softens. You'll never find security in good resolutions. Sin will reduce them to crumbs. *Place yourself under new Management.* Your very nature demands an Employer.

"Yield yourselves unto God, . . . and your members as instruments of righteousness unto God" (Romans 6:13). Treasure every instinct, every emotion, every gift you have now. Place them at the disposal of a new Administrator. Dedicate them to a better Executive. The same earth mixture that makes the weed can make the flower. Carbon makes charcoal, but it makes the diamond. Give yourself—all of you—to Jesus Christ. He will make the right production out of your life. It is not abandoning your talent, instinct, or gift. It is placing them under the best employ possible.

John understood it and experienced it when he said: "This is the victory that overcometh the world, even our faith" (1 John 5:4). That same victory is yours for the asking!

A REVIVALTIME TESTIMONY

"We are Baptists, but surely enjoy those minutes with Brother Ward on *Revivaltime*. I am a public school teacher and appreciate the high standards C. M. Ward sets for the young people we teach."

CALLOUSES

Text: *"That which hath been is now; and that which is to be hath already been; and God requireth that which is past."* *Ecclesiastes* 3:15

THERE is a proper and challenging sense to the word *evolution.* Everything we are and everything about us must be tied into what has gone before. The future will spring out of the present. *How can you join it all together and make it count?* That is the supreme challenge.

History is important. Research is important. There's more to it, fellow, than just cramming dates and names. What are the *prevailing influences?* Every stage of life becomes a record and a prophecy. Every state of being is at once fruit and seed.

The principle of this text is working in my life whether I care to admit it or not. "That which hath been is now; and that which is to be hath already been; and God requireth that which is past." *That adds to something called character—me.*

In the kingdom of God, as in all other realms, the law is, first the blade, then the ear, and after that the full corn in the ear. It isn't *magic,* mister! There's no Pandora's box and suddenly you are a saint. There are battles to be fought and victories to be won.

There is a shelf of "instant foodstuffs" marketed today. Many would like to believe that character can be obtained the same way. That is wishful thinking. Success is earned. A reputation is built.

Every man's present is the fruit of his past. You can't sow carelessly and reap carefully. Back of every character, whether noble or evil, there have been *causes* that must produce such goodness or badness as is now revealed. A *Hitler* or a *Luther* are a long time in the making, and will be felt for a long time to come.

It is something to be a parent. There is the force of heredity in this world. There is a chain of genes and circumstances. Every physician in town will attest to it. You are going to affect your child just as your parents affected you. Think about it! God says one thing to you, sir. "*Train* up a child in the way he should go: and when he is old, he will not depart from it" (Proverbs 22:6). That is your God-given burden, parent.

I'll tell you this in an argument for *supervision.* There has not been an impulse however strong or feeble, a motive high or low, a thought whether base or noble, a companionship slight or intimate, a book either wholesome or harmful, a journey either pleasant or sad—there has been nothing that has not left on us its mark and indelible stamp.

I have often stood at the rim of our Grand Canyon in Arizona and marveled how the mighty Colorado River, during centuries past, has cut that canyon deep and wide. It has written its history on the sides of the canyon.

What I am has been etched in the same manner. Every story heard has left its imprint. Every person met has touched my life for good or bad. Every scene has registered. Every religious service has motivated or discouraged me. The record is complete.

Think what coarseness and vulgarity are doing to you, sir! Your life has become a cesspool. You drip with obscenities and smut. How can it be otherwise? Paul knew. He said, "Be not deceived: evil communications corrupt good manners" (1 Corinthians 15:33).

You rub in rot, sir, and you will produce rot. You can't be one thing at the club, Wednesday noon, and another thing in the church, Sunday morning. Christ put the lie to that kind of crooked thinking. He said: "Do men gather grapes of thorns, or figs of thistles? . . . A good tree cannot bring forth evil fruit, neither can a corrupt tree bring forth good fruit" (Matthew 7:16, 18).

We are all recorders. I, myself, keep the most accurate account of me that is possible in the universe. *Every incident is written irrevocably into my life.* It is impossible for me to cheat.

Pontius Pilate knew it. He said, "What I have written I have written" (John 19:22). That was the awful burden his conscience bore. History can never ease it. Pilate, and no other, gave the crucifixion order. That is what my text says, "That which hath been is *now.*" It is as heinous and as inexcusable in 1970 as it was in '33. There is something attached, personally fixed, to your life. *You are producing* an *individual composite—like no one else's on earth.*

Hold in your hand a glass of mineral water! It appears absolutely clear. Until you taste it, you would not expect the presence of minerals. Even taste cannot separate the ingredients. Take it to a chemist. He discovers a dozen salts. He can trace the life-story of that glass of water. He can tell you how one drop was filtered through a particular mineral, and another drop through a different mineral. The record is positive. It is *there.*

So, to the eyes of men we may be crystal clear. We may even deceive ourselves and think we are acceptable. One day there will be a complete analysis. Nothing will be hidden. This is what the Bible says: "Therefore judge nothing before the time, until the Lord come, who both will bring to light the hidden things of darkness, and will make manifest the counsels of the hearts: and then shall every man have praise of God" (1 Corinthians 4:5). *Yes, sir, we carry the story with us!*

There is something else in this text to prod us. *Just as our todays reveal our yesterdays, so they are the prophets of our tomorrows.* The warnings are buzzing in your life and mine.

You aren't going to outgrow some evil tendency you have cultured. You aren't going to outrun some agent you have invited into your life. It's like joining the Communist Party. You are in for *life.* You carry a mortgage that can be closed at any moment.

"I am" is the child of "I have been," and the parent of "I will be." *Only God can break the law of continuity.* It is like a set of railroad tracks. They fix distance and direction. You will go where they take you.

I ask you to examine the habits that bind you. Do you honestly believe for one second that any habit in your life will ever lessen its demand upon you? No habit, indulged, will ever have mercy upon you. It is well named a *vice.* It holds you powerless. It is well named a *passion.* The intensity is like high voltage. You can't let go. You are a *slave.*

What are the chances that a drunkard will reform? What are the percentages that a narcotic will kick the habit? "Can the Ethiopian change his skin, or the leopard his spots? then may ye also do good, that are accustomed to do evil" (Jeremiah 13:23). It becomes your *nature.*

Paul notes this. "And were by nature the children of wrath" (Ephesians 2:3). That's why it takes God to change you, mister. It takes a miraculous rebirth. *You and I need the Supernatural.*

I'll tell you something. *Few begin evil late in life.* It will be a rare exception to discover anyone who has been Christlike since early teens, then in his late fifties or early sixties chucks it all, and decides on a life of sin and reckless prodigality. The vine can be trained on the trellis when it is young and tender, but grown old and brown it cannot be twisted. I have always respected these four lines:

"A pebble in the streamlet scant
 Has turned the course of many a river.
A dewdrop on the tiny plant
 Has warped the giant oak forever."

Sinner, I must warn you. Every day you put off your duty decreases the probability that you will ever serve God. *Hell yawns for you.* The riptide has you in its grip.

That is the *warning* of this text. "And that which is to be hath already been." Judgment has already begun in your life, sinner! *God is allowing you a full-dress rehearsal of what a final hell will mean.*

That is a *predestination* that I can understand. It is the kind of predestination I make for myself. Where are the aspirations, the lofty plans, you had for yourself ten years ago? What has happened to your dreams? Promises! Promises! The shambles mock you. The devil lies. He whispered, "You can quit any time you wish." So you gave in.

Ask the narcotic. The withdrawal is hell. So, instead, you plunge deeper. It is a *fix.* That is the right tag. There is no variety—no letup. You do it again and again.

Character takes on *permanence.* You have become a helpless addict. At last it is a wild, resistless abandonment. You don't even think about it any longer. Nothing can save you. You are caught in a Niagara. "Reproach hath broken my heart; and I am full of heaviness: and I looked for some to take pity, but there was none; and for comforters, but I found none" (Psalm 69:20).

Has God forsaken you? No! "Thou hast known my reproach, and my shame, and my dishonor: mine adversaries are all before thee" (Psalm 69:19). Believe that, in your agony, sinner! *Turn to God.*

This text has at least one more thing to say to us. What if everything I have said leaves you unmoved? You say: "What of it? It will all work out. I think I'm doing alright as it is." What of it? This text says this to you: "God requireth that which is past." Another version says, "God seeketh again that which is driven away." *You are responsible for the efforts you have felt.*

Christ told Jerusalem, "How often would I . . . and ye would not!" (Matthew 23:37). *That could be the story of your life.* How many times have you driven your Saviour away—how many times?

He came back to ask men for the talents—the one with ten for his ten—the one with five for his five—and, yes, the man with only one for his one. *You will have to report.* Be sure of that.

There are professing church members in this audience who have spent more on one week's fishing trip—more on one night's entertainment—than they gave to the church all year. He'll come back, mister! You better have that report ready.

Sinner, what you say is already printed in the New Testament. Another sinner said it. "Go thy way for this time; when I have a convenient season, I will call for thee" (Acts 24:25).

You have already marked that "more convenient season" on your calendar. You and your family plan to be in the Sunday morning service next Christmas Sunday—weather permitting. Mister, He may have "a more convenient season" for you before Labor Day. God can make a date with you without consulting you.

Let me tell you what this text says one more time. "God seeketh again that which is driven away." You have driven those vows you made right out of your memory. You have driven those promises you made to mother on her deathbed right out of your heart. God will come back for them as certainly as this nation collects taxes.

There is salvation. God has a standing offer to cancel your past. He guarantees to stand with you in the present. He offers you a redeemed future. Make that your choice.

"Let the wicked forsake his way, and the unrighteous man his thoughts: and let him return unto the Lord, and he will have mercy upon him; and to our God, for he will abundantly pardon" (Isaiah 55:7).

UNTOWARD

Text: *"Save yourselves from this untoward generation."*
Acts 2:40

I WAS ministering recently in the Redwood Section of California, several hundreds of miles north of San Francisco. While there Dr. Fred Greve, professor at Bethany College, Santa Cruz, California, brought my attention to this passage.

Charles Dickens says in a memorable passage in The Tale of Two Cities:

> "It was the best of times, it was the worst of times; it was the age of wisdom, it was the age of foolishness; it was the epoch of belief, it was the epoch of incredulity; it was the spring of hope, it was the winter of despair; we had everything before us, we had nothing before us . . . It was the year of our Lord one thousand, seven-hundred-and-seventy-five."

And thus he speaks of an "untoward generation." The direction is not determined. They are neither *for* nor *against*. It is an alarming *drift*.

This is not the "hippie" or the "panther" or the "addict" or the "commie." They are *committed*. They are motivated and dedicated to either the extreme left or the extreme right. It is what is tabbed today as the "great silent majority"—the business-as-usual crowd—the it-can't-happen-to-us crowd—that float easily with the times. It is the *unconcerned*. It is the *unalarmed*. "Save yourselves (from that crowd, says Peter) from this *untoward* generation."

Christ pinpointed this *abstraction.* "Blessed are those servants, whom the lord when he cometh shall find *watching*" (Luke 12: 37). It is the lack of *aim* that is condemned. It reminds me of the navigator who told the pilot that they were lost, "But, sir," he added, "we're really making good time." The big crowds today *are going nowhere fast.* They are content to be "untoward."

A winner is he or she who has a goal in sight. This is the keynote in the 11th chapter of Hebrews. *Greatness is never an accident.* Abraham *"looked* for a city." Noah *"prepared* an ark to the saving of his house" (Hebrews 11:7). The author says of pilgrims, "they *seek* a country." He says of the intrepid, "now they *desire* a better country" (Hebrews 11:16). He says, later, of children of faith: "here have we no continuing city, but we seek one to come" (Hebrews 13:14). There is no question of *listlessness.* Mister, if you aren't *toward* anything, you won't make it.

Bishop Gerald Kennedy of the United Methodist diocese of Los Angeles, not long ago, reflected this about *sects.* He believes beginning groups or movements, sects, are distinctive. They are *toward.* They are pronounced and distinctive. Then, he believes, the developing and broadening period sets in when this forward movement is *diluted.* That is followed by the ecumenical pattern, where the movement gives place to the *untoward.*

Andy used to describe it to Amos in the former days of radio: "We is all lovin' brothers in the Mystic Knights of the Sea." It is a format of *anything goes.*

It isn't liberty, mister, it's license. It is a state of intoxicated carelessness. It can wreck a nation. It can wreck a church. It can wreck a marriage. It can wreck a soul. "Save yourselves from this untoward generation." It sounds like a general alarm at sea—"To the boats!"

Elijah, in his famous Carmel address and demonstration,

called a generation like that to order. "How long halt ye between two opinions? if the Lord be God, follow him: but if Baal, then follow him. And the people answered him not a word" (1 Kings 18:21). They weren't *toward* anything. Elijah called for a division of the house.

Edmund Burke reduced it to a sentence when he said: "For evil to triumph, it is only necessary for good men to do nothing."

Love is always a direction—a committed force. You love *someone* or *something.* It is definite. You don't fall in love "in general." There is a specific. There is an *attraction.* You are *involved.* It isn't a matter of cold, machine-like calculation. It defies *logic.*

Why should a tall man feel as he does toward a short girl? Why should a woman from a privileged class give her heart to a practically unknown? This mystery cannot be solved by the computer. Thank God, it can't!

There are forces which *command* us. Suddenly, I *care.* I care in excess of my need to sleep or my need to eat. I am possessed. Like a magnet draws, I am *drawn.* I feel responsible. There is a conviction that my sense of well-being, my fortune, even my desire to live are interwoven with another. I am no longer the master of my own destiny. I am overwhelmed. I feel respect. I want to treat her like a queen. I solicit her preferences. I protect her entrances and exits. No, sir, you can't be in love and be *untoward.*

There is an ominous warning sounded by our Lord in Matthew 24:39: "and *knew not* until the flood came, and took them all away; so shall also the coming of the Son of man be." *That is the cost of indifference.* Noah *knew.* They didn't. Noah knew that society had become rotten ripe. Noah knew that a flood tide of violence and unrestrained lawlessness and profane and vulgar patterns could not go on indefinitely. Noah knew there is always a season for the Holy Spirit to *strive,* and that there is a deadline. "They *knew not.*"

It's the Titanic running full speed ahead into the iceberg. It is France and Britain blissfully ignoring the signs of impending World War II. It is George III losing the American Colonies. It is the man smiling at the cough that warns him that cancer is attacking his lungs. "They *knew not.*" If people would fight sin like they fight old age, we could have a paradise.

An "untoward generation" *destroys values.* The attitude of I-don't-care-what-happens shreds priorities. Value is based on *how much something is wanted.* The more a painting or a piece of art is wanted, the more value is attached to it. When no interest is shown, the article is practically worthless.

No one is born with values. These must be declared. They must be *chosen.* There is no future for an indefinite generation. The attitude of I-don't-know-what-I-want, or it-doesn't-matter-to-me, or I-can't-make-up-my-mind is a *diaster route.*

"Set your affection on things above, not on things on the earth" (Colossians 3:2). There's some "setting" to do. That is an operation God assigns to me. I must, by deliberate choice, turn my soul heavenward. *No man on earth will ever land in heaven by mistake.*

God "set" Himself toward our redemption. "In whom also we have obtained an inheritance, being predestinated according to the purpose of him who worketh all things after the counsel of his own will" (Ephesians 1:11).

My salvation, mister, isn't a happenstance, some lucky break in history. My salvation is a *plan.* God wills it. "But with the precious blood of Christ, as of a lamb without blemish and without spot: who verily was *foreordained* before the foundation of the world, but was manifest in these last times for you" (1 Peter 1:19, 20).

It is said of Jesus: "Therefore have I set my face like a flint, and I know that I shall not be ashamed" (Isaiah 50:7). That is the price of victory, sir!

"Save yourselves from this *untoward* generation," was Peter's rallying cry as he preached at the Day of Pentecost. It was a generation that could shout "hosanna" one day, and 24 hours later "crucify." It was a generation that could prostitute itself before Caesar, and curse him under its breath. It was a generation that could for a pretense make long prayers and at the same time devour widows' houses (see Matthew 23:14). It was a generation that could crowd out to hear John the Baptist, and abandon the Messiah he was born to proclaim. It was a *wind-blown* generation, "tossed to and fro, and carried about with every wind of doctrine, by the sleight of men, and cunning craftiness, whereby they lie in wait to deceive" (Ephesians 4:14). It was a generation without a *rudder*.

It's peril, sir, to be sucked in to such a maelstrom. It's a lackadaisical attitude of "neither cold nor hot" that brings the divine rebuke, "I will spew thee out of my mouth" (Revelation 3:16).

Be *toward* something in this hour! Have convictions! Stand up and be counted! "Whether it be right in the sight of God to hearken unto you more than unto God, judge ye. For we cannot but speak the things which we have seen and heard" (Acts 4:19, 20). *That attitude became a powerhouse.* Civic leaders said, "These that have turned the world upside down are come hither also" (Acts 17:6). They became "more than conquerors."

It's an interesting injunction, *Save yourselves!* You and I must make that move. We can be smothered by another "untoward (aimless) generation." There is a drift in morals and standards of conduct.

Styles are indiscriminate—"without form, and void." Ambition is scorned. The "mod" is the unwashed body, unshaven, unpressed, undistinguished, indeterminate lounger and scrounger. A no-win policy is the order of the way. The laissez-faire doctrine is embraced. Accumulated debt is encouraged. The schoolroom has surrendered to "anything goes" attitudes. Father turns the discipline of the family to the paid social worker in the community. Preachers think of security. The courts of the land wrangle and delay. Society offers its bosom to the criminal. Abroad are "seducing spirits, and doctrines of devils; speaking lies in hypocrisy; having their conscience seared with a hot iron" (1 Timothy 4:1, 2).

And the cry rings out, "Save yourselves!" It is an *alarm,* sir! You should do something about it. Joshua survived an "untoward generation"—a generation that rebelled and died in the wilderness. He survived an "untoward" committee. He survived "untoward" tactics that sought to shackle him.

How did he do it? He gives the secret in the farewell address to Israel: "Choose (be toward something) you this day whom ye will serve; whether the gods which your fathers served that were on the other side of the flood, or the gods of the Amorites, in whose land ye dwell: but as for me and my house, *we will serve the Lord*" (Joshua 24:15).

God can do something with such a choice. I ask you to reach a decision.

A REVIVALTIME TESTIMONY

"I am stationed on a remote Coast Guard station in Alaska, but am fortunate that *Revivaltime* tapes are sent to us here. It is a bit of home!"

ESAU AND ISHMAEL

Text: *"And Esau said, I have enough, my brother; keep that thou hast unto thyself. And Jacob said, Nay, I pray thee, if now I have found grace in thy sight, then receive my present at my hand: for therefore I have seen thy face, as though I had seen the face of God, and thou wast pleased with me."*
Genesis 33:9, 10

ISRAEL is the heir of a strange, historical *tandem confrontation.* These two lingering "accounts payable" have had long sizzling fuses that have threatened a world holocaust since the Book of Genesis. They are (1) *the quarrel between Isaac and Ishmael,* and (2) *the blood feud between Jacob and Esau.* Both have carried bitterness. God is involved in each dispute. They are woven into the history of this planet.

I believe one of these threats is about to be miraculously solved. I believe the 33rd and the 34th chapters of Genesis foreshadow astounding developments in the Middle East that are ready to unfold before us. John M. Hightower, veteran reporter and analyst of foreign affairs has written:

"The cease-fire in the Middle East . . . is a rare and unexpected triumph . . . over deep fears and bitter hatreds matured by 22 years of . . . conflict. . . . *The chances of success were rated by top Washington policy makers as near zero.*

"Prolonged attempts at peace-making, including the yearlong joint U.S.-Soviet effort that collapsed in December, had already failed."

We are witnessing a rare turnabout. A few years ago the solidarity of the Communist world was cracked when Mao Tse-tung of China and the Kremlin leaders broke fellowship over dialectics. A bitter and resolved doctrinal dispute has followed.

Now *a deep fissure* threatens to divide the Pan-Arab world. The fact has been incorporated in our Bible all along. *Esau's problem is different than Ishmael's problem.* And Esau will come to terms before Ishmael. There is an *"inner periphery" and an "outer periphery" to Israel's dilemma, and her struggle to find acceptance.*

These Genesis chapters describe Jacob's return to the land after exile. They reveal material resources on both sides. They speak of a *threat* and a *fear* and *maneuverings* that bring unreconciled parties to the brink. The motive is a long-simmering desire for revenge. It is the revenge of a relative who feels he has been shamed before a world audience and made to look weak and stupid.

Israel's pride and strength—her confidence that she can even wrestle with Almighty God and write history in her favor—*is about to be touched.* There is a reconciliation in the offing. Let me read these wonderful lines from Scripture to you again:

"And Esau said, I have enough, my brother; keep that thou hast unto thyself. And Jacob said, Nay, I pray thee, if now I have found grace in thy sight, then receive my present at my hand: for therefore I have seen thy face, as though I had seen the face of God, and thou wast pleased with me. Take, I pray thee, my blessing that is brought to thee; *because God hath dealt graciously with me, and because I have enough.* And he urged him, and he took it" (Genesis 33:9-11).

Mister, watch that scene come into focus! Note these prophetic words: "I have seen thy face, as though I had seen the face of God, *and thou wast pleased with me.*" Israel's problems, as tension grew, seemed almost insurmountable.

The peace-making formula of Secretary of State William P. Rogers, Soviet Foreign Minister Andrei A. Gromyko, Assistant Secretary Joseph J. Sisco, and Soviet Ambassador Anatoly F.

Dobrynin lay in wreckage. Israel's pressure to buy 125 new jet fighters from this country was relentless. It was a step that would bring any further relationship of this nation with the Arab to a final breaking point. That became crystal clear.

In the meantime the Soviet became more deeply involved in the conflict. Israel's economy and manpower could not stand a war of attrition. It is what Defense Minister Moshe Dayan told a Tel Aviv audience that Israel was strong enough to reject directives from her friends "but she is not so strong that she can afford to lose allies."

There was that specter—a possible nuclear-power confrontation in the Middle East. Russian pilots began flying defensive patrols along the Suez. Then, suddenly, this turn in events—a move toward understanding!

Could you choose a better description, "I have seen thy face, as though I had seen the face of God, and thou wast pleased with me"?

And, now, *this cleft in the Arab world!* Remember! There is the story of *Esau,* and there is the story of *Ishmael.* These stories are different. *The story of Esau is the story where diplomacy prevails.*

Esau *sold* his right. Ishmael was *driven* out. Go back to the story of Esau! Isaac said: "What shall I do now unto thee, my son? And Esau said unto his father, Hast thou but one blessing, my father? *bless me, . . . also,* O my father. . . . And Isaac his father answered and said unto him, Behold, thy dwelling shall be the fatness of the earth, and of the dew of heaven from above; and by thy sword shalt thou live, *and shalt serve thy brother*: and it shall come to pass when thou shalt have the dominion, that thou shalt break his yoke from off thy neck" (Genesis 27:37-40).

It's a strange contract. I'll tell you this. Unusual events are in the making.

And there is another interesting corollary to this strife between twins. It is a detail that a casual Bible reader can miss. "And Esau seeing that the daughters of Canaan pleased not Isaac his father; *then went Esau unto Ishmael,* and took . . . wives" (Genesis 28:8, 9). So, you see, it has been an old alliance.

But a point of live-and-let-live must be reached, *where each must go his own way.* That is Isaac's promise to Esau: "It shall come to pass when thou shalt have the dominion, that thou shalt break his yoke from off thy neck" (Genesis 27:40). *That moment in history seems to be approaching.* It's always exciting to live in Bible prophecy.

The words of Moses to Israel, found in Deuteronomy 23:7 are enlightening. "Thou shalt not abhor an Edomite; *for he is thy brother*: thou shalt not abhor an Egyptian; because thou wast a stranger in his land."

Others about Israel were not treated with the same deference. The most amazing summary is found in Hebrews 11:20: "By *faith* (so there was no possibility of error) Isaac blessed Jacob *and Esau* concerning things to come." The time in history has arrived for fulfillment of those "things to come."

Every Bible student should read the amazing directive found in Deuteronomy 2:4, 5. "Ye are to pass through the coast of your brethren the children of Esau, which dwell in Seir; and they shall be afraid of you: take ye good heed unto yourselves therefore: *meddle not with them; for I will not give you of their land, no, not so much as a footbreadth*; because I have given mount Seir unto Esau for a possession."

Russia is going to discover that Jacob and Esau are *twin brothers,* and that there is a limit to what misunderstanding and strife can be promoted between them. That is what this story in Genesis prophetically forecasts. This world is in for a surprise. "And Esau ran to meet him (Jacob), . . . and fell on his neck, and kissed him: *and they wept*" (Genesis 33:4).

There are land promises to Esau which cannot be *abrogated.*

That is why the Suez and Sinai will be negotiated. Joshua 24:4 says: "And I gave unto Isaac Jacob *and Esau*: and I gave unto Esau mount Seir, to possess it."

Seir is the great fortress city, Petra, of modern-day tourist attraction. In past history it has been known as "The Rose Red City" and "The Rainbow City." It once had an organized culture of 267,000 inhabitants. It stood above and guardian at the crossroads of the old caravan routes that moved east to west and north to south. It is one of Nature's great landlocked fortress areas. Its history is an exciting story, both past and future. Cleopatra gave it to Mark Anthony as a wedding present. Genesis 36 records: "These are the generations of Esau the father of the Edomites in mount Seir (Genesis 36:9); "And these are the *kings* that reigned in the land of Edom, before there reigned any king over the children of Israel" (Genesis 36:31).

Daniel gives us an amazing prediction before he closes his prophecy. He tells us that the Man of sin, Antichrist, will not infest the Sinai or Petra. Here it is, Daniel 11:41: "He shall enter also into the glorious land, and many countries shall be overthrown: but these shall escape out of his hand, *even Edom, and Moab,* and the chief of the children of Ammon."

Isaiah and Jeremiah reveal even more amazing details! When sin has reached its zenith and Antichrist has set himself forth in the Temple, *a great counterinsurgency will arise*. "Behold, he shall come up and fly as the eagle, and spread his wings over Bozrah: and at that day shall the heart of the mighty men of Edom be as the heart of a woman in her pangs" (Jeremiah 49:22).

The sense of expectancy and fulfillment will reach their final crescendo. It will be the knowledge *that He has come.* Let Isaiah add further detail. "Who is this that cometh from Edom, with dyed garments from Bozrah? this that is glorious in his apparel, traveling in the greatness of his strength? I that speak in righteousness, mighty to save" (Isaiah 63:1).

So the outlines of the Lord's return grow more and more firm, sir.

Balaam, who was hired to curse Israel, but who was made to bless Israel under the duress of God, prophesies in Numbers: "There shall come a Star out of Jacob, and a Sceptre shall rise out of Israel, and shall smite *the corners* of Moab (just the corners), and . . . Seir also shall be a possession *for* his enemies; and Israel shall do valiantly" (Numbers 24:17, 18). That pattern is now forming as messianic prophecies are being fulfilled. Mister, God gave you a Bible to read!

The pattern, now emerging again before the councils of Earth, has long been set. Numbers gives the account of the impasse: "Thus saith thy brother Israel, Thou knowest all the travail that hath befallen us: . . . We will go by the high way: and if I and my cattle drink of thy water, then I will pay for it: I will only, without doing any thing else, go through on my feet. And he said, Thou shalt not go through. And Edom came out against him with much people, and with a strong hand. Thus Edom refused to give Israel passage through his border: *wherefore Israel turned away from him*" (Numbers 20:14, 19-21).

Jephthah, the judge, recalls this incident. "When Israel came up from Egypt, and walked through the wilderness unto the Red sea, and came to Kadesh; then Israel sent messengers unto the king of Edom, saying, Let me, I pray thee, pass through thy land: but the king of Edom would not hearken thereto. And in like manner they sent unto the king of Moab; but he would not consent: and Israel abode in Kadesh. Then they went along through the wilderness, and compassed the land of Edom, and the land of Moab, and came by the east side of the land of Moab, and pitched on the other side of Arnon, but came not within the border of Moab" (Judges 11:16-18). Moab is the legacy of Lot's seed, the nephew of Abraham.

There are *blood ties*. They will be sorted. There are *multiple contracts* of God to these varied, interrelated seeds. Each contract will be kept. God is not confused. History will be written God's way. Military and geographical adjustments will be made to conform to prophecy. God deals in what mankind thinks impossible.

Never reckon without counting God in! *He is in the business of turning hatred to peace.* There had been days when Esau hated Jacob. "Esau said in his heart, The days of mourning for my father are at hand; then will I slay my brother Jacob" (Genesis 27:41). That changed! "And Esau ran to meet him, and embraced him, and fell on his neck, and kissed him: and they wept" (Genesis 33:4).

God wants to make the same change in your life. So, give a little and God will give a lot! There's a better day available.

A REVIVALTIME TESTIMONY

"It is like having God talk to me when I listen to *Revivaltime*. *Revivaltime* is the living Word of God in action to me."

RELIGION PAYS

Text: "*Godliness is profitable unto all things, having promise of the life that now is, and of that which is to come.*"
1 *Timothy* 4:8

GODLINESS means belief in God and a daily practice of that belief.

First, you have to *know* that God *is*. David's assurance, "I shall not want" was predicated on his knowledge, "The Lord is my shepherd" (Psalm 23:1).

God doesn't ask for faith without *evidence*. That doesn't mean you can explain everything. But God always furnishes a *reason* for faith. Take the Bible! God asks us to believe that it is like no other book—that it is infallible. So, you comb the pages. You test each verse. The evidence is there.

Without such evidence religion could not sustain itself. I would buckle under temptation. I could not live a godly life, mister, if I had to keep pretending there was a God.

Superstition can never support godliness. I must have an unshakable foundation. I need more than family tradition, fable, legend, or a mystic's reverie. I need *fact*.

I see this so plainly in the 119th Psalm. "I have more understanding than all my teachers: for thy testimonies are my meditation" (Psalm 119:99). In the New Testament you have it again. "This is life eternal, that they might *know* thee, the only true God, and Jesus Christ, whom thou hast sent" (John 17:3). You have to *know*. "I know that my Redeemer liveth" (Job 19:25).

Second, there must be *sincerity*. There is no godliness without sincerity. And yet it is the best counterfeited item on earth. That is why there are so many hypocrites in the church. A hypocrite can talk like a saint. A hypocrite can be as precise as a saint. A hypocrite can dress like a saint. He can be outwardly pious, yet all the time at heart be a devil. The Pharisees were professionally pious men. Their total design, however, was to gain influence—to impress those who judged by outward appearance.

When God gives Himself to us, it is not in mere appearance—outward show—but *wholly* and without reservation. *God means it!* Godliness isn't sham or imitation. It isn't "tinkling cymbal" or "sounding brass." It is more than *form,* sir. There is a *power* to it. It has authority—grip!

Third, there must be *zeal.* Godliness—that something that is profitable—is founded upon knowledge, manifests itself in sincerity *and operates by zeal.* There must be *fervor.* A godly man will let his light shine.

David *danced* before the Lord. He was a successful politician, a popular general, married into society, *but he danced.* Nothing could cool his ardor.

Paul knew every affliction in the book, but nothing could keep him from *glorying.* He made headlines wherever he went.

Solomon knew wealth and prestige as few will ever be privileged to know it and he said: "Many waters cannot quench *love,* neither can the floods drown it" (Song of Solomon 8:7). Read the Song of Solomon, and you will feel exuberance. It will take you back to your honeymoon.

Religion is meant to be like that. When it becomes irksome, cold, and boring, it is no longer godliness or profitable. So, now, what are the *advantages?*

"Godliness is profitable." How? If I were to ask you what, above all else, you desire in life, it would be interesting to note where you would place godliness on the list. But, note! "Godliness is profitable *unto all things.*" There is a relationship.

There are many things we can have and not have godliness. A wicked man may have health and wealth, education and fame. But, not one of these, or a combination of these, is capable of being profitable unto all things.

A man's health may fail at any moment, and then what does that man have? This is the problem with great athletes. In an unfortunate second an athlete's entire life can be shattered. A man's wealth may vanish. Then, what does he have in his poverty? A man's fame may recede. Then, what does he have in his obscurity? This is the problem with stage and screen stars. They are soon forgotten. Their names are dropped. What do they have that is "profitable unto all things?"

How can you tackle the sorrows of life? How can you equate the injustices? Where can you find compensation? You can't liquidate every sorrow with your bankbook. You can't right every injustice with your education. You can't answer every mystery with your personal reputation.

I think you shortchange yourself, sir, when you leave godliness out of your life. Your bank account needs to be geared to faith. Your education needs to point you to God. Your health needs a foundation of thankfulness. Otherwise, you can be the most miserable, rich, erudite, popular, healthy man on the block. "What is a man profited, if he shall gain the whole world, and lose his own soul? or what shall a man give in exchange for his soul?" (Matthew 16:26).

Godliness is also profitable *unto all times.* Paul says, "having promise of the life that now is, and that which is to come."

Eternity is so long and residence on earth so short, that "that which is to come" must have precedence. Paul thought so. In comparison, he said: "Our light affliction, which is but for a moment, worketh for us a far more exceeding and eternal weight of glory; while we look not at the things which are seen, but at the things which are not seen: for the things which are seen are temporal; but the things which are not seen are eternal" (2 Corinthians 4:17, 18).

Is that how it *weighs* out with you, sir? Let me look at your scales! What weight have you placed upon these few, paltry years of residence upon earth? What are your *investments?* How many thousands do you have tied up in the house? What extra thousands do you have in the accessories—that boat, that automobile, that ranch, those stocks, those antiques, those rare furnishings, that art, that expensive education, those memberships? Let me see what is tipping the scale in your life! Is it *time* or *eternity?*

You forget, sir, how fleeting the moments are—how your existence on earth is suspended one breath at a time. So you grab grab for money, thinking that you may reach for godliness at any time. Because God makes salvation free, you propose to take it when you please. That is like a child going to his father and saying, "Because I can love you any time I will not love you now." "That which is to come"—the big existence—is always a very narrow step away.

But godliness has even something to say for the present and now. There are apparent advantages for the man who is centered on the here and now. The godly man is even better off right here on this earth. I'll tell you this. The godly man has a better conscience than the sinner. I would rather have a toothache or a backache or a tummy ache, than I would to have a conscience ache.

The godly man has a peace of mind that no sinner can ever enjoy. The believer enjoys a pardon and a confidence. Now let me list some of the other *advantages*:

First, *godliness influences health.* Ask your insurance companies. Lusts and hellish habits take their expensive toll. They will rob a man of sleep and spill his energy in every Satanic pigpen. The writer of Proverbs knew what he was talking about when he said, "The fear of the Lord prolongeth days" (Proverbs 10:27). It is a fountain of life, to guard us from the snares of death (see Proverbs 14:27).

Second, *godliness influences our reputation.* Every parent recognizes this. No father wants his son to get in with the wrong crowd. Every mother warns her daughter to avoid the fast set. Employment agencies are still looking for church memberships when interviewing applicants.

Third, *godliness influences happiness.* What real pleasure does a man have, who can't stand being left alone for one minute? He needs perpetual dissipation. He has to drink. He has to tell and hear dirty stories. He has to gamble. He has to dance. He is a *fugitive.* He has to hide from himself his real condition. He doesn't want to meet himself as he really is. So he buys excitement. He seeks the crowd. He caters noise to numb his soul. He gets drunk to avoid looking into the future. Mister, *godliness will free you from torment.*

Fourth, *godliness influences contentment.* I could correct all the social troubles between rich and poor in five minutes could I make men believe Paul's words: "I have learned, in whatsoever state I am, therewith *to be content.* I know both how to be abased, and I know how to abound: every where and in all things I am instructed both to be full and to be hungry, both to abound and to suffer need" (Philippians 4:11, 12).

Like a ball player you ride the *slump* and you ride the *crest.* Godliness enables you to live happy and die easy.

Godliness is *profitable,* sir. Have you made that decision? What grounds have you for postponement? You can't always go on sowing. *Soon you must reap.* There must be a full audit of your life—an eternal evaluation, to see whether or not you are worthwhile and fit for eternal service.

Yes, you are adventuring—finding out what life is all about!

But there is always the return journey. And when you finish the trip, what will be profitable? I have a conviction it is in these words:

"A charge to keep you have,
A God to glorify;
A never-dying soul to save,
And fit it for the sky."

A REVIVALTIME TESTIMONY

"Although I am of the Catholic faith, I listen to *Revivaltime* every Sunday. I am physically handicapped and unable to attend church services very often. *Revivaltime* is my 'church.' "

MOTIVATION

Text: *"The life which I now live in the flesh I live by the faith of the Son of God, who loved me, and gave himself for me."*

Galatians 2:20

THIS is Paul's *personal testimony*. Something must motivate you to choose right instead of wrong. There are only *two* ways to live—*right* or *wrong*. What are the *incentives* toward righteousness?

Paul experienced both kinds of living. He speaks from personal involvement. He *explored*. He tasted deeply. He is a giant character. He can talk to any of us. He was the first great missionary of our religion. He was the liberator of Christianity, its great emancipator from the outer shell, the chains of Judaism. *His life was totally remade.*

When you ask for examples of purity of purpose, nobility of soul, complete devotion, untiring energy, dauntless courage—you look to Saul of Tarsus. He wrote them into the record. They have become a part of the *history* of this planet. What this one man accomplished is too big to deny or ignore.

The questions are: "How did he do it? What was the impelling force of such a career?" The answer is in this text: "The life which I now live in the flesh I live by the faith of the Son of God, who loved me, and gave himself for me." *In substance, he fell in love, and never fell out.*

If you are content to drift, I have no message for you. If you are without hunger and thirst to make your life count, I am wasting your time, and you are wasting mine. There is no interest in what I shall say to the person who lives for self and sin. You and I are on different sides.

I'm addressing myself to the person who wants to *climb*. This service is directed to the person who means to have *victory*. I can't do a thing for the person who grovels in failure. I believe there is something better than wallowing in sin. I believe there is a Power that can substantiate your personal decision when you say, "I will *arise*." I believe it, or I wouldn't preach it.

I want to live as successfully for God as I lived, one time, for the devil. I want to head as surely toward heaven, as one time I headed toward hell. This man, Paul, tells me how he did it.

I know this. I can't do it *in* myself. I am a sinner *by nature*, the same as anyone else. It isn't *in* me to sacrifice, to spend my resources for the gospel, to say "no" to the chatter and the conduct of this world. The *pull* is too strong. I get carried away like others.

I know people *try*. God knows they do! They discipline themselves. They pledge themselves. They organize societies to channel themselves toward noble purposes. They flee to retreats and shut themselves off from worldly contact. Oh, yes! Thousands in every generation bravely set out to climb "the highest hill."

What happens? Where are the *champions?* Who dares to enter the ring and face his besetting sin? Where is the winner —the person whose life is the epitome of self-control? Suddenly circumstances provoke a full-scale attack and that person is ravaged—and self-control, his poise, lies shattered, and a respected life is shambles. The work of weeks and months is undone. That person is covered with shame, filled with despair, and debates within whether it is worthwhile to ever try again. I am speaking to many in this audience.

But the "highest hill" is there to climb! It challenges you. Every day you have the feeling. You want to know what it is like at the *top*. You already know what it is like *below*. What can sustain your climb? That is the question.

History is filled with suggestions. One school tells me there is latent in man himself all the necessary power; that there is no need for Christianity, or for that matter, any other religious impulse. They believe like Socrates that *ignorance is the cause of sin.* I wish it were. I would vote to make education compulsory all the way through university level. This group promotes the idea that men will do right if they *know* right. It sounds promising.

There's a gulf between good *resolutions* and good *living.* If every marriage adhered to the vows groom and bride swear to keep at the altar, the divorce courts would go out of business. Knowing what to do, and *doing* it are two different matters. Gazing at beauty doesn't make me beautiful. Sin began in a *garden.*

Paul knew all about that school. "The good that I would, I do not: but the evil which I would not, (which I hate) that I do" (Romans 7:19). That is the sad experience of humanity.

Not one resident of the state penitentiary ever planned to go to prison. Not one gambler ever planned to throw good money away after bad money. Every thief plans to get his capital, and then quit and go honest. Why doesn't it work out that way? "Therefore to him that *knoweth* to do good, and doeth it not, to him it is sin" (James 4:17). Knowledge only increases the guilt.

I'll tell you this. Any prescription of "thou shalt" and "thou shalt not," will never work. It may provide temporary relief. That is like prescribing skin salve for malignant, organic cancer. It's an *outward* remedy, and my malady is *inward.*

I need something to get down inside. I need a determination—a *will.* Putting me behind bars won't make a good man out of me. The "want" inside of me has to be changed. Paul put it plainly: "For the flesh lusteth against the Spirit, and the Spirit against the flesh: and these are contrary the one to the other; so that ye cannot do the things ye would" (Galatians 5:17). It becomes sham and mockery.

It is like repeating incantations over a corpse. Something inside of me has to be *awakened.* It is like a boy who sees no use or purpose for girls suddenly thinking about and wanting nothing else.

Ethics have no power to resurrect. Seminars don't produce saints. There must be an electric current of God's grace. There must be an *infusion.* The Law may say, "Thou shalt." Conscience may add, "Yes, I should." But it takes Christ within to say, "I will."

I know all about the Sermon on the Mount. Read your New Testament and you will discover that Jesus spent all the previous night in prayer. If it took prayer to fit Him to even *preach* it, how much more prayer must it take to *practice* it?

There is a particular school of objectors who cry: "Hold up His spotless life, His busy, philanthropic life; preach the duty of imitation of Christ and leave theology in the background. Get back to the Christianity of Christ," they say. "The Sermon on the Mount should be good enough for anyone," they plead. That sounds very, very reasonable.

Don't be shocked! *Where is there any gospel, any good news, in the Sermon on the Mount?* What Christ outlined in that sermon is *tougher* than anything Moses outlined. Jesus gave us God's interpretation of the Law by which we must be judged.

He tells me that unjustifiable anger against my brother makes me a murderer in God's sight. He tells me that unchaste thinking makes me an adulterer in God's sight. A sermon like that makes me want to go back into the Old Testament for relief. It only makes my burden heavier to bear. That *Mount* isn't half as easy to climb as Mount Sinai. You and I need more than the Sermon on the Mount, mister! You better get that through your head right now.

I want to tell some of you liberal-minded preachers that the gentle Lamb of God you love to preach can become the Lion of the tribe of Judah roaring in the ears of conscience, all the thunders of God's perfect, inexorable law.

When we do not appropriate the effects of Christ's death, the life of Jesus is powerless to save us. I need more than to *reflect* on the goodness and perfection of Christ. I need to experience the *redemption* He offers. The menu and the meal may be the best culinary art can afford. But I am still a starving, dying man until I exercise knife and fork and personally receive the meal. Smelling flowers doesn't make me a flower.

True, His name is Emmanuel, "God with us." He was the brightness of the Father's glory, the spotless image of God's person and character; but as such, He would have only *dismayed* and *dazzled* us by making it perfectly clear the infinite distance between man and God, unless His name had also been called Jesus, the *Saviour*. Without His atoning death, breaking down the barriers of sin and guilt, what I need, sir, would have been beyond reach. It is His death and resurrection that are victory for me. All roads lead to Calvary. That is what makes Jesus Christ different to any other in history.

Through Paul, Jesus continues to teach mankind the full meaning of this victory. He "loved me, and gave himself for me." So Paul says, "Look at me! It *worked* in me. It is not just theory. 'The life which I now live in the flesh.'" It is more than contemplation, more than admiration, more than imitation, sir! It is Christ "*in* you."

One-fifth of the Gospels is taken up with the account of that one dark day of crucifixion, and were the entire earthly life of Christ told with a proportional minuteness, it would take two hundred volumes the size of our Bible. That is the importance of Calvary! That is why Paul makes justification by faith his central theme. He believes everything pivots on that truth.

Yes, mister critic, I agree that *conduct* is indeed three-fourths of life. It is like the three-fourths of a tree *above* ground, but *underneath* are the roots of faith in the soil, watered by the rain and dews of divine grace. It is like a house where three-fourths is above ground, but beneath are the foundations.

The life of Jesus gives us an *ideal,* a standard of perfection and beauty, but no *power.* Calvary and the Resurrection provide that power. He "loved me, and gave himself for me." That is what *changes* me.

You know that when you would lift a heavy weight with a power which we call a lever, you must have a point on which to rest the lever as you bear down upon it. We call that point a *fulcrum.* The great Syracusan mathematician Archimedes once said: "Give me a place where I may stand (a fulcrum), and I will move the world."

I have a moral problem to lift. Where shall I find that fulcrum? Where shall I stand in order to bring the lever of effort to its most effective use? Will I stand on the Sermon on the Mount? Will I stand on Christ's miracles? Will I stand on His patriotism?

The apostle directs us to the green hill without the city wall. I will stand at the Cross and the Open Tomb. My victory is there. He "loved me, and gave himself for *me*."

That, mister, is saving, lifting, redeeming faith. Exercise it, and immediately something *moves.* You experience *power.* Head knowledge becomes heart experience. There is no substitute for falling in love. Paul knew it. He said, "the love of Christ constraineth me" (2 Corinthians 5:14).

Now, say it with me, "He loved *me,* and gave himself for *me*."

A REVIVALTIME TESTIMONY

"We are Mormons. We enjoy hearing your sermons on Sunday and make it a duty to wake up at 8 a m. to turn the broadcast on."

ACCURSED

Text: "*But though we, or an angel from heaven, preach any other gospel unto you than that which we have preached unto you, let him be accursed. As we said before, so say I now again, If any man preach any other gospel unto you than that ye have received, let him be accursed.*"

Galatians 1:8, 9

YOU meet an undercover attempt to formulate a "new gospel" for this hour—*a relevant religion.* We might as well talk of adding new elements to the earth and the air. Every element of nature which man needs for the health of his body, the enlargement of his thought and of his resources, is beneath or around us. New models? Yes! New combinations? Yes! New discoveries and applications? Yes! But *new material*—never!

God stored in the gospel of Jesus Christ all that mankind needs or ever will need for his social, intellectual, and spiritual life.

I'll tell you this, mister! The God who made the material world perfect did not make that which is higher imperfect. Put the gospel to the test, sir!

The power of the gospel is not limited to the rapture of pardon in a human soul; its vitality is not confined to meditations upon the divine love. Christians are not called to be shutaways who build for themselves cloisters. The Church of Jesus Christ is not a Tower of London to preserve mementos and guard crowns. *It is a vital force applied to this generation.*

The gospel never *smothers.* It *directs.* The science of navigation cannot tell a wheelsman how many times in an hour he is to move the wheel to the right, and how many times he is to move the wheel to the left.

How shall this vital force—the gospel—be applied today? What is needed?

First, *an increase of faith in the Bible, and in the unlimited power of the gospel it proclaims.* The tendency in our highly developed laboratory research is to magnify the wonders of nature, and lose sight of the personal being, until God becomes only "a Law" around which all other laws coil.

Mister, God is not a law. He is the *life* of all that is. "My soul thirsteth . . . for the *living* God" (Psalm 42:2)—not some equation, but for a God of revelation who feels my heart throb into His, and who hears prayers and answers them.

We are not experiencing anything new in these troubled times. Where there is *progress,* there will be *questions;* and where there are questions, there will be aspiring and scoffing men withstanding the truth.

Exploded forms of error are always taking new forms and new names. Paul called them in his day, "babblings, and oppositions of science falsely so called: which some professing have erred concerning the faith" (1 Timothy 6:20, 21).

The *authority* is in that Bible, mister! And the triumph of Jesus Christ—His death and resurrection—establishes that authority. The Bible rises or falls with Jesus Christ. It is as simple as that.

Second, *an awakening to holiness and righteousness is needed.* The only real Christianity is Bible Christianity. It is defined there. Holiness means likeness to God. Holiness means a godly walk and conversation. You cannot separate holiness from righteousness. A cultural acceptability is not enough. God is the fountain, and holy living is the stream. Preacher, I must have a mighty inspiration from God. I cannot produce Bible righteousness *in,* or *of,* or *by* myself. Any kind of self-righteousness is obnoxious.

Preacher, *some form of godliness is not godliness.* Our

churches are full of forms. "By the deeds of the law there shall no flesh be justified" (Romans 3:20). Are we not called to "the righteousness . . . which is *by faith*"? (Romans 3:22). It isn't something I produce. It is something that is *imparted.* An emotional experience should never be placed above *character.*

Love toward man is joined eternally to love toward God. "What . . . God hath joined together, let not man put asunder" (Matthew 19:6). I must live and move and have my being *in* God. And if God isn't in that service, preacher, I'm not going to get one thing out of it—no matter how well run the service may be.

Let me offer this piece of advice. *Don't wait for feelings.* The feelings which have character are those which come *after* the soul is consecrated to God. If I owe a man $5,000, due today, and I have in my pocket a checkbook and in the bank the money, what nonsense—worse than nonsense—for me to plead delay because my *feelings* are not aroused. Pay the debt! Right feelings will *follow.*

In so many of our services we are trying to get *feelings.* "He that keepeth my commandments, he it is that loveth me" (see John 14:21). What does the Bible say? Preach it! Urge action toward it.

The pulpit has no authority to make allowances, any more than a baseball umpire behind home plate has authority to make allowances. Preach the *Word!* Set forth the distinction. Wrong is wrong. Right is right.

Third, *there is need to adjust the relations between rights and obligations.* I have certain *rights,* and I have certain *obligations.* These personal rights were won through struggle. Brave men led the battle. Freedom is a precious legacy.

Our national existence and character were formed under a declaration and maintenance of rights which the exigencies of the times demanded. We have held out to all nations the invitation: "Come, for here are equal rights to all men." It has an invitation unequaled in history.

An American, today, boasts of his rights and stands protected by his rights; and well he may, for they have been won by the courage and self-denial, and prayers and blood of godly ancestry. But this spirit which claims rights is getting beyond bounds; is being debased and is running riot toward our destruction. The lawless have seized upon it, and are hurrying liberty into license.

There is no gospel without *obedience* or *duty,* mister. Melville wrote something that will stand the test of time:

"What we call faith when considered as waiting upon God, we call obedience when considered as going forth at his bidding. The cherub with the wing folded in the presence of the Almighty is Faith. The cherub with the wing expanded to execute his commission is Obedience. *But the wing is the same* whether folded or expanded, and the cherub in its burning flight through immensity, and in its silent standing before the throne of the Creator, *acts on one principle and yields but to one law.*"

The Good Samaritan did a *duty,* but a sense of duty did not drive him. He had "compassion" upon the wounded man. Love in his heart drew him, and in love he did his duty. In the Christian, "I must" is changed to "I love to." Thus our duties and responsibilities become our best privileges. And when this operates, the great questions of social life arrange themselves and find solution.

What are the rights and the obligations of *property?* Human law, based upon divine law, secures each of us the absolute control and use of our property as against any and every other mortal claimant outside our families. But the gospel makes us "stewards" and requires us to hold our property as God's gift, and to use it—*all of it*—in God's service.

My brain and my influence are rights, but the rights of responsibility—responsibility to God, responsibility to man. *God never gave the right of self-indulgence.*

Face the gospel, sir, and you will discover that the possession of endowments of mind or soul: the possession of property, be it large or small, for one's own self is pagan—*awfully pagan.*

The gospel comes to us with the proclamation of enlarged privilege and opportunity for doing good to others. Talents are to be *invested.* That is what Christ taught.

"Have just laws," says someone. Yes, but the letter *without the spirit* killeth. The gospel destroys the aphis of status. You see others as brethren. If there is special blessing or more talent, these are bestowed only to sanctify others.

God chose one day and hallowed it, in order that man might be helped to hallow every day. Tuesday is as truly God's day as is Sunday. A plumber is as Christian as a preacher. The gospel explodes distinctions. "Whether therefore ye eat, or drink, *or whatsoever ye do,* (tailor, letter carrier, delivery man, lawyer, schoolteacher, cook), do *all* to the glory of God" (1 Corinthians 10:31).

That is what the gospel says. The smoke that rises from a factory dedicated to God, is as typical of praise and service as incense that mounts from a cathedral altar.

Without the gospel, sir, wealth can become mean and ugly. *Prosperity with consecration is the answer.* My rights are maintained by my obligations. My worship is only as strong as my obedience.

The dignity of man does not depend upon *accumulation.* Christ had not "where to lay his head" (Matthew 8:20). "He who though rich for our sakes became poor, that we *through his poverty* might become rich" (see 2 Corinthians 8:9).

Christ is just as much Saviour and Benefactor to the person on unemployment insurance, as He is to the business executive; to the uneducated as He is to the literate.

You have as many rights in Him as any other person. And you have as many obligations as one of His, as the apostle John discovered he had. *The hope of any advancing society is in Jesus Christ.*

Let the law of the jungle prevail—might makes right—and the larger brain will crowd down the smaller; the stronger will oppress the weaker; the rich who are proud will ride upon the shoulders of the poor; and the skilled will supplant the unskilled and starve them. The gospel says something different. Be helpers of each other—"Bear ye one another's burdens" (Galatians 6:2). *It insists upon a brotherhood.*

No, sir! The gospel of Jesus Christ has not come to the limit of its strength. It is not worn out. The gospel is "the *power* of God," and it is "the *wisdom* of God."

Let me tell you something, preacher! God forged a key that unlocked the door of the tomb, and He did it all alone. He picked that padlock all by Himsef. This planet doesn't need a new gospel. *God has already discovered the combination.*

This man, because he continueth ever, hath *an unchangeable priesthood.* Wherefore he is able also to save them to the uttermost that come unto God by him, seeing he ever liveth to make intercession for them" (Hebrews 7:24, 25).

Believe it, preacher! There is "an unchangeable priesthood." That gospel is as good in 1970 as it was in 1870. It will save and cleanse and rectify to the uttermost. God has given us His answer!

A REVIVALTIME TESTIMONY

"I continue to listen to *Revivaltime* and have received too many benefits to try to list them here."

WORK

Text: *"Son, go work today in my vineyard."*

Matthew 21:28

THE word *work* is a word coined in heaven. Both the law and the gospel advise: "Six days thou shalt work" (Exodus 34:21). Haggai preached, "Work: for I am with you, saith the Lord of hosts" (2:4). A believer and an idler should never be mistaken for each other. A believer is a worker.

God's approbation is seen in the animal kingdom. The highest-ranking animals are those who do the most. Nature is everywhere an unceasing worker, and wherever any of her creatures voluntarily cease from labor they suffer for it. Birds must build their nests. Large animals must catch their food before they eat it.

Three reasons enforce this call to work. Work is a means of *discipline.* Work is a means of *possession.* Work is *obedience to God's command.* The questions now remain: "Where shall I go forth to work? How shall I invest my life?"

First, I must labor for *material things.* The option is poverty. I must earn a living. God has laid down the rule. It covers preachers and laymen. "In the sweat of thy face shalt thou eat bread" (Genesis 3:19). "If any would not work, neither should he eat" (2 Thessalonians 3:10).

That rule hasn't been rescinded. The Bible commends industry and thrift, and even business acumen. The Bible never condemns a man for being successful or wealthy. *It only condemns improper methods used to obtain such ends.*

Yes, I have read what Jesus says, "Be not therefore anxious for the morrow" (see Matthew 6:34), and "Labor not for the meat which perisheth, but for that meat which endureth unto everlasting life" (John 6:27). But read their contexts! They do not provide excuses for laziness. They are not grants to condone nonsupport.

Rightly used material things are blessings. *They are meant to render us service but never to make us slaves.*

Yes, danger lurks! It is possible for a man to give himself so completely to this field of labor that both sense and soul are absorbed in earth, the better channels of thought are clogged with earth; and all the noblest powers are buried in earth. Oh, yes! *Material things can get the best of you.*

Second, I must labor for *intellectual things*. No one is born educated. I must learn. That takes *work*. The brain demands as the stomach demands—to be fed. This planet is as dependent upon the *engineer* as it is upon the *farmer*.

The engineer multiplies wealth. The educated brain has opened the possibilities of steam, electrical energy, and nuclear power. Time is saved. Distances are shrunk. People and products of all nations are interchanged. Had there been no schools, no research, no mental labor, we would have remained in the Stone Age. *Mind* and *matter* are linked toward greater profit. I have never believed that God is on the side of ignorance.

God's Word speaks of the poor wise man who by his wisdom delivered the beleaguered city; and declares that *wisdom is better than strength*. It pleased God when Solomon asked for wisdom. The New Testament emphasizes *study*.

Again, danger is present! It is right for us to think for ourselves. *But it is not best for man nor woman to be all intellect and nothing else.*

Mister, it is possible for a fellow to dwell in this field until his reason is his only guide, his opinion is his right, his desire is his law, his intellect is his god. That is tragedy. Mister, it is possible to be educated beyond your intelligence. You can become a danger to mankind.

Voltaire had brilliant intellectual powers, but who that is familiar with the story of his life will say that Voltaire labored for the highest things? *There is a better end than to become a cultured skeptic.*

Third, I must labor for *moral qualities.* I am not born good, any more than I am born educated. *Morality is an achievement.* I must discover ethics. I must acquire right and wrong, external rectitude, just as a baseball batter learns the strike zone. That takes work!

I discover that liberality is better than stinginess. I realize that honesty is superior to fraud. I calculate that sobriety is a winner over drunkenness, and that chastity is better than prostitution. I decide against dirty language. I enhance myself by honoring my parents. I must make all these decisions. It's work!

Let me remind you. There is no loving-kindness in intellectuality when it exists alone. Intellect without principle or heart is as wicked as Satan and cruel as the grave. God wants us to work in this field. "All things whatsoever ye would that men should do to you, do ye even so to them: for this is the law and the prophets" (Matthew 7:12). That is an assignment. Go to work on it, lady!

This entire field of moral effort suffers because the laborers are so few, so indifferent, so political, so cowardly, and so slow.

Yes, I will entertain your questions: "Is my mission fulfilled when I have done to men all things which I would have man do to me? Is it enough to do the works of honesty and sobriety and philanthropy? *Can I be totally and eternally satisfied in such fulfillment*?"

No. There is a thirst *unquenched.* I have discovered deeper longings in my soul. I have worked hard in these vineyards of material gain, intellectual achievement, and moral attainment.

But I have always felt there must be something better, a worthier end, a greater accomplishment. The Divine hurries to answer: "This is the work of God, that ye believe on him whom he hath sent" (John 6:29). *I learn there is a work of faith.*

I learn that through faith it is possible for weak stumbling mortals "to subdue kingdoms, work righteousness, obtain promises, stop the mouths of lions, quench the violence of fire, escape the edge of the sword, out of weakness be made strong, wax valiant in fight, turn to flight the armies of the aliens" (see Hebrews 11:33, 34).

I learn that all things are possible to him that believeth. Now I have a vista that sets me tingling. I am going to go to work in that field.

Is this a *dream* or a *distinct possibility* for a human being like myself? The Creator gave me a physical capacity by which I can earn a living. He gave me a mind by which I can learn. He gave me a soul by which I can discern good and evil. In like manner He furnishes me with a capacity for *faith.* God reaches toward me in full partnership. *Thus I become a laborer together with Him.*

This gives glory and purpose and success to all my other labor. Faith is the hand that reaches out through the unknown and lays hold on God. It is expressed in the lines of this old hymn:

> "Oh that the world might taste and see
>   The riches of His grace
> The arms of love that compass me
>   Would all mankind embrace."

This work of faith is my salvation. I may learn *about* God by physical labor, the sweat of my brow, or as I delve into the libraries of accumulated wisdom, or as I acquaint myself with law. But only the work of faith will acquaint me *with* God. Through Christ I have a meeting. I consider His offer to cancel my failure, to liberate me from all that degrades me, to love and provide for me eternally. I find the right to say, "I believe!"

Have you begun to labor in this field, sir? You pride yourself in the hard work you do, and rightfully so. Have you started this "work of God" to "believe on him whom he hath sent"? (John 6:29). *This is the work that supports you all the way into another world.*

Why should you get busy? Why should you pay any attention to me? Because "the night cometh, when no man can work" (John 9:4). There is a cutoff point. Certain human labors can only be done in this world. If you would erect buildings or accumulate stocks you must get at it on this side of the grave. If you would go to Hong Kong, Saigon, or Singapore you must travel now. If you are going to study philosophy, write books, or discover the intricacies of the law, every moment counts. No spirit once departed ever returns to lay stone upon stone, make discoveries in science, or feed the starving.

So it is with the work of faith by which the soul lays hold upon God through His Son Jesus Christ. *There is a deadline.* You better go to work on it now, sir! That would be the advice every damned soul would give you. Do it *now.*

You ask me: "Brother Ward, don't you think there may be a possibility for a man to do in eternity what he should have done on earth?" I answer you. God has given us no promise of that opportunity in His Book. Look toward Nature, sir! It accurately reflects the mind of God. If one neglects to start his corn crop in June, can he successfully start it in October? If a person neglects to harvest his apples in the mild autumn days, can he pick them in good condition at Christmas? If a father fails to train his son in the right way, can the lad be as easily led toward righteousness when he has reached maturity? If you throw away your health in your youth, can you get it back later? *The weight of evidence points in one direction.* Your chance is now.

No preacher on earth can assume the responsibility that a Christ-rejecter will be given a further chance in eternity. It isn't my mission to threaten you. It is my job, however, to warn you. "The night cometh, when no man can work" (John 9:4). There is a sunset for you, sir!

The greatest thing you and I will ever do is to exercise personal faith in Jesus Christ. That is mankind's supreme accomplishment. That confession will stand, mister, when everything else you may have achieved can crumble. That is worth more in eternity than all the stocks acquired, all the libraries multiplied, all the assembly lines lengthened, and all the laws written. Because God will finally decide what is important and what is minor. What profit to gain the whole world and lose one's soul?

You need more than clothes, automobiles, college degrees, and club memberships, sir. *You need a healthy soul.*

Your big job on earth, lady, is to get yourself ready for the life to come. It will take more than style and sophistication. It will take a bridge.

Jesus Christ makes that offer to you. "I am the Way." Take it! That will be the smartest decision you will ever make. A power will go to work for you in that moment of decision with saving energy beyond anything you have ever labored to realize on earth. God will do something for you that you can't do for yourself. "This is the work of God, that ye believe on him whom he hath sent" (John 6:29).

Reach out for personal salvation!

HATRED

Text: "*We know that we have passed from death unto life, because we love the brethren. He that loveth not his brother abideth in death. Whosoever hateth his brother is a murderer: and ye know that no murderer hath eternal life abiding in him.*"

1 *John* 3:14, 15

TAYLOR Caldwell, in her new book, *Great Lion of God*, an account of Paul, as she views him as a man and in the framework of the period he lived and wrote history, makes this comparison of the times:

"The Roman Empire was declining in the days of Saul of Tarshish as the American Republic is declining today—*and for the very same reasons*: Permissiveness in society, immorality, the Welfare State, endless wars, confiscatory taxation, the brutal destruction of the middle class, cynical disregard of the established human virtues and principles and ethics, the pursuit of materialistic wealth, the abandonment of religion, venal politicians who cater to the masses for votes, inflation, deterioration of the monetary system, bribes, criminality, riots, incendiarisms, street demonstrations, the release of criminals on the public in order to create chaos and terror, leading to dictatorship 'in the name of an emergency,' the loss of masculine sturdiness and the feminization of the people, scandals in public office, plundering of the treasury, debt, the attitude that 'anything goes,' the toleration of injustice and exploitation, bureaucracies and bureaucrats issuing evil 'regulations' almost every week, the centralization of government, the public contempt for good and honorable men, and, above all, the philosophy that 'God is dead,' and that man is supreme. *All this Saul confronted in his own world, where the word 'modern' was deeply cherished.*"

That is a remarkable summary by one of the great writers of the hour! *It affords a looking glass.*

There is a vein of destructiveness very evident among us. A fevered generation, bent toward chaos, cannot be understood in rational terms.

Peering into the unconscious, *Freud saw that man had both a death instinct and a life instinct.* There was, he said, an inherent drive in man to destroy himself and the world he created. Freud could not explain the fact, he could only state what he saw.

Dr. Karl Menninger, in his classic—*Man Against Himself*—has documented a terrifying catalog of the human capacity for *self-hatred and self-destruction.* These philosophers and investigators arrive at one word again and again—*frustration.* The primary meaning is to thwart. It is a picture of meaninglessness, an inability to accomplish. It produces, in many forms, tendency toward suicide.

Permit a personal observation for anything it may be worth. It seems to me it is operating, like a spreading virus that can reach epidemic proportions, in our young people as follows: We have raised a generation that has never known hardship. This, paradoxically, makes them incapable of tolerating even mild setbacks or obstacles of any kind.

If a nation refuses to bow down and accept absurd fantasies about instant equality, this self-destructive quality flares. The madness to kill, burn, riot, annihilate becomes rampant. *It is a strong, insane, uncontrollable urge.*

You should ask yourself, "Why this death urge?"

John, like Paul, never wanders far, in his ministry, from the miracle of his own transformation as a young, headstrong, riotous Galilean, with an urge to burn and destroy into an apostle of love, vision, and creativity. He cannot, and will not, deny what has happened in his own life.

In this New Testament letter, John equates *love with life and hate with death.* He says they are recognizable, telltale symptoms. He says: "He that loveth not, knoweth not God; for God is love" (1 John 4:8).

John knows that once he *hated.* Tagged "a son of thunder" by his community, John was in conflict with the society of his day. His ambitious parents prospered but John felt bemeaned, bedeviled, and frustrated in the fishing business. He rankled under the protective custody of Rome. A religion that sought compromises held no interest for him. He wanted more from life than comfort and sophisticated values. *He wanted answers.* Neither Sadducee, the liberal, nor Pharisee, the recalcitrant, held interest for him. He felt provincial, discriminated against as a Galilean, caged, shadowboxing with life, a victim of the establishment.

Hatred coiled within him. He wanted to lash out, *to hurt.* All the paranoiac tendencies were there. John might have left a trail of bloodshed and riot. Instead he gave to mankind a record of spiritual excellence and moral splendor. *Something happened to effect that change.* It became John's message. "Beloved, let us love one another: for love is of God; and *every one that loveth is born of God,* and knoweth God" (1 John 4:7).

John experienced a new birth. One Person was responsible—Jesus Christ of Nazareth. Jesus took all the hate out of John. The Son of God quelled the death that was storming through the young fisherman. Jesus accomplished the switch that Freud saw from "a death instinct" to "a life instinct."

John testifies, "In this was manifested the love of God toward us, because that God sent his only begotten Son into the world, *that we might live through him*" (1 John 4:9). That is when John began living, when he met Jesus.

Christ silenced the rage in John's soul. He turned *contempt* to *compassion.* "But whoso hath this world's good, and seeth his brother have need, and shutteth up his bowels of compassion from him, how dwelleth the love of God in him?" (1 John 3:17).

It hadn't always been that way in John's life. He thirsted for a shortcut to be first and foremost. He didn't really care who got mangled in the process. *Jesus made the difference.* So, John says: "Let us not love in word, neither in tongue; but in deed and in truth" (1 John 3:18).

Hatred is *death,* young adult! That frenzy of self-disgust that turns you to violence—that commands you to destroy the "system" which has created the freest, most prosperous nation in history—is a warning. *You are in the throes of death.* Freud so testifies. Menninger so testifies. John so testifies. *The urge toward self-destruction is the promise of more hell to come.*
Taylor Caldwell, in her foreword, also notes:

"Christ was not concerned with this world, which now so engrosses those who claim to be His followers . . . He was not preoccupied with 'social problems' and injustices. He constantly preached that justice and mercy would flow *from a changed heart,* and love, not by man's laws and ordinances."

It is profound to note Taylor Caldwell's conclusion and conviction:

"Man's nature cannot be changed in any particular—*except by the power of God,* and religion. All the 'education' in secular institutions and all the secular exhortations will never succeed in civilizing man. As Christ said, 'Who *by taking thought,* can add one cubit to his stature?' No one, of course."

Christ provides *creativity.* It is "life more abundantly." It can embrace affluence and prosperity. But more than anything else this new and vital direction in living provides *achievement.* You *arrive.* You know where you've been, what you are, and where you're headed. *The quarrel is gone.* The challenge that grips you is, "Follow me . . . and I will make you to become."

The authority of that Friend grips you. You *believe* He is

able to do it. Then you watch it accomplished in your life, and your life begins to affect the lives around you. John watched it in his own record. "Herein is our love made perfect, that we may have boldness in the day of judgment: because as he is, so are we in this world" (1 John 4:17).

No one strikes out who allows Jesus to have the mastership in his or her life. The future, or "the day of judgment" will confirm that His plan for you was the *best* and *eternal* choice.

Every truly happy person has learned this—that there is a *love* for life. Every moment is redeemed. Every opportunity is redeemed. Every tool is redeemed. Every experience is redeemed.

Christ makes your sojourn on this planet meaningful. You stop castigating, throwing away youth and opportunity, wasting your substance and reducing life to a pigpen existence in the name of getting even.

It is the greatest moment of joy, this side of paradise to "pass from death"—to have all the venom swabbed out of your soul, to have the darkness rebuked. God never intended your existence on earth to be a graveyard.

Hell will make it that, mister. Look at yourself! Do you see murder there? What stygian caverns encompass you? What hate enthralls you? What lackluster boredom handcuffs you? What discontent churns inside? The urge to destroy yourself is upon you. Why? The true answer that the devil hides from you is that at the root of it all, *you hate yourself*. That is why the answer is the new birth. Christ has provided it for you. John says: "Whosoever shall confess that Jesus is the Son of God, God dwelleth in him, and he in God" (1 John 4:15).

Many years ago, as a young evangelist in the city of Owen Sound, Ontario, Canada, there came to the altar in my meetings a woman whose countenance and personality bore all the marks of a survivor from a slave-labor penal camp. *If ever I saw a life bound by hell, it was this woman.*

Suddenly the Holy Spirit revealed to me that she was full of hatred. And I asked her, "Will you *forgive*?" The struggle was short and decisive.

I learned that a brute had taken her in marriage and treated her worse than he would handle an animal. He sent her into the forest to cut timber, and set a daily work quota for her. Everything that had been womanly and fine soured in her. She existed for revenge. She communed with death. Life was a decoy. It was hollow—*gutted.* But some flickering spark struggled against that gloom. Deep within her soul there was a whisper—a promise of something better. It had brought her to the altar. I saw that woman "*pass* from death unto life."

You can cross over lady! A way has been opened. John found it. John remembered how it happened to him: "In this was manifested the love of God toward us, because that God sent his only begotten Son into the world, *that we might live through him*" (1 John 4:9).

ABRAHAM, THE PIONEER OF FAITH

Text: *"And he believed in the Lord; and he counted it to him for righteousness."*

Genesis 15:6

ABRAHAM is the *pioneer.* Isaiah thought so. Centuries later he reminded his generation: "Hearken to me, ye that follow after righteousness, ye that seek the Lord: look unto the rock whence ye are hewn, and to the hole of the pit whence ye are digged. *Look unto Abraham* your father, and unto Sarah that bare you: for I called him alone, and blessed him, and increased him" (Isaiah 51:1, 2). Christ acknowledged it. He observed that "Abraham rejoiced to see my day"—*he caught the meaning of his life and Mine*—"and was glad" (John 8:56).

It was revealed to Paul that Abraham was the progenitor of those "who are not of the circumcision only, but who also walk in the steps of *that faith of our father Abraham,* which he had being yet uncircumcised" (Romans 4:12).

It all adds to this. *Abraham knew and enjoyed the grace of God.* "By faith Abraham, when he was called to go out into a place which he should after receive for an inheritance, obeyed; and he went out, not knowing whither he went" (Hebrews 11:8). That is the "rock" from which the believer is "hewn."

Your righteousness depends upon one fact—*God's call to you, and your unswerving obedience to that call.* "I called him." "When he was called." You can't find God. God finds you.

Why did God select Abraham? That must always be an

interesting question. Is the choice made *indiscriminately?* No. God must have reasons. One is suggested in the narrative. We have a report of a conversation with angelic attendants: "*For I know him,* that he will command his children and his household after him, and they shall keep the way of the Lord, to do justice and judgment; that the Lord may bring upon Abraham that which he hath spoken of him" (Genesis 18:19). Evidently God knew something else about Lot.

There had been preliminary testing. He had followed the voice of faith and searched for the land of promise. He had been blessed with goods and the goods had not strangled his faith. These steps prepared him for the *vision* and the *faith* that henceforth was to be *counted to him for righteousness.*

Piety is never magic, mister! It seems fascinating to a lot of folk to see John and James dropping their nets and running after Jesus at His sudden call. They forget that they had seen Him before, and had beheld His "first of miracles in Cana of Galilee, when he manifested forth his glory; and his disciples believed on him" (see John 2:11).

Abraham wasn't born differently than I am born. He had the same choices to make. He faced the same infirmities. There is nothing synthetic or unnatural about him. If there were, I could not do what he did. *My exercise of faith must be based on the same probabilities and the same possibilities.*

There were things this man had to do. First, he had to cross the River Euphrates. That is when he took on the name of *Hebrew,* which means one who has crossed over. *That is where he turned his back on the Chaldean world and its idolatries.* That was something Abraham had to do. That was not imputed to him. He showed his faith *by his works.*

You must do the same. "But as many as *received* him" (John 1:12)—that is something you must do. God cannot and will not do that for you. "If any man *hear* my voice, and *open the door*" (Revelation 3:20)—that is up to you, alone! You must take that first step.

Abraham *heard*. He opened the door. Abraham received God. He made room for His presence. That is how it started.

He wasn't an innocent child. For 75 years he had *vexed* his righteous soul with the unlawful deeds and filthy conversation of the wicked around him. Something within the man rebelled. He was nauseated. He choked on the moral rot of his day. He was ready when the "call" came. Yes, sir! Abraham made an *adult decision*. It was free will all the way. *He made up his mind to travel toward a better life.*

This man wasn't a perfect man. He had his problems. Even the *sun* up there, mister, has its black spots. But I love it just the same. Abraham had his problems, but he inspires me, nevertheless. He was an imperfect man—just like me—when he heard God calling him, and simply obeyed the call, just as I am trying to do. *That call never left him, nor has it left me*. Abraham found it good and profitable to obey. So have I!

There comes that great moment when God asks you to *believe*. God didn't ask Abraham to do anything. *He asked him to trust Him*. God counted that trust for righteousness. It's what I do when I look at a seed of corn, and impute to it, the blade, the green leaf, and the full corn in the ear. *I see in that seed the finished product*. God saw in Abraham's act of trust the whole life of obedience that was to follow. That is a great moment of the soul!

When a recruit takes the oath of allegiance, this same thing happens. Loved ones, neighbors, government, officers *impute* to that recruit all the deeds that follow—long marches, endurance, sacrifice, fierce battles, hand-to-hand combat, valor, and willingness to die for what he believes.

In fact, it is a way of life. We all exercise this trust. I impute my future, with all my obligations, upon the pledges redeemed by those who contract to support me. We live and move and have our being upon these promises to pay.

That is what God did to Abraham. He honored his check his promise to pay. He *imputed* right results to the courage, fidelity, the trust, the gratitude of that Chaldean. *He extended him credit.* He smiled on him and endorsed his note, and told him of "a shield, and an exceeding great reward" (see Genesis 15:1), and pointing him to the innumerable stars that then were shining in the sky, promised him, that like them, innumerable and glorious in their orbits, should his seed be.

Believer, the same God spreads a vision before you. God offers you *credit.* That credit is the power and victory of Calvary. Use it! There is no limit to what you can become, and what you can accomplish through it. Remember this! If I can make an *investment* in some earthly child of mine, the Eternal Father has every right to make an investment in you or me. I'll quote it to you. "If ye then, being evil, know *how* to give good gifts unto your children, how much more shall your Father which is in heaven *give* good things to them that ask him?" (Matthew 7:11).

That credit sustained him. Abraham had his *highs.* He "entertained angels unawares." He generously allowed his nephew first choice. He gathered his household and waged war against marauders. He paid tithes to Melchizedek. You could run him for bishop in most denominations—*until you balance his highs with his lows.* There is his lie to Abimelech about his wife. There was his polygamy. There is enough shame in Abraham for anyone. Isaiah describes it correctly. God was hewing out of a rock, and digging out of a pit, *a man.* That is the story of this mighty salvation.

God can't save perfect people. He can't extend credit to those who don't need credit. When you stand and affirm that you are *not* "as other men," you have just canceled your credit. You don't need Calvary. You need a shrine.

Well, mister, I would like to see your business records for the past week. I would like to see the percentage of profit you took over and beyond a fair amount of rightful gain on your investment. I would like to see the rent you charged. I would like to talk to your children and gauge their respect for you. I would like to see what you left the waitress. I would like to see how you treated the employee. I would like to discover how much Sunday religion you have. So, don't be too quick to cast a stone at Abraham!

What you have to do, mister, is simple. *Put your hand in the hand of God.* Do the same as this man! "By faith Abraham, when he was called to go out into a place which he should after receive for an inheritance, *obeyed;* and went out, not knowing whither he went" (Hebrews 11:8).

That is your business. *Turn your life over to God.* Don't argue. Obey! You are weary of a sense of condemnation. Move out. If there were not a better life, you wouldn't feel a call to a better life. God won't let you down. "What, O man, doth the Lord require of thee, but to do justice, to love mercy, and to humble yourself to walk with God?" (see Micah 6:8).

Make that start now, and the *vision* God will give you, will sustain you. I promise you divine fellowship. Without such fellowship you would be walking in a trance. Salvation is more than an Alice-in-Wonderland fantasy. God will come to you again and again. Promises are redeemed. You achieve victories. The impossible is realized. That is the New Testament to you.

There is an *Isaac*—Christ is a fact. And God makes this New Testament Isaac to you "wisdom, and righteousness, and sanctification, and redemption" (1 Corinthians 1:30). There are no limitations in Christ—and Christ is yours. What a big checkbook God gives you!

Head down that aisle! Start, not knowing whither it may lead you. Simply head God's way. It isn't church programs you need—washings, oracles, ordinances. You need God to speak to you. "I called him *alone.*" Your salvation is something person-to-person.

You'll have to *trust* all the way sir! Abraham was an old and contented man when God asked for his Isaac. His love and adoration for this boy was a worldly temptation to the old man. Somewhere along the line it's easy to settle down and "set your affections on things *below*" (see Colossians 3:2). This may be good and wholesome and the very best category in town, but they can get in between you and your trust and obedience toward God. You can start building dream kingdoms of your own. Soon, it becomes *your* home, and *your* estate, and *your* family, and *your* future. And God is a sweet memory and a powerful Friend to have in an emergency. *And then the big test comes!*

Is it as easy to obey, to step out at God's command, to give Him your all, when you have achieved wealth and success and comfort? *Well, God has to know!* It's par for the course.

It was as tough on Abraham as it was on Job. It came suddenly like a black tornado. He was to offer unconditionally his pride-and-joy, everything he had ever lived for, everything he had ever hoped to be—*sacrifice it.* Would faith survive? No one will ever know the anguish inside that tent. God has hidden it. It is too sacred to a man's soul and record to ever be publicized. I'll tell you this. God *understands.* He gave His Only Son.

Did Abraham's faith *save* him? That is what I want to know. Yes, it did! He "accounted that God was able to raise him up, even from the dead" (see Hebrews 11:19). He *accounted.* It's what a sea captain does when he leans on his compass for direction amid storm and fury. "My son, God will provide himself a lamb for a burnt offering" (Genesis 22:8).

That is saving faith, lady—faith in God's adequate provision for you. It is your faith in Calvary. "God will provide . . . a lamb." It is your affirmation, "God has resources for my need."

That is your victory, mister—your only victory—*faith in the grace of God.* Go all the way! Hold nothing back. Something in the recesses of your soul will whisper, "It is well with my soul."

A REVIVALTIME TESTIMONY

"It was during one of the *Revivaltime* broadcasts that I was saved."

CHEATED

Text: *"O Lord, thou hast deceived me, and I was deceived."*
Jeremiah 20:7

MANY years ago, the great pulpiteer, George H. Morrison, drew attention to this text. It says something out in the open that every preacher has thought. And it's comforting to find preachers who have experienced what you have experienced, especially one in the Bible such as Jeremiah.

I asked, 41 years ago when Mrs. Ward and I were starting out in the ministry and we were existing hand-to-mouth on five dollars a week that a boarder-roomer paid us, "Where were the promises of success that I felt when I was set apart for the ministry?" I have asked, "Why did people die when I have prayed for their healing?" I have asked, after preaching, "Why didn't the unsaved respond?" *So many times you feel that God has let you down.*

Jeremiah had been a prophet for 20 years. He had been arrested as a public nuisance and placed under protective custody. He thought of the glorious promises God had made him, and he compared them with all he had suffered. God had said, "I will be with thee to deliver thee." God had said, "I will make thy word a word of power." *The promises seemed to mock him.* Melancholy filled his soul.

Of course, we can see now what he couldn't see then. He was preserved. His word is heard today. But, at that moment, Jeremiah felt *cheated.* And I think every Christian must feel that way at times. So, the question is this. *Why should it happen to me? What good is there in it for me?*

Disillusionment seems an integral part of life. Young zealots always feel that their "movement" is hand-carved by God Himself. We claim the messianic touch. Didn't the young Nazi? He believed that he was a member of the super race, raised at a point in history to correct and direct the entire human program. It was a dream that fell apart in the blizzards of Russia and succumbed in the ruins of Berlin.

It is one of the sweet illusions of the *child* that father and mother has neither fault nor flaw. Deep within, all of us want to believe in Santa Claus. We thirst for *magic* more than we do for *miracle.* I hear prayers offered repeatedly by wishful thinkers in public auditoriums, that God will save and fill the altars of that service with the unsaved, when not a single sinner has been brought to the meeting.

We love our illusions, but they cannot always last. You and I do not live in an "Alice-in-Wonderland" world. We are always reaching moments when we pass from the age of innocence to the age of accountability, and suddenly things are never again what they seemed to be. The aura of the honeymoon may dissipate in a few days, but that doesn't mean the marriage need be any less effective. *You do awaken from dreams.*

These are perilous moments. I have always had a world of sympathy toward the teen-ager when I pastor. This moment arrives like a thud for them. Nature suddenly changes their bodies. They are as *unsure* of themselves as they are about the uncertainty of voice level, the fuzz on the cheek, or the signs of femininity emerging on the girl's body. They need understanding, *not condemnation.*

So many young people are lost to the Church right there. *Everyone levels criticism.* So the devil whispers "Everybody thinks you are a sinner. *You might as well be a sinner.*" The channel to adolescence is the most peril-infested passage in the entire human orbit. Great pastors understand this.

Mankind survived the discovery that earth was round, not flat.

We've been to the Moon and our romance has been revised. I haven't heard any new songs heralding the love potion of this sphere. You learn that the sun doesn't rise in the east and sink in the west. Poetry is one thing, *fact* another. The stars don't twinkle, and the sky is not blue. It isn't a *hoax.* No! There is no question of morality involved. We enjoy and cling to make-believe. The movie industry has made a fortune supplying the unreal and the impractical.

Abraham could have joined Jeremiah in his complaint. He was promised the land of Canaan. He went westward with that hope. He thought of milk and honey. He thought of enemies subdued and evicted. *The strange thing is that to his dying hour Abraham did not possess one county in Canaan.* He was a stranger there, dwelling in his tent, and forced to haggle about a grave for Sarah. It took *faith,* mister. It took faith. Faintly, at first, then with clearer vision his eyes were opened to a better country.

Here is the danger! So often, if a promise is not fulfilled as we have made up our minds beforehand that it should be fulfilled, we are unwilling to accept God's design of fulfillment. *It is easy to claim foul.* I am inclined to narrow God to my interpretation. And if it doesn't happen like I want it to happen, I too can say, "I was deceived."

We all start with fancy blueprints for living. When I wrote the script for my life at 16 and 17, *I really wrote a script of triumphs without testings.* It was fanciful the way I thought I should live. I allowed no place in the script for sickness, weariness, failure, financial pressure, desertion by friends, or closed doors. I was ready to conquer the world. Ah, such is the mirage of youth!

The script has had to be rewritten a number of times. I have served God in fields of effort that I never intended to include in my itinerary toward heaven. I have slept in barns and the back seats of automobiles and in tents that let more rain in than they ever kept out. I have eaten food, on the free-will offering plan, that needed a Blue Cross and a Blue Shield hospital insurance program to go with it. I have waited for offerings that never were taken. I have preached sermons that were better never to have been preached. I have been the target of criticism. I never planned it that way. I have wanted to quit. I have wanted to run away. I have been ashamed. I have been confused. I've known the same *blues* as Jeremiah, "O Lord, if *this* be life, thou hast deceived me, and I was deceived."

I have looked at the challenge of the gospel, "Come unto me, . . . and I will give you *rest*" (Matthew 11:28). I'll tell you this. You'll work harder and longer hours in the kingdom of God than you ever dreamed of working. You'll *fight.* You'll *wrestle.* You'll *run.* You'll *climb.*

The Christian life is neither a picnic nor a slumber party. No, sir! You are not tricked at this altar. It's just different than you think it will be. Your imagination is one thing. God's schedule is another.

You will survive. You will grow *stronger.* Joseph did. All his dreams seemed to mock him. David did. His reverses made him the outstanding general that he became. God knows better than to let you continue to be spoon-fed.

Jeremiah's sorrows deepened his life and ministry. *What seemed to baffle him made him search further until he made new discoveries of faith.* My father would say so often, "God will pull you through anything if you can stand the pull." General MacArthur, beaten on Bataan, comes back to receive the unconditional surrender on the battleship *Missouri* in Tokyo Bay. You look back and say, "I have fought a *good* fight." You wouldn't plan it that way. But when you look back, you wouldn't change a thing. You wouldn't have had it any other way.

I think it is the great heart of God that allows us time for *dreams.* I wouldn't change a thing about youth or young adulthood, although I work among them in many classes of instruction. I'm still opposed to putting old heads on young shoulders. Let them dream a bit! Life will catch up with them soon enough. Their plans will have to be revised, but let them plan.

I like to hear a young preacher. He knows all the answers. No one is more sure of himself. In another 25 years he will be tempered and restrained. Don't take it away from the young. Let them enjoy their thrills. They will pass soon enough.

Jacob, the young and reckless adventurer, and Jacob, the patriarch, have little in common. The stern realities of life took care of that. There's always a chocolate coating to the medicine. The blue sky will always be a joy, and sunrise and sunset will be beautiful, although we know that sunrise is a phantasm and that sunset is but an illusion of the eye. I have discovered this. God is a *Charmer* as well as a *Creator*. I felt that divine charm reach out toward me more than once in my life.

I know this, looking back a bit as I can over the course, it will make you *valiant*. I remember leaving home with a five dollar bill in my pocket. My father felt it was time for me to *git*. I know, now, that he loved me nonetheless. It was because he loved me more than I could ever realize, that he adopted stern measures for my own good. The first night out for Jacob, away from home, with a hard rock for a pillow, helped to make a man out of him. God is that kind of a Father.

When this Movement began, Christ's return was expected before World War I. So, we met in temporary and inexpensive buildings. Insurance policies were allowed to lapse. The pursuit of education was restricted. Were we *deceived?* No! The Blessed Hope never ceases to serve its purpose. Christ is coming!

My wishes were not always in turn with His timetable. But I'll tell you this. I have never regretted that *burning hope* that consumed me, as a young evangelist, and turned my eyes away from a world system. It made me dare and face enemies that I would never have challenged otherwise.

I believe God strengthens us by what He *hides* as much as by what He *reveals*. If He showed a young preacher at 20 what that preacher will have learned by the time he is 40, that young preacher might never have the courage to start.

So, God leads us on! I don't think Israel would have ever left Egypt and started the journey through the Wilderness had they known what those 40 years would mean. The start is always romance and drama. That is how we begin school. That is how we enter marriage. That is how we start the job. The toil, the sweat, the tears come soon enough. *But we survive, and we are the better for it.* The dream takes shape. Our trust is not misplaced. God's contract with our lives is kept in full.

Jeremiah's life is redeemed. His message is a text for this day. And we learn that God in His infinite wisdom always knows how to bring the best out of us. Time will tell, and time is on God's side.

A HUNDRED YEARS FROM NOW

Text: *"Of the increase of his government and peace there shall be no end."*

Isaiah 9:7

EVERY sign indicates that one hundred years from now the Great Tribulation will have come and gone, *and Earth will be well into its period of* 1,000 *years of peace.*

What will it be like? Take your Bible and follow me!

By that time Jerusalem will become "The joy of the whole earth" (Lamentations 2:15). Christ, personally, will administrate a world government. "This same Jesus, . . . shall so come in *like manner* as ye have seen him go into heaven" (Acts 1:11). He went personally, visibly, suddenly. He will return personally, visibly, suddenly. His feet left the Mount of Olives. His feet will touch the same Mount when He returns.

"Every eye shall see him, and they also which pierced him" (Revelation 1:7). *His personal presence is required on Earth.* "I will overturn, overturn, overturn it: and it shall be no more, until he come whose right it is; and I will give it him" (Ezekiel 21:27). God's promise to Earth shall be redeemed, "And the *government* shall be upon his shoulder" (Isaiah 9:6).

The "*ladder*" that Jacob saw will become a reality. There will be unbroken communication between two worlds. "Hereafter ye shall see heaven open, and the angels of God ascending and descending upon the Son of man" (John 1:51).

Everything will center in Jesus Christ. "The earth shall be full of the knowledge of the Lord, as the waters cover the sea" (Isaiah 11:9).

Daniel told Belshazzar about it. "And there was given him dominion, and glory, and a kingdom, that *all people, nations, and languages,* should serve him: his dominion is an everlasting dominion, which shall not pass away, and his kingdom that which shall not be destroyed" (Daniel 7:14).

Every member of the redeemed family of God will be *employed.* There will be different spheres of service with graded responsibilities. Christ gave us a clear outline of this. "Who called his own servants, and delivered unto them his goods . . . to every man according to his several ability" (Matthew 25: 14, 15).

It is a question of gift and ability. These are conferred upon the believer, and we are exhorted to "receive not the grace of God in vain" (2 Corinthians 6:1). The man who hid his pound lost his *pound.* The man who hid his talent lost his *soul.* You will find the one in Luke 19:24 and the other in Matthew 25:30. There is a day of accounting. *Those who will reign with Christ will have earned that right.*

The resurrection of the righteous is an extended resurrection. It began with Christ. He became "the *firstfruits*" (1 Corinthians 15:20). There were those who arose immediately after Him. "And the graves were opened; and many *bodies* of the saints which slept arose, and came out of the graves *after* his resurrection, and went into the holy city, and *appeared* unto many" (Matthew 27:52, 53).

This number will be increased. "The dead in Christ shall rise first: then we which are alive and remain shall be caught up together with them . . . to meet the Lord" (1 Thessalonians 4:16, 17).

There are others. "And I saw thrones, and they sat upon them, and judgment was given unto them: and I saw the souls of them that were beheaded for the witness of Jesus, and for the word of God, and which had not worshipped the beast, neither his image, neither had received his mark upon their foreheads, or in their hands; *and they lived and reigned with Christ a thousand years*" (Revelation 20:4).

The resurrected will pass in review. Each is known. Each has ministered. Mary's ointment, Dorcas' garments, Epaphras' prayers, Paul's testimony, Peter's preaching—all will be reckoned and totaled. The apostles will have a special duty. "Ye also shall sit upon twelve thrones, judging the twelve tribes of Israel" (Matthew 19:28).

For every faithful pastor a distinct award is waiting. "When the chief Shepherd shall appear, ye shall receive *a crown of glory* that fadeth not away" (1 Peter 5:4). No one will make fun of a preacher in that day.

For every soul winner there will be a mark of distinction. "For what is our hope, or joy, or *crown of rejoicing*? Are not even ye in the presence of our Lord Jesus Christ at his coming?" (1 Thessalonians 2:19).

There will be peace on earth. Conferences and treaties can never produce peace. Jesus can. "He maketh wars to cease unto the end of the earth" (Psalm 46:9). I believe it. "Nation shall not lift up sword against nation, neither shall they learn war any more" (Isaiah 2:4).

Creation shall enter into rest. The dream of the ecologist will be realized. The unbalanced elements will be adjusted. The groaning of nature will subside. "For we know that the whole creation groaneth and travaileth in pain . . . waiting for . . . redemption" (Romans 8:22, 23).

This threat of man's impiety toward the forces of nature is very real to us today. It will take more than the taxpayers' billions to change this "sin against heaven"—*the waste of a prodigal.*

"The wolf and the lamb shall feed together, and the lion shall eat straw like the bullock: . . . They shall not hurt nor destroy" (Isaiah 65:25).

Mankind will be relieved of its two most crushing burdens—*traditional and ritualistic religion and standing armies.* The wasted energies of men will be turned into other channels. The arid and impoverished soils of earth will be turned to profit. *The hinterlands of Australia, Asia, and Africa will support an exploding population.* "The wilderness and the solitary place shall be glad for them; and the desert shall rejoice, and blossom as the rose" (Isaiah 35:1).

The refurbished land between the Jordan and the Euphrates —designed to form a part of Emmanuel's land, a great triangle nearly as large as India, south of Calcutta and Bombay, will gladden the hearts of Ishmael and Isaac alike. *There will be enough, and to spare, for every Palestinian refugee.* "In that same day the Lord made a covenant with Abraham, saying, Unto thy seed have I given this land, from the river of Egypt unto the great river, the river Euphrates" (Genesis 15:18).

Moses explained it to the nation in detail. "Every place whereon the soles of your feet shall tread shall be yours: from the wilderness and Lebanon, from the river, the river Euphrates, even unto the uttermost sea shall your coast be" (Deuteronomy 11:24).

The plan of Jesus Christ for this planet will be realized. "His dominion shall be from sea even to sea, and from *the river* even to the ends of the earth" (Zechariah 9:10).

Everyone will have *equity.* "His name shall endure for ever: his name shall be continued as long as the sun: and men shall be blessed in him: *all nations shall call him bessed*" (Psalm 72:17).

Earth will experience *righteousness.* "Behold, a King shall reign in righteousness" (Isaiah 32:1). Note! This could not have been had an *unrepentant Israel* made Him their King. The same Blood that bought redemption, purchased the inheritance. He will reign because He won the right to reign. *That right was disputed at Calvary.* The total power of a world system cried out against Him. "But his citizens hated him, and sent a message after him, saying, We will not have this man to reign over us" (Luke 19:14). *That message was delivered at the Cross.* Christ defeated His adversary. Jesus is the legal and victorious Heir to this planet. His victory assures a new earth.

No opposition will be countenanced. "He shall rule them with a rod of iron" (Revelation 19:15). Today men's sins are not imputed in the sense of being summarily dealt with, but then, "I will *early* destroy all the wicked of the land; that I may cut off all wicked doers" (Psalm 101:8).

Sin simply will not be allowed. There will be no drunkenness, no theft, no crime, no dishonesty, no embezzlement, no fraud, no adultery, no divorce, no child abandonment, no narcotic traffic, no political chicanery, no customs violation, no industrial cartel and price fixing, no substandard merchandising, no exorbitant interest rate. "For if *the word spoken by angels* was steadfast, and every transgression and disobedience received a just recompense of reward" (Hebrews 2:2)—*then imagine what the spoken command of Jesus Christ will mean.* Sin will not be tolerated. Christ's rule will be a blessing to the righteous and a scourge to the wicked.

The power of evil will be throttled at its source. Antichrist is apprehended and consigned to the lake of fire. *Satan is placed under bond.* "And he laid hold on the dragon, that old serpent, which is the Devil, and Satan, and bound him a thousand years, and cast him into the bottomless pit, and shut him up, and set a seal upon him, that he should deceive the nations no more, till the thousand years should be fulfilled" (Revelation 20:2, 3).

Can you imagine what it would be like to be able to live just 24 hours without having the devil bothering you?

There can be no Millennium without *two things,* mister—(1) Christ's personal presence on Earth; (2) the devil's imprisonment. The great seducer is placed under lock and key. The lie will be taken out of this world. His demons, his angels, his evil spirits, his principalities will be exiled. They will be bound without the power to escape. For 1,000 years, mister, this planet will be perfectly free from satanic influence.

That is relief beyond comprehension. The billboard will not lie to me. The theater marquee will never be allowed to appeal to a base instinct. No selfish demagogue will create a movement to enhance personal interest. There will be absolute truth in advertising. No discriminatory practice will be permitted. That pressure will be lifted for 1,000 years.

I believe that 100 years from now, Earth will be well into Christ's reign upon earth.

But you can miss it all, sinner! "But the rest of the dead lived not again until the thousand years were finished" (Revelation 20:5). Who are they? Jesus answered that question. "Marvel not at this: for the hour is coming, in the which all that are in the graves shall hear his voice, and shall come forth; they that have done good, unto the resurrection of life; and they that have done evil, unto *the resurrection of damnation*" (John 5:28, 29).

There is a separate "call-up" for you, sinner. If you *waste* one life, why should you be given an opportunity to waste another?

Let me read this from God's Word to you! "For as the Father hath life in himself; so hath he given to the Son to have life in himself; *and hath given him authority to execute judgment* also, because he is the Son of man" (John 5:26, 27).

Your personal appeal to Jesus Christ can decide your destiny. His word is final. Turn to Him now.

SILENCE

Texts: *"And the chief priests accused him of many things; but he answered nothing. And Pilate asked him again, saying, Answerest thou nothing? behold how many things they witness against thee. But Jesus yet answered nothing; so that Pilate marveled."*

Mark 15:3-5

"In quietness and in confidence shall be your strength."

Isaiah 30:15

THIS is the majesty that shames our pettiness.

"Blessed quietness, holy quietness,
What assurance in my soul;
On the stormy sea, Jesus speaks to me,
And the billows cease to roll."

It's easier to sing than to experience!

Pilate marveled. He was not the first to marvel at Jesus. Soldiers marveled at His control of language. Disciples marveled at His control of nature. Skeptics marveled at His control of disease and demons. *Now the Roman marvels at His control of Himself.*

There is only one answer to Jesus Christ. "What manner of man is this, that even the winds and the sea obey him!" (Matthew 8:27). "How knoweth this man letters, having never learned?" (John 7:15). Sir, He is God. Now it is the Governor's turn, "Answerest thou nothing? behold now many things they witness against thee." *That is a greater miracle than silencing the sea.*

It *identified* Him. Isaiah had prophesied: "He was oppressed, and he was afflicted, yet he opened not his mouth: he is brought as a lamb to the slaughter, and as a sheep before her shearers is dumb, so he openeth not his mouth" (Isaiah 53:7). He was that Man.

A world system believes there are ways to make a person talk. So, the soldiers, past-masters in the art, led Him away. They clothed Him. They placed a reed in His hand. They cover Him with spit. They bow in mock obeisance. It is practiced scorn designed to bring a victim to a boiling point. But Jesus Christ opened not His mouth.

At Golgotha the executioners offered Him wine mixed with myrrh—a potion to dull the senses to pain. He brushed it aside. They stretched Him upon timber. They tore flesh and muscle. He maintained silence. Then they thumped the cross into a standing position. The fresh wounds are further lacerated. His body twists in unspeakable agony—but not a word escapes His lips.

Mental cruelty is added. "Ah, thou that destroyest the temple, and buildest it in three days, save thyself, and come down from the cross" (Mark 15:29, 30). But he stays there in silence.

Professed servants of God add a word, "He saved others; himself he cannot save" (Mark 15:31). They revile Him. "Let Christ the King of Israel descend now from the cross, that we may see and believe" (Mark 15:32). He made no acknowledgment. He stayed there. And I am here because He did.

Finally He speaks. It is not a word of denunciation. It is not even gentle reproof. Through parched and fevered lips, He breathes a prayer for those who place Him there. "Father, forgive them; for they know not what they do" (Luke 23:34). That was His reply.

He is regal. The splendor out-glitters the jeweled crowns of Earth's emperors. Dripping with spit, He is the epitome of kingliness. All the cheap trappings and noisy sway of earthly acclaim pales into discount in comparison. Today's cheap publicity is tawdry beside His eternal glory. His nonresistance makes my threats and bridling offense impudent and impotent in retrospect.

How quick we are to vent our feelings. The least slight, the lightest wound brings a howl. I want to justify myself. I want to talk back. I don't want to take the blame for anything. We find it difficult to take rightful reproof. It is man's nature to shift the blame—to find some scapegoat.

Jesus kept silent under all the lying accusations of evil, malicious men. He would not dignify their gross disrespect. He would not murmur. They heaped the sin of the world upon Him. And men marveled at Him.

Our tendency is to strike back in the same vein—to return blow for blow. *And thus we delegate power to others to move us.* And the world looks on, but does not marvel.

I need to do more than *talk* about Jesus. I need to manifest something beyond *liberality.* Visiting the sick is not enough. *The world wants to see me under pressure.* How will I react under provocation? That is the language that convinces the ungodly. Sinners either marvel, or they do not marvel.

So, I need to ask myself an important question. *Why do I not hold my peace?* I had better go to the Word. Here it is! "Out of the abundance of the heart the mouth speaketh" (Matthew 12:34). Mister, it isn't a state of the mind. *It is a state of the heart.* My quick retort can mirror abominable pride and contemptible self-love. It is wounded pride that causes us to seek to humiliate another who belittles us. It is wounded self-love that causes us to rise up in self-defense at the least intimation of unjust criticism. *And the world does not marvel.*

What an empty void there is left in the heart after a volcanic eruption of self-defense! How often words *humiliate* us before people because we do not *humble* ourselves before God! The answer is heart cleansing. I must not question His instruments any more than I would those of a surgeon. *And very often His instruments are those of our own household.*

Wife, He will use your husband! Parent, He will use your child! Preacher, He will use your deacon! Employer, He will use your employee! *We all postpone this surgery of the soul.* We try every other method but God's method.

We seek to suppress the seething corruption within our hearts, only to find that if the circumstances last long enough the heart will belch forth that which is within. We recoil at the sharp instruments that we recognize must be used. We turn toward psychology and psychiatry. I must face it. I cannot avoid it. "Out of the abundance of the heart the mouth speaketh" (Matthew 12:34). *If my heart isn't right, my mouth won't be right.*

Blessed is the man whom God leads up a dead-end street, where there is no way to turn. Thank God for the Throne of Grace!

My solution is in Him. "Looking unto Jesus the author and *finisher* of our faith" (Hebrews 12:2). He, alone, has run the exact race I am called upon to run. He has been "in *all* points tempted like as we are" (Hebrews 4:15). Others' experiences may not be mine. *But He understands exactly what I am experiencing.*

I know this. I want to be like Him. I don't want to be like Pilate. I don't want to be like the chief priests. I don't want to be a mocker or a scourger. *I want His victory.*

I must let Him reign in me. Self cannot be trusted. Christ must rule my spirit. Only then can my lips remain silent before men.

The fact is, sir, that Jesus never asks me to be *like* Him. That would be an impossibility. I would have to be born of a virgin. He asks me to *surrender* to Him. He will share with me. It is not *self-control* I need. I need *God-control.* He proposes to do in me what I cannot do in myself. You will know it, sir, when He has that control. If you speak at all, it will be within the secret place of prayer where you, too, can pray for those who despitefully use you.

Many years ago, Henry Suso, a saintly man of God, was standing on a street corner in a little town in Germany talking to a group of men about Christ, when suddenly a woman appeared and vehemently thrust a very young baby into his arms, saying, "Here! Take the child of your lust!"

As the woman hurriedly turned and fled, Henry Suso simply stood there, holding the child in his arms—stood there inarticulate with wonder and amazement. First a look of consternation and then a deep condemnation stole over the countenances of the men as, one by one, they turned and walked away, leaving the man of God standing there alone with the child. *But —abandoned by men, Henry Suso was not abandoned by God.*

Henry Suso took the child to his humble home, cared for the child, and reared the child with all the love of a father. Many summers and winters passed, and the lad grew to be 12. And whereas men had once beaten a path to the door of Henry Suso for spiritual counsel—they had long since cast his name out for evil. For 12 long years his name was anathema to the community. *Yet in all that time, Henry Suso never spoke a word in self-defense.*

Then one day a woman came to the little town to search for the boy—a woman whose mother-heart could no longer endure. She went about the village and made it known that she was the mother of the lad; that she had never even known Suso except for his reputation for godliness. She told with deep contrition of heart how she had been as one possessed, in that far-off day, *with a devilish desire to destroy this man of God.*

Needless to say, the holy reputation of Henry Suso spread quickly throughout all Europe. He had remained silent under most severe provocation. *He had placed the burden of his justification upon his Saviour and Master.*

The world may not care about my doctrine, but it does care about my life. It is asking for a flesh-and-blood revelation of the gospel in me. That is the text they best understand.

Jesus said, "And I, if I be lifted up from the earth, will draw all men unto me" (John 12:32). *That is the mainstream of evangelism.*

So I ask myself: "How can I best lift Jesus before others, in my home, in my office, on my stream?" Here is an opportunity! The self-defense of heated words men understand; but silence under mistreatment and unjust dealings causes them to *marvel.* That will gain their attention.

I seek that stillness of God within the soul. *It is incomparable power.* In the moment I can remain silent under cutting, slashing criticism, with the silence of Him who answered His accusers with never a word, I share His majesty. Then I know the authority of His great salvation.

SALVATION IS NOT FOR SALE

Text: "*Dwell with me, and be unto me a father and a priest, and I will give thee ten shekels of silver by the year, and a suit of apparel, and thy victuals.*"

Judges 17:10

G*OD'S message is not for sale.* It is not a commodity that can be packaged and priced. Yet a world system never quits trying to make it so. "Dwell with me, and be unto me a father and a priest, and I will give thee ten shekels of silver by the year, and a suit of apparel, and thy victuals."

A popular entertainer in this nation, described it in a song he sang, "Sixteen tons, and what have you got? *I owe my soul to the company store.*" The gospel of Jesus Christ, sir, can never be a "company store" product.

The heart of the matter is this. "But seek ye first the kingdom of God, and his righteousness; and all these things (salary, clothing, groceries) shall be added unto you" (Matthew 6:33). You cannot *seek* "all these things" and *add,* at your convenience, "the kingdom of God, and his righteousness." It won't work.

You want proof of acceptance in another world. That must be the most important evidence this side of the grave for anyone. Can I trust Someone I have not seen, but whose Word I have in black and white? It adds to this. If He cannot care for me down here, He cannot care for me up there. So He offers me physical proof! You must have a salvation stronger than a theory or a philosophy. There must be a blood relationship. *I must experience evidences of His responsible care.*

Hell dedicates itself to destroy this life of trust. The path of

Hell's target is to destroy faith. Hell can do nothing about Calvary or the Open Tomb. They are *facts*. The subtle invasion is this. Can you really trust God? Isn't it better to work out your own salvation?

Play it cagey! Don't place all your eggs in one basket. This world has good things to offer. Hedge your wager. Don't withdraw entirely from the system. "Dwell with me, and be unto me a father and a priest, and I will give thee ten shekels of silver by the year, and a suit of apparel, and thy victuals."

We can always use a good man, and you have no need of worries. Leave your future in our hands. It's an old and time-tested offer. Accept it, and you'll lose your trust.

Paul could say to the Galatians, "Do I seek to please men? for if I yet pleased men, I should not be the servant of Christ" (Galatians 1:10). Our national leaders cannot be caught in a conflict of interests. They must divest themselves of properties and positions that could compromise their decisions as public servants. The Levite, under the law of God, was pledged to that commitment. They were separated to look toward God alone. The gentleman in my text had other ideas. "And the man departed out of the city from Beth-lehem-judah to sojourn where he could find a place" (Judges 17:8).

He decided there was nothing more propitious than to draw his breath and his salary. He felt the call of God should never get in the way of a steady supply of cash, clothing, and groceries. It was no longer God's will for his life that was uppermost. It became a matter "where he could find a place" (see Judges 17:9). *And, mister, there is a difference between God's leading for your life and looking toward man.* When God is your supply and direction you don't have to "tickle ears."

When you make money your goal, you are a lost soul. The Levite in this story lost his. Presently a committee waited on him, and said, "Hold thy peace, lay thine hand upon thy mouth, and go with us, and be to us a father and a priest: is it better for thee to be a priest unto the house of one man, or that thou be a priest unto a tribe and a family in Israel?" (Judges 18:19).

He knew where advancement lay in his chosen profession. He was quick to realize the advantages offered. His loyalty became a question of the highest bidder. So will yours when you place money before the Master. God and greed cannot dwell in the same heart. "For the love of money is the root of all evil: which while some coveted after, they have erred from the faith, and pierced themselves through with many sorrows" (1 Timothy 6:10).

Avarice is the infection that breeds everything that is despicable and devilish. It will turn simplicity and sincerity into superficiality. You'll become an *actor* instead of a *witness.*

Salvation is utter dependence upon Jesus Christ. The Twelve were given a chance to prove it. "Provide neither gold, nor silver, nor brass in your purses; . . . for the workman is worthy of his meat" (Matthew 10:9, 10).

There's not one moment or one experience when I do not need His help. "In him I live, I move, I have my being" (see Acts 17:28). You can't make it by yourself. The gospel is that good news that God doesn't require it. *He furnishes you help all the way.* It is dependence that provides intimacy between the believer and his God. The important factor is to *know Him*—far more important than knowing *about* Him.

I learned to sing this gospel song, and seek the experience it describes, early in my Christian life:

"You have longed for sweet peace,
And for faith to increase;
And have earnestly, fervently prayed.
But you cannot have rest,
Or be perfectly blessed;
Until *all* on the altar is laid.

"Is your all on the altar of sacrifice laid?
Your heart, does the Spirit control?
You can only be blessed,
And have peace and sweet rest,
As you yield Him your body and soul."

If Jesus Christ only means to you "ten shekels of silver by the year, and a suit of apparel, and thy victuals"—you haven't got much, mister. You haven't got nearly enough to deliver you from sin and habits of evil. You are a long, long way from that "abundant entrance" Peter describes. You are only a *peddler*—a huckster of religion. You'll never go to the stake for it as John Huss did in Bohemia. You wouldn't face a firing squad rather than betray Jesus Christ. Your comfort on earth means more to you than your gain in heaven.

No! *Salvation is not for sale.* Christ put no price on what He did for me. "As poor, yet making many rich" (2 Corinthians 6:10). The strength of my redemption is the great, eternal heart of God. He *loved* me. The answer to my own soul is this. *Do I love Him?* Jesus is still asking, "Lovest thou me more than these?" (John 21:15). Do you?

THE MAJORITY OPINION

Texts: *"For they have consulted together with one consent: they are confederate against thee."*

Psalm 83:5

"But the chief priests and elders persuaded the multitude that they should ask Barabbas, and destroy Jesus. . . . Pilate saith unto them, What shall I do then with Jesus which is called Christ? They all say unto him, Let him be crucified."

Matthew 27:20, 22

JAMES Reston of the New York Times observed recently that forces "try to persuade, or coerce the people into believing." He continued, "debate seems to get more and more like a noisy advertising campaign designed to persuade the doubters that 'a majority' favor such and such a policy."

We should take a look at history. There was a time when "a majority" favored slavery. That didn't make it right. There was a time when "a majority" opposed granting a franchise to women. They believed women should not be allowed to vote. That didn't make it right. There was a time when "a majority" favored strict isolation. That didn't make it right.

Isaiah had something to say about this. He said, "All we *like sheep* . . ." (Isaiah 53:6). It is so easy to surrender personal conscience. The easy way is to choose to believe that because the crowd is doing it—*it must be right.* This nymphean idea about cigarettes is being corrected right now by our Federal Government. *Because smoking was popular didn't make it right.*

The biggest question surfacing right now in this nation is *personal conscience.* Individuals are being forced to take a look at themselves. And most of us do not like what we see. We see fabrication—*packaging that goes on unceasingly.* We are computerized. We are polled. We are herded. Today, we have serious doubts about war. We have serious doubts about the atomic bomb. *We need time with our own souls.*

It seems to me young people are inclined to leap from the frying pan into the fire. While questioning the morality of war in Southeast Asia and ever-expanding cemeteries, they move with green-light speed into the use of drugs. There were 4,200 deaths caused by drug addiction in New York state alone last year.

Why protest the waste of young life in Vietnam and accept it at home? What makes it right to befuddle the mind, to sink in filth and squalor, to puncture vein after vein? What is this strange popularity—this hallucination? The plain answer to the epidemic is this. *Drug-taking is a fashion,* picked up from contemporaries or from pushers (who may themselves be teen-agers).

Paul lays down a rule for Christian conduct. He says, "Let every man be *fully persuaded* in his own mind" (Romans 14:5). That must be the foundation for character. Paul says, "So then every one of us shall give account of himself to God" (Romans 14:12). *You and I cannot escape personal responsibility.*

There is a remarkable illustration of this, documented for us, by Marshal Rommel's Chief of Staff, Lieutenant General Hans Speidel. His book is called Invasion 1944. He deals specifically with the tortured doubts of the popular German Marshal toward Hitler. He recalls:

"Rommel struggled to determine at what point obedience must end for a general who feels responsible for the fate of his nation, and at what point *human conscience* would demand insurrection.

"He did know the difference between *obedience to God* and *obedience to man.* For the sake of the people he must assume an extraordinary burden of responsibility.

Rommel accepted personal responsibility for decisions and rejected Hitler's demand that he be responsible only for executing orders. He wanted to save his country and the world from further bloodshed.

"Rommel was quite aware that independent action might lead to self-destruction, and possibly be the pretext for a new legend of 'the stab in the back,' *but he never recoiled from the thought of personal sacrifice.*"

Can you respect yourself? That is the answer. There are answers beyond the computer. Had the question of whether or not there might be an independent United States been submitted to the computer in 1776—undoubtedly, the answer would have been, "No." Had the question whether States torn by Civil War might become an even stronger nation, been submitted to the computer in 1864—undoubtedly, the answer would have been, "No." Had the question whether a Pearl Harbor could become a complete victory for a depleted nation been submitted to the computer right after the Japanese attack—undoubtedly, the answer would have been, "No."

The computer cannot add an *intangible*—the strength of man's spirit. It is there in the story Jesus told, "I will arise." I cannot escape personal decision and expect to survive.

There is always the temptation to *drift.* I do not wish to challenge the claims of advertising. So advertising adopts *the technique that this is the voice of the majority.* And since the majority approves, it must be right.

Lieutenant General Hans Speidel also cites the example of Major General Henning von Tresckow. He was involved in the Russian section of World War II. This General had long recognized Hitler's accumulation of senseless greed in its most brutal form; desire for renown; the conqueror's dream of power; lust for killing and destruction; vainglory and paralyzing fear; thirst for vengeance; and boundless despair.

Major General Henning von Tresckow wrestled with his

conscience. He left this will and testament:

"When I appear a few hours from now before the Throne of God to render account for my deeds and omissions, *I believe I will be able to answer with good conscience* for all that I have done in the struggle against Hitler.

"As God told Abraham that he would not destroy Sodom if only ten righteous men were to be found in the city, it is my hope that, for our sake, God will not destroy Germany."

Yes, you and I carry this burden—*what must I do?* The Government cannot be my conscience. The Church cannot be my conscience. The chief priests and elders were wrong about Jesus. The Family cannot be my conscience.

The entire family of Jesus Christ, including four brothers and several sisters, would have persuaded Him to have taken a different course. I'll read it to you from Mark 3:31, 32: "There came then his brethren and his mother, *and, standing without,* . . . And the multitude sat about him, and they said unto him, Behold, thy mother and thy brethren *without* seek for thee." The family stood on the outer periphery, disassociating themselves from this mad Son. They believed His course was reckless tragedy.

The story of this text is repeated in every generation, "they have consulted together . . . they are confederate." There are always those who are ready to do your thinking. They become "blind leaders of the blind." The result must be, "And if the blind lead the blind, both shall fall into the ditch" (Matthew 15:14).

This nation grew powerful defending the sanctity of the individual. Sir, you count very much! You are not just a digit on some list. You are more than a social security number. You are not merchandise to be traded or discarded. You will always be what you were created, made "in his own image, in the image of God" (Genesis 1:27). You may foul that image. You may betray that image. You may disregard that image. *But that image will always be there to testify to you.*

Look into your own soul! Elijah did, and it brought him to Mount Carmel and the historic confrontation with Baal. Joseph did at Potiphar's house, and it led him in and out of an Egyptian prison, and at last into the Royal Court. Daniel did, and it sustained him on death row, and returned him to a high seat in government. Esther did, and she said, "If I perish, I perish" (Esther 4:16). In the final analysis, you have to live with yourself. *Can you stand the man or woman you are?*

Majority opinion is essential for business. Without it business comes to a standstill. However, that is a different question than the question whether or not "majority opinion" *is the right opinion.*

Majority opinion would have told Gideon to go home and forget the Midianites. That opinion was 31,700 strong. Every poll and every computer favored withdrawal. Majority opinion would have told David he was too young and too inexperienced to go up against Goliath. Walter Lippmann wrote 40 years ago: "Nobody can seriously maintain that the greatest number must have the greatest wisdom or the greatest virtue."

What does your own conscience say about Jesus Christ? Your own soul is asking this question, "Whose Son is He?" *That is a question for you to answer.* Don't shift it to the seminary. The theologians will debate while you perish. Don't submit it to your denomination. You can't rest your soul on stained-glass windows or expensive organ. Don't take it to your club. In one-half hour His Name will be used both for an invocation and a dirty story. *You answer!*

Simon Peter did. After a brief canvass of public opinion, "Whom do men say that I, the Son of man, am?" (Matthew 16:13)—there came the necessity of personal conviction, "But whom say ye that I am?" (Matthew 16:15).

That is what will save you or destroy you, sir. "And Simon Peter answered and said, Thou art the Christ, the Son of the living God" (Matthew 16:16).

Stop hiding behind others. Make this the hour when you declare yourself. Let the record state that you, yourself, *believed.*

You may stand alone on your street, in your family, or in the congregation. But in that moment you will feel dignity. You will no longer feel like a pawn, moved at the convenience of another. Contend for your right to make up your own mind. You will be judged on that basis. "Let a man examine himself!" (1 Corinthians 11:28).

Do that now. Put questions to your own soul,, and decide to exercise yourself daily "to always a conscience void of offense toward God, and toward men" (Acts 24:16).

SIX BIG "IFS"

Text: *"If it be thou."*

Matthew 14:28

ONE thing is certain. *There is no sense in praying if God doesn't answer.*

Can anyone ask? Under certain conditions, yes! What are those *conditions?* There are six, and they are spelled out in the Word of God.

FIRST, "If ye abide in me, and my words abide in you, ye shall ask what ye will, and it shall be done unto you" (John 15:7). This condition appears in every Bible. Jesus made this plain. "If ye abide in me!" This is where the *if* is. Christ, Himself, placed it there. I cannot expect an answer *if* I do not "abide."

Webster says to abide "is to remain *fixed* in some state." Jesus described it as branch and vine. It is more than an occasional contact. *It is total.*

I must be honest with you. What I want to do and what I might do under given circumstances could differ. Could I "abide" under excruciating pain? Could I "abide" were I taken to the stake and burned like John Huss? Could I "abide" in the midst of financial panic? God's answer to me is this—*others have.*

Some of you "abide" for only an hour on Sunday morning. Where are you on Wednesday and Sunday nights? Why didn't the evangelist see you on Friday night? Where were you "abiding" that night? Some of you have been in and out of marriages that God solemnized. You stopped "abiding" after five, ten, fifteen years. You started "abiding" with Hollywood and Madison Avenue patterns. You don't *believe* what you formerly believed. And you are not getting the same results, spiritually, that you formerly experienced.

So, my friend, read it again—"and my words abide in you" (John 15:7). That means seeing it as God sees it. Too many of us cherish our own viewpoints. We would have it read, "and *my own words* abide in me."

That won't work, sir. God may say something to me that I don't like. His word deals with a personal failure. Will I receive the heavenly counsel? Will I submit? Will I harbor the divine message? *God seeks that life in which His will is uppermost.*

It means more. To abide in Christ is to have no interest into which He is not brought, no life which He cannot share. Is your Lord welcome and respected in the company you keep? He isn't if His Name is taken in vain. And you shouldn't be there either! The rule is simple, young person. If you can't take your Lord with you, you shouldn't go. There shouldn't be any argument—what harm is there in it?

I must acknowledge His presence at all times. I have no right to keep anything from Him. I must respect His decision. I must seek His counsel in all things. I think many of us are *visitors* rather than *residents* in the grace of God.

SECOND, "And this is the confidence that we have in him, that, if we ask any thing according to his will, he heareth us: and if we know that he hear us, whatsoever we ask, we know that we have the petitions that we desired of him" (1 John 5:14, 15). *This is the second big "if"—"if we ask any thing according to his will"* (1 John 5:14).

It is apparent that I must discover the will of God. That takes reading, listening, and inquiring. He is the *parent.* I am the *child.* Childlike, I am full of desires. He knows best. It must be that way.

The most desirable thing in this world must be what is *eternally good* for me. So, I must submit to His judgment. God is too much of a Father to permit me to be hurt or turned aside spiritually by indulging me in some selfish desire.

Many of us have learned that it is wasted effort trying to bend God's will to suit our own. The only effective prayer is, "Not my will, but thine, be done" (Luke 22:42).

I have always liked this story. A little girl prayed for another doll to add to her already large collection. But when another doll was not forthcoming, her brother taunted her, "So God did not answer your prayer, did He?"

"Oh, yes, He did," she was quick to reply.

"Well, what did He say?" came the retort.

With an air of finality and sweet acceptance, the little sister replied, "He said, 'No!' "

The best prayer is prayer that is soaked in the Word of God. There are times when, though we know that we are praying according to God's will, the answer does not seem to come. *This is often true in prayer for loved ones to be saved.* I am helped by knowing His will. It is God's will that none should perish.

It is also His will that none should be forced. He will woo. He will let that one reap the harvest of his or her evil years, but He will never storm that loved one's life. I must come to terms with this. The love and power of an omnipotent God can be held in abeyance by the strong will of puny man. The Word of God teaches me these facts.

THIRD, "Whatsoever ye shall ask in my name, that will I do, that the Father may be glorified in the Son. *If* ye shall ask any thing in my name, I will do it" (John 14:13, 14). Here is the third big "if"—"if ye ask any thing in my name."

Have I a right to use that Name? There is only one woman in this world who has a right to use my name. She has *earned* that right. Any other woman, attempting the same privileges, is masquerading.

Many a professed believer is *masquerading.* He hasn't earned the right to that blessed Name. The world knows you are not a Christian. There is no separation. There is no common interest with One you profess to love above all others. You have more right to the name of some downtown club, some college fraternity, some labor union, some political party, some denominational membership than you have ever earned to carry His Name. You have to *belong* before you can *ask.*

It is more than a ritual, mister. To end a prayer with the words, "for Jesus' sake," may only serve to let others know you are finished. I am talking about *authority.* Has that authority been invested in you? His Name is above every other name.

Paul met those who were trying to use that Name without the authority to use it. "Then certain of the vagabond Jews, exorcists, took upon them to call over them which had evil spirits the name of the Lord Jesus, saying, We adjure you by Jesus whom Paul preacheth. And there were seven sons of one Sceva, a Jew, and chief of the priests, which did so. And the evil spirit answered and said, Jesus I know, and Paul I know; *but who* are ye?" (Acts 19:13-15). *The checkbook is for the family only.*

FOURTH, "Ask in faith, nothing wavering: for he that wavereth is like a wave of the sea driven with the wind and tossed. For let not that man think that he shall receive any thing of the Lord" (James 1:6, 7). Here is the fourth big "if." It is called *wavering.*

It starts with *conviction*—"God . . . *is,* and that he is a rewarder of them that diligently seek him" (Hebrews 11:6). *Prayer is not an experiment.* It is direct communication.

I am a child of God. I have that assurance, I believe my request will be heard. Without faith it is impossible, sir!

Someone *believed* there was radio. Someone *believed* there was television. Someone *believed* there was the jet engine. I am even more thankful for those who believed God. Joshua *believed.* The sun stood still. Elisha *believed.* The Jordan parted. Peter *believed.* Dorcas was brought back from the dead. A believer takes God at His Word.

FIFTH, "And when ye stand praying, forgive, if ye have aught against any; that your Father also which is in heaven may forgive you your trespasses" (Mark 11:25). Here is the fifth big *if*—"if ye have aught against any."

I am asking for a *favor.* Have I granted a *favor?* There is an exchange. Besides, the channel to heaven and to the Throne of Grace must be *clear.* That channel, sir, leads through the powers of darkness. Count on it! Satan will make it his business to interrupt. There will be opposition. Hell only needs the slightest occasion to blackmail you. An unforgiving spirit provides that occasion.

I can pray effectually for another, only, when I have forgiven that person. My heart isn't right with God if there is resentment, jealousy, malice, greed, envy present. Yes, sir! There are *hindrances* that I can remove.

SIXTH, "Truth, Lord: yet the dogs eat of the crumbs which fall from their masters' table" (Matthew 15:27). This is the *importunity* that Christ so often commended. It's the final big, *if.* The answer is there *if* I will stay with it through obstacle and discouragement. "O woman, great is thy faith: be it unto thee even as thou wilt" (Matthew 15:28). So many of us quit too soon.

Faith holds on. Faith *persevers.* George Mueller of Bristol, England, prayed some 50 years for a certain man to be saved. He went home to be with the Lord not seeing that man saved, but that man was saved two weeks after the death of the Lord's servant.

The walls of Jericho tumbled the seventh day, the seventh time around. Elijah prayed until a "crumb" appeared, "a little cloud out of the sea, like a man's hand" (1 Kings 18:44). General Naaman washed seven times. It is recorded of Jesus in Gethsemane, "And (He) prayed the third time, *saying the same words*" (Matthew 26:44).

Lord Alfred Tennyson placed his conviction in writing:

"More things are wrought by prayer
Than this world dreams of. Wherefore,
  let thy voice
Rise like a fountain for me night and day.
For what are men better than sheep or goats,
That nourish a blind life within the brain,
If, knowing God, they lift not hands of prayer
Both for themselves and those who call them friend?
For so the whole round earth is every way
Bound by gold chains about the feet of God."

A RADIO INVITATION

This altar reaches into Thailand and Vietnam and Formosa and Okinawa. It has stretched in these 17 years of services until it has become one of the longest altars on earth. And I am sure that it passes so near to where you are that a single step can bring you to it. So kneel with us.

This is the moment to open your heart and share your deepest longings with God. The Holy Spirit will guide you. It is His mission to lead you "into all truth" and "glorify" Jesus—to make the Saviour personally real to you. Prayer isn't fancy words or a learned speech. It is an expression of the soul—the language of the spirit—*a release.* I find there is no *substitute.* Inner peace comes when I commune with God. Then I am calm and hopeful, and my life assumes a joy and radiance. I know this. *God will hear you when you pray in the Name of Jesus.*

"I come in that Name. Lord, make this one of our greatest altar services.

"Receive the sinner at this altar who is now repenting. Strengthen that determination to go all the way—to receive water baptism and communion, to honor Thee with a tenth, to begin a systematic study of the Bible, to be present and support a Bible-believing and soul-winning Sunday school and church, to witness daily for Thee. In Thy Name, we receive into this fellowship those who kneel humbly before Thee. *They are now our brothers and our sisters.*

"We pray for our nation. *Arrest our sin.* Encourage righteousness from the White House to the humblest home. Let us honor Thee, that Thou mayest honor us. Amen."

Praise God with me, folk! Go in God's Name and strength. You are *secure* because the victory is in this fact that it is "not by might, nor by strength, but by My Spirit, saith the Lord."

IS IT REASONABLE?

Text: *"If a man die, shall he live again?"*

Job 14:14

NO *other question is as important.* It won't go away. You may not want to think about it, but it will face you constantly.

I believe there are five apparent *reasons* for answering in the *affirmative.* You may check these wherever you are in this audience.

First, *every living thing serves some useful purpose.* That is true from a blade of grass to an elephant. Nothing is placed on this planet without purpose. This fact affords the search and excitement of our laboratories.

A blossom may feed some insect which in turn is devoured by some game bird, which, flying across space, comes within the reach of the hunter's gun, later to provide sustenance for his body. *Nothing is without destiny.*

You may observe this with me. In the case of every single order known in this universe, *the life purpose of each is fulfilled by the time of its death.* Man is the only exception to this rule.

Certain creatures fulfill their purpose *by* death. Edible animals are a case in point. They die to provide food. Other animals provide fertilizer, and in death, cause other things to grow.

How can you fit into that category? Do you really believe man was created deliberately for worm food, or to fertilize the soil? What value to wait 70 years for 175 pounds of fertilizer? We do not believe this is destiny. We place our dead in lead-lined caskets and seal the caskets in air-proof vaults. Nature has provided for more extensive and cheaper methods to enrich the soil.

Use common sense, sir! Man has not accomplished his purpose for being by the time of his death. *Therefore it must carry over.*

Second, *education is never without purpose.* You may go to school endlessly. Some do. They have no particular goal except to put in time. Education is different. *I prepare myself.* Critics conclude that it takes a person 60 of his years of living to be able to function to his highest power the following ten years. Even Christ spent 30 years preparing for a three-year ministry.

Do you, for a moment, conclude that life is over when you graduate from college? It is well named when graduation is named the *commencement.* You are barely equipped with modest essentials to begin. And the demand for further and further training increases.

What purpose can this investment and expense serve, if we plunge so soon into nothingness? It is fraud and waste to encumber humanity with so many years of schooling and then abort it all.

Again, use common sense, sir! The purpose of education must be bigger. Its usefulness does not stop with the grave.

Third, *all forms of matter are indestructible.* An example is coal. Coal is complex. Expose it to flame, and the action of the flame destroys its *form*; and apparently its *substance* as well. The residue is called ash.

Ask the chemist! He will tell you that not one element of the coal has been lost. He has been able to capture and analyze every element *in the higher forms of gases. There has been a change, not annihilation.*

Let's take another very simple and common example—the example of *dry ice.* This is a solid substance produced from a gas by man's ingenuity. Suddenly the solid disappears. It is invisible. What has happened? Is there total *nothingness?* No. The same gas that was once condensed into a solid, may again be captured and condensed *again* into a white, ponderable form in which we once possessed it. *So, the visible can be changed to the invisible and back to the visible.*

All matter serves mankind. Am I to believe that the servant is potentially greater than the master? Will all forms of matter continue and man perish? I need proof, that has not yet been forthcoming, before I could believe that. I shall be *changed.* Yes! But I shall not be eliminated.

Fourth, *there are the findings of ethnology.* Ethnology is the science of living races.

The fact is every race with recorded history has believed in life beyond the grave. The ethnologist concludes that, as a basis for this universal faith, there is somewhere an established fact. Something provides the ground for such belief.

The late Dr. Harry Rimmer, who dealt extensively with this subject, provides this illustration. He recalls an excavation of Mongoloid burial mounds. This is his testimony:

"Although the ossi in all these mounds were buried generally in the embryonic position, we found one small deposit startlingly different. Fourteen magnificent specimens of battling manhood had been buried sitting up in a circle around the ashes of a camp fire.

"It was the custom of this people, when on the war trail, to sleep sitting up around the embers of their dying flames. They drew up their knees, wrapped their arms around their knee-caps, and peacefully dozed. Their weapons were placed by their right hands and their left, in a position of instant convenience. Sleeping thus in a circle, if any alarm was given, instantly alert, their combined vision covered every point of the compass. If disturbed by an enemy, they but dropped their hands to the hafts of their weapons, sprang alertly to their feet, and began battle.

"These fourteen had been buried in this position, with their weapons handy to their grasp. In the study of the position of these sleeping warriors, with mute eloquence that is sometimes heard from the clarion voices of the dead, *they testified that they waited a call to spring erect and take up the battle where it had been concluded by their deaths.*"

The same story is told from the tombs of Egypt. Viking legends tell the same thing. Nineveh and Babylon join with the others.

It is an undying hope in the breasts of men. What sustains such hope? Nothing erases it.

Fifth, *there is the amazing sense of balance.* This says that every earthly need is met by a source of supply.

This planet houses a myriad of *noises. Ears* have been provided to detect and interpret these noises. This planet is filled with motion and *color. Eyes* have been created to note and distinguish these colors and motions.

Lungs would be meaningless were it not for the atmosphere which girdles this planet. There is *thirst,* and there is water. There is *hunger,* and there is food. *Check the longings—the desires!* Every yearning of which man is capable has possibilities of satisfaction.

Man wanted to *fly.* That desire has found satisfaction. Man wanted to go to the moon and return. That desire has been satisfied. Man wanted to reproduce himself in picture. He has found the answer in photography. Man wanted to converse, instantly, anywhere in the universe. That desire led to radio.

For every desire there must be an answer. Name the fulfillments! There is the submarine, the answer to man's desire to swim like a fish. There is radar, the answer to man's desire to see beyond the clouds and through the night.

The Creator built man with *desire.* I know this from the

evidences provided, it is not placed within to either mock or torment. It is there to discover *the answer.*

To each of us come moments of love. They are irresistible. They drive us. Life becomes arid without response. Someone, somewhere, fits that need. Some calling, some profession, some avocation answers that quest.

The strongest yearning of all is for life after death. I don't want to perish. *That desire has been planted in my bosom by a higher Power.* Why should it be there?

Reason is that *calm* voice. That is why I have directed this question toward reason. The Creator has provided it as a further checkpoint alongside conscience, imagination, emotion, and will. "Come . . . let us *reason* together" (Isaiah 1:18). So, ask yourself, "Is it reasonable?" I have named five challenges that reason provides.

I have outlined certain obvious *effects.* Reason demands a *cause.* A headache is an effect. So, immediately, the physician seeks a cause. This calls for an *examination.* This is what you should do.

You are going somewhere. You are on your way. You cannot mark time. You cannot turn back the clock.

Are you ready? God has not left Himself without witness in any generation, for the visible things of creation *testify* to the invisible Creator.

I have named five daily experiences that "testify" to you. You have the choice of *unbelief,* but you cannot find comfort in *doubt.* Reason won't let you any more than conscience, imagination, feelings, will, or the Word of God permit you.

So, then, the answer is *preparation.* God has given instructions. They are in His Book. Follow them!

Paul told Timothy that it all became manifest to him "by the appearing of our Saviour Jesus Christ, who hath abolished death, and hath brought life and *immortality* to light through the gospel" (2 Timothy 1:10).

Reach out toward Christ, and He will do the same for you.

GAMES PEOPLE WOULD LIKE TO PLAY WITH GOD

Text: *"How long shall thy vain thoughts lodge within thee?"*
Jeremiah 4:14

A WHILE back, Darrell Logue, a fine associate minister at the First Assembly, Tyler, Texas, brought this theme to my attention. I have thought about it since. *To so many, religion is a game to be played.* It is exciting and demanding.

Dr. Berne, in a best seller he authored, Games People Play, has stated: "Most people in most of their family and business relationships, are constantly playing games with each other." It forms a unique study in human relationships. *Strangely, this is carried toward a more important relationship.* It's an old habit.

Jeremiah sensed it in his day. *There was a lot of motion and little reality.* His generation wanted to be religious, but they didn't want to be pure, holy, or separate. *They wanted to be accepted by God and enjoy, at the same time, the pleasures of idolatry.* Jeremiah gave God's verdict: "But thou shalt say unto them, This is a nation that obeyeth not the voice of the Lord their God, nor receiveth correction: truth is perished, and is cut off from their mouth" (Jeremiah 7:28).

"For my people have committed two evils; they have forsaken me the fountain of living waters, and hewed them out cisterns, broken cisterns, that can hold no water" (Jeremiah 2:13).

Jeremiah's generation convinced itself that it could play both ends toward the middle. "Will ye steal, murder, and commit adultery, and swear falsely, and burn incense unto Baal, and walk after other gods whom ye know not; and come and stand before me in this house, which is called by my name, and say, We are delivered to do all these abominations?" (Jeremiah 7:9, 10).

A favorite game people would like to play with God, is one called, *LET'S MAKE A DEAL.*

I have wanted to play that game myself. Usually we are most anxious to play it when we find ourselves in serious trouble. The sick, the bankrupt, the apprehended, the loser are always ready to play. They are ready to make a deal.

I have found myself in terrible pain, and I have offered to increase my giving, or accept the burden of some additional Christian service, or do more Bible reading, or endure a little fasting, *if God will only lift the pain.* We bargain with God. To lots of people, religion is simply bargain hunting—getting the best deal possible.

Let me remind you, folk! When God enters an agreement, it is in *contract form.* And if you *cheat,* you will face the *penalty.* So, don't bargain unless you mean it!

Adam made this discovery. His deal went like this: "Of every tree of the garden thou mayest freely eat: but of the tree of the knowledge of good and evil, thou shalt not eat of it: for in the day that thou eatest thereof thou shalt surely die" (Genesis 2:16, 17). That was the deal! Man had a garden, and God asked for faith.

God is prepared to listen. He listened to Jacob. "If God will be with me, and will keep me in this way that I go, and will give me bread to eat, and raiment to put on, so that I come again to my father's house in peace; then shall the Lord be my God: and this stone, which I have set for a pillar, shall be God's house: and of all that thou shalt give me I will surely give *the tenth* unto thee" (Genesis 28:20-22). Why don't you try tithing? Make a deal, sir! But don't *play* games.

Another favorite game people would like to play with God, is one called, *charades.*

This is a game where *you assume an identity.* You pretend to be someone and ask people to identify the character you assume.

So I make all the moves like a robot. I sing. I pray. I give. I make an *impression.* But the real me, my heart, is a million miles away. I'm an *actor.* I'm an *actress.* Jesus made a note of this. He said, "This people honoreth me with their lips, but their heart is far from me" (Mark 7:6). Jesus said you must serve God "*in truth.*" Motions, parades, statistics, audiences, efforts are not enough.

People play this game at communion. They dress. They kneel. They partake. God says, "Let a man *examine* himself!" (1 Corinthians 11:28). Why? Because you can *pretend.*

People play this game with baptism. A prominent personality in Samaria did. "Then Simon himself believed also: and when he was baptized, he continued with Philip, . . . But Peter said unto him, . . . thou hast thought that the gift of God may be purchased with money. Thou hast neither part nor lot in this matter: *for thy heart is not right in the sight of God*" (Acts 8:13, 20, 21).

People play this game with *giving.* Ananias and Sapphira did and were caught. It cost them their lives. You can really get into trouble assuming false identities.

Another favorite game people would like to play with God is one called, *hide and seek.*

As long as they can hear God's voice calling, "Where art thou?" they feel everything will turn out favorably. So, they go fishing on Sunday morning, counting on hearing that Voice. They watch television on Sunday night, counting on hearing that Voice. They train for money instead of souls, counting on hearing that Voice. They never want to get so far from God that they miss His presence entirely. They don't want to come out into the open for God.

Let me ask you, sir! *What if God left you there?* Suppose He didn't seek. Suppose He were absolutely indifferent. But, He does *seek*. He does *call*.

He kept on the trail of Saul of Tarsus. He said to him, "It is hard for thee to kick against the pricks" (Acts 9:5). He kept on the trail of Peter. He said to him, "I have prayed for thee" (Luke 22:32). You may hide, but He will find you. He found Jonah. He found Moses. Jonah hid in the Mediterranean. Moses hid in Midian. The eyes of the Lord cover sea and land, sir.

David played games with God. He discovered something. He said, "Whither shall I go from thy Spirit? Or whither shall I flee from thy presence? If I ascend up into heaven, thou art there: if I make my bed in hell, behold, thou art there. If I take the wings of the morning, and dwell in the uttermost parts of the sea; even there shall thy hand lead me, and thy right hand shall hold me. If I say, Surely the darkness shall cover me; even the night shall be light about me. Yea, the darkness hideth not from thee; but the night shineth as the day: the darkness and the light are both alike to thee. For thou hast possessed my reins: thou hast covered me in my mother's womb" (Psalm 139:7-13). *You may hide, sir, but God will find you.*

Another favorite game people would like to play with God is one called *concentration*. It goes like this. "Look, God, I'm religious!" The Pharisees were master players. They fasted twice a week. They prayed long prayers. They kept accounts down to the penny. They were careful about their religious appearance. Jesus said about them, "Ye compass sea and land to make one proselyte; and when he is made, ye make him twofold more the child of hell than yourselves" (Matthew 23:15).

Religion was *total business* with them. They tied in real estate, high rents, expensive clothes, rich furnishings, choice menus, difficult ritual, complex study, restrictive degrees. It was something to be a Pharisee. *It was status.*

Jesus made a note of this. "I say unto you, That except your righteousness shall exceed the righteousness of the scribes and Pharisees, ye shall in no case enter into the kingdom of heaven" (Matthew 5:20).

Mister, it takes more than *show!* Your church attendance flash and sweep may be spectacular. You are ushered to the family pew. The minister has a choice bit in his sermon related to you. *Your attendance is duly noted and publicized.*

Jesus was explicit about this. "Take heed that ye do not your alms before men, to be seen of them: otherwise ye have no reward of your Father which is in heaven" (Matthew 6:1).

And again He warned, "Do not sound a trumpet before thee, as the hypocrites do in the synagogues and in the streets, that they may have glory of men. Verily I say unto you, They have their reward" (Matthew 6:2).

The Master observed: "And when thou prayest, thou shalt not be as the hypocrites are: for they love to pray standing in the synagogues and in the corners of the streets, that they may be seen of men. Verily I say unto you, They have their reward" (Matthew 6:5).

You can be so *religious,* and at the same time so *ungodly.* It may be a game with you. It's a popular one. Millions play it every Sunday morning. There are rich prizes.

Let me say this to you as your evangelist. *You may play games with God, but God is not playing games with you.* Your relationship with God is deadly serious. Samson learned the hard way. He trifled. He had his fun. He turned *coy,* then he turned serious. It became a highly amusing game to him. He flirted with the enemies of God. He said, "Bind me with seven green withes that were never dried, then shall I be weak, and be as another man" (Judges 16:7). He counted on God going along with him.

So, when Delilah shouted: "The Philistines be upon thee, Samson. . . . He brake the withes, as a thread of tow is broken when it toucheth the fire.... And Delilah said... Behold, thou hast mocked me, and told me lies" (Judges 16:9, 10).

Mister, *you can play that game too often.* Samson played until he thought he was master. He was mistaken. He said, "*I will go out as at other times before,* and shake myself. And he wist not that the Lord was departed from him" (Judges 16:20).

God is not going to *play* with you, lady. You may pretend with others, but don't *pretend* with God. That's why I don't want anyone to play with my soul. When I go to church, I want a serious service. I want the preacher to be honest with my mind and my conscience. I don't want to be misled. I'm on a one-way trip to eternity, and I want the directions clear and concise. I don't want to be lost in church suppers, fund-raising drives, musical entertainment, social issues, or athletic benefits. I want the preacher to prepare me for "that day" when I must stand before God, and *give an account of myself.*

Jeremiah came to Judah, saying, "It's time to stop playing games with God." God asked pointed questions through His servant, "Why *trimmest* thou my way to seek love?...Why *gaddest* thou about so much to change thy way?" (Jeremiah 2:33, 36).

Stop your fancy detours, preacher! Stop your denials, church-board member! God won't adjust to anything that is tricky.

Jeremiah told Judah there was *one way.* "Thus saith the Lord of hosts, the God of Israel, Amend your ways and your doings" (Jeremiah 7:3). So, do it *now*—this side of the grave!

SALVATION IS SO SIMPLE

Text: "*Whosoever therefore shall confess me before men, him will I confess also before my Father which is in heaven.*"
Matthew 10:32

I HAVE used this text more often in my campaigns, giving the invitation, than I have used any other. *It reduces salvation to one step.*

God undertakes the entire transaction—*everything.* The cost is all underwritten. Calvary erases your sin-bill—paid in full. So, that leads you to this one thing. *Acknowledge your Benefactor.*

Everyone who comes face to face with Christ must make a decision—either *confess* Him, or *deny* Him. There is neither room for postponement or compromise. It would be foolish to say, "I do not confess Him, but on the other hand, neither do I deny Him."

I'll tell you what the Book says. "He that is not with me is against me; and he that gathereth not with me scattereth abroad" (Matthew 12:30). One thing is certain—*you cannot have an open mind about Jesus.*

Don't even permit me to confuse you. You are not asked to confess your *denomination.* To say, "I am a Lutheran," or "I hold membership with the Christian Church," or "I attend services at the Salvation Army" won't save you. It isn't confessing a creed or a code of ethics. It isn't even confessing that you are a sinner. Here it is! "Whosoever therefore shall confess *me* before men." That is what it takes, mister.

There is no transfer of Calvary's victory to your mismanaged life without it. "That if thou shalt confess *with thy mouth* the

Lord Jesus, and shalt believe *in thine heart* that God hath raised him from the dead, thou shalt be saved. For with the heart man believeth unto righteousness; and with the mouth confession is made unto salvation" (Romans 10:9, 10). The sooner you say, *Jesus saves me,* the better.

Salvation is like marriage. When something has happened to your heart, it won't take long to talk about it. Mark talks about it. "He that believeth and is baptized shall be saved; but he that believeth not shall be damned" (Mark 16:16).

You wouldn't want it more straight than that. You have to come *out* for Jesus Christ. God is prepared to cancel every moral debt you owe on the basis of your confession of His Son. It isn't bribery or blackmail. It is your salvation.

There are no undercover Christians. I have never been secretly married. I have been publicly married for 41 years. "Let all those that seek thee rejoice and be glad in thee: let such as love thy salvation say continually, The Lord be magnified" (Psalm 40:16).

"Let the redeemed of the Lord say so, whom he hath redeemed from the hand of the enemy" (Psalm 107:2). Jesus Christ is too meaningful to *quibble* about.

Peter told the public, "For we cannot but speak the things which we have seen and heard" (Acts 4:20). To deny Christ is to deny Calvary, and to deny Calvary is to deny history. *You call God a liar.*

Public confession is God's plan for world evangelization. The militancy is in the words, "I believe." They did it in the New Testament. "Therefore they that were scattered abroad went every where preaching the word" (Acts 8:4).

So often, we want our expensive church properties and our programs to do the confessing. No, sir—*it is personal involvement.* "What shall *I* do then with Jesus which is called Christ?" (Matthew 27:22). God places that question before *you.* It isn't a group decision. It must be your decision.

It is binding at the day of Judgment. "Him will I confess also before my Father which is in heaven." Look at the far-reaching effects! "But whosoever shall deny me before men, him will I also deny before my Father which is in heaven" (Matthew 10: 33).

Do you know of any way to circumvent that denial? And there will be a full audit of your residence on this planet. "So then every one of us shall give account of himself to God" (Romans 14:12).

One thing will stand out above every lie you have told—every piece of property you have stolen—every filthy thought—every hateful feeling—every mistreatment of your parents—*your denial of Jesus will stand out above all else.*

I'll tell you what the Book says. "Because he hath appointed a day, in the which he will judge the world in righteousness *by that man* whom he hath ordained; whereof he hath given assurance unto all men, in that he hath raised him from the dead" (Acts 17:31).

You are going to face Him on "that day," sir. Will He, or will He not, recognize you? That is for you to determine.

Christ went all the way for us. Every humiliation—every stroke of the whip—every painful step—every second of agony *were for me.* The purchase wasn't cheap. Jesus was ashamed *for* me, but never *of* me. God asks as much from me.

You ask, "How can I confess Him before men?" I give you five ways.

1. *Start your Christian life by open confession.* Rise from your knees and face the people present. Jesus told the man, out of whom He cast a legion of devils, "Go home to thy friends, and tell them how great things the Lord hath done for thee, and hath had compassion on thee" (Mark 5:19).

Business is accomplished by vote—by a division of the house. Very legal minutes and records keep such decisions available. "Then Moses stood in the gate of the camp, and said, Who is on the Lord's side?" (Exodus 32:26). Your decision *for Christ* must be a matter of eternal record.

2. *Constantly confess Christ before others.* Never miss an opportunity. If you love Him, you will talk about Him. Paul told Timothy, "I am not *ashamed;* for I know whom I have believed, and am persuaded that he is able to keep that which I have committed unto him against that day" (2 Timothy 1:12).

3. *Do it by water baptism and the Lord's Supper.* This isn't a denominational matter. It is a New Testament matter. This is what they did in the evangelism Philip conducted. "But when they believed Philip preaching the things concerning the kingdom of God, and the name of Jesus Christ, they were baptized, both men and women" (Acts 8:12).

The Ethiopian official felt he should do the same thing. "And as they went on their way, they came unto a certain water: and the eunuch said, See, here is water; what doth hinder me to be baptized? And Philip said, If thou believest with all thine heart, thou mayest. And he answered and said, I believe that Jesus Christ is the Son of God. And he commanded the chariot to stand still: and they went down both into the water, both Philip and the eunuch; and he baptized him" (Acts 8:36-38).

4. *Do it by the life you live.* Go to your neighbors and make things right. That will confess Christ before men.

We make Christ known by what we do not do and by what we do not say. There are times when that is the loudest possible way to witness. Jesus made this plain. "I am the light of the world: he that followeth me shall not walk in darkness" (John 8:12).

You can't engage in questionable things and confess Him before men. "Let your light so shine before men, that they may see your good works, and glorify your Father which is in heaven" (Matthew 5:16).

My attitude when I am *losing* will let men know whom I

serve. Paul kept that in mind. "But I would ye should understand, brethren, that the things which happened unto me have fallen out rather unto the furtherance of the gospel" (Philippians 1:12).

5. *Do it by definite association with a company of the Lord's friends.* Be seen with the right crowd! Not forsaking the assembling of ourselves together, as the manner of some is; but exhorting one another: and so much the more, as ye see the day approaching" (Hebrews 10:25).

Your church membership and regular attendance and support is a very real testimony. It is said of the disciples, "They went to their own company" (Acts 4:23). Lions don't run around with polecats, and eagles don't fly with buzzards.

Your salvation depends upon an open and unreserved confession of Jesus Christ. *As long as you are ashamed of Him you are unsaved.*

I'm not ashamed to own my Lord
Or to defend His cause,
Maintain the honor of His word,
The glory of His cross.
Then will He own my worthless name
Before His Father's face;
And, in the New Jerusalem,
Appoint my soul a place.

I believe it is as simple as that.

THE KISS

Text: *"Mercy and truth are met together; righteousness and peace have kissed each other. Truth shall spring out of the earth; and righteousness shall look down from heaven."*
Psalm 85:10, 11

WHAT seemed impossible and irreconcilable, held a "Big Four Meeting" at Bethlehem, and changed the history of the universe. *Mercy, Truth, Righteousness,* and *Peace* met in Jesus Christ.

Before the manger scene, these four were hopelessly split. *Mercy* and *Peace* pleaded for mankind. *Righteousness* and *Truth* condemned the race. The pleadings of *Mercy* are a matter of record. "Wherefore hast thou made all men in vain?" (Psalm 89:47). "What profit is there in my blood?" (Psalm 30: 9). "Will the Lord cast off for ever? And will he be favorable no more? Is his mercy clean gone for ever?" (Psalm 77:7, 8).

That was the case Mercy made.

But *Truth* was heard as well. "In the beginning was the Word, . . . and the Word was God" (John 1:1). So the Word spoke, "The soul that sinneth, it shall die" (Ezekiel 18:20). *God cannot alter His Word.*

Righteousness stands with *Truth.* God is "righteous in all his . . . works" (Psalm 145:17). "The wages of sin is death" (Romans 6:23). *The Judge of the world must never judge unjustly.*

It became the *deadlock* of time. What use of justice of God will do no justice? Forget the word! "But what use of me," saith Mercy, "if God spare not sinners?" It all waited a *settlement. Truth* went into exile. Heaven, alone, provided a sufficient clime. *Truth* dare not look down upon this wretched planet. *Mercy* alone pleaded for mankind.

Peace sought, if possible, to work out terms—to find a solution—to bring about a settlement. So, that became the question! When would the meeting be held, and on what grounds? Our judgment could not be postponed indefinitely. Two were *for* us. Two were *against* us. Something had to be done to bring them into oneness.

Mercy was always ready. *Righteousness* would not look down upon what appeared to be an "open-and-shut" case for the prosecution. There was no question of guilt. It was proven beyond reasonable doubt.

There could be no meeting without *Truth*. The problem must be explored. *Truth* must ask, "Can nothing be done?" On that basis, *Righteousness* must be involved. Centuries of argument have produced a *stalemate*. What is needed is forgiveness—*the kiss of eternity*. Only that kiss can save us.

Like a song, *four-part harmony is required*. And that is why, sir, Christianity is a *song* as no other religion upon earth can be a song.

What can Muhammad's prayers do to effect a reconciliation? Who will satisfy God's justice? That takes more than *prayers*, mister! Justice is not moved by prayers. Try it in the court sometime!

What can the heathen offer? They offer endless *sacrifices—blood without ceasing*. The answer is always this. "It is not possible that the blood of bulls and of goats should take away sins" (Hebrews 10:4). Why should a beast die for a man's sins, any more than a man die for a beast's folly? It doesn't make sense. What then? Can man offer himself? Micah asks that question, "the fruit of my body for the sin of my soul?" (Micah 6:7).

I will ask a Jew. Is it in an endless search of the *Law*? After all his generations, why hasn't my Jewish friend found the answer? None has hunted more zealously than he.

Here is the answer! "Sacrifice and offering thou didst not desire; . . . Then said I, Lo, *I come*" (Psalm 40:6, 7).

Mercy, Truth, Righteousness, and *Peace* can all find room, and to spare, for a meeting in *Jesus Christ.* Give the Son of God a *body* and it can be done. "For what the law could not do, in that it was weak through the flesh, God sending his own Son in the likeness of sinful flesh, *and for sin,* condemned sin in the flesh" (Romans 8:3). He is Mercy. He is Truth. He is Righteousness. He is Peace. *They gather and harmonize in no other.* Every claim is satisfied.

Among the ancients, Job saw it by faith. You will read, "Then he is gracious unto him, and saith, deliver him from going down to the pit: I have found a ransom" (Job 33:24).

Jesus meant it when He said, "I am *the way.*" What a meeting the Bethlehem Morn provided! There is an *honor* about the Christian religion that no other philosophy or ethic in the universe can touch.

The scoffer and the critic will ask, "Cannot an Almighty God forgive, of His free goodness, of His abounding mercy, *without putting His Son to all this pain?*" If He were to abandon His justice or waive His truth, He could. But then He would cease to be God. Mercy pleads. Yes! But justice groans to be satisfied. Is not justice as important to our well-being as mercy?

This Christmas text says, "And righteousness shall look down from heaven." Every report of the Saviour's birth includes this item. An outer world was stirred. What focused the attention of heaven? The text states it plainly. "Truth shall spring out of the earth."

Something happened on this planet *that could not have happened in heaven.* "But when the fulness of the time was come, God sent forth his Son, *made of a woman*" (Galatians 4:4).

"And there shall come forth a rod out of the stem of Jesse, and a Branch shall grow out of his roots" (Isaiah 11:1). Heaven saw something that it hadn't seen on this planet since the collapse in the Garden of Eden.

Truth hurries to the meeting. *Every fulfillment is in Jesus.* Every prophecy is meticulously honored. Jesus cannot be denied. He is *certified* beyond any possible reservation. This is "the woman's seed" designated in Genesis three and verse 15. Nothing like it had been seen on Earth before. "Which things the angels desire to look into" (1 Peter 1:12).

What could *Righteousness* say? *Righteousness* says "yes" to a clean birth, a holy life, an innocent death, a spirit and a mouth without guile, a soul and a body without sin. That is what *Righteousness* beheld. *Righteousness* cannot detect the slightest variation. It is enough. *Righteousness* is ready to kiss—to embrace *Mercy, Truth,* and *Peace.*

The impasse is broken at the manger, sir! Joy unspeakable and full of glory breaks forth. My salvation is in the ascendancy. "Righteousness shall go before" (Psalm 85:13). There is no uncertainty—no holding back. "If God be *for* us, who can be *against* us?" (Romans 8:31).

Yet it could not be either a complete or authoritative meeting without *Peace.* "And, having made peace through the blood of his cross, by him to reconcile all things unto himself; by him, I say, whether they be things in earth, or things in heaven" (Colossians 1:20). Hell cannot win, mister.

Millions have experienced this peace. I have. Nothing can void this reconciliation. *He is our Peace.*

These same four must meet in every one of us if we are to enjoy His birth—*the new birth.*

There must be *Truth.* This is manifest in open and complete *confession.* "If we confess our sins" (1 John 1:9). When this *Truth* appears, *Mercy* will embrace it. "He is faithful . . . to forgive" (1 John 1:9).

David discovered this. "And David said unto Nathan, I have sinned against the Lord. And Nathan said unto David, The

Lord also hath put away thy sin; thou shalt not die" (2 Samuel 12:13).

Truth is on your side, sinner! *Truth* pricks you to confess your sins. And the moment you do, *Mercy* moves toward you.

Righteousness measure all of us. There are no favorites and no exceptions. I do not meet the requirements. I have come "short of the glory of God" (Romans 3:23). But as soon as I cry, "Lord be merciful to me a sinner," I can go to my house "*justified*" (see Luke 18:13, 14).

I'll tell you this. You will never have this harmony outside of Jesus Christ. These four must meet if you are to enjoy the miracle of redemption.

Recently I was the guest of the great Eglin Air Force Base on the West Coast of Florida. It was my privilege to examine at close range the mighty F-111, the flying arsenal of our Air Force, each ship worth millions. I was fascinated at the cockpit where the pilot sits in the midst of this labyrinth of computerized electronics. He may be locked in at two-and-one-half times the speed of sound. *Where are his eyes focused?* In front of him are coordinating factors. They spell out safety or danger. But when they cross in a perfect "magic T," the pilot rests in the knowledge that all is well.

There are *four factors* that must meet in a perfect cross for me. Otherwise I am a lost man. Where shall I look? I ask you, "Where other can I look?" The miracle is in Jesus alone. That Cross at Golgotha meets every requirement. I feel the magic "kiss" of Christmas in my soul.

The *order* is not an accident. *Mercy* leads to *Truth*. *Truth* leads to *Righteousness*. *Righteousness* leads to *Peace*. Who needs them? You do, mister!

Christianity is a meeting. That is why you will know it when this meeting takes place in your life. The moment of assurance and joy strikes when *all four* factors coordinate. That is the "kiss" you seek. That is the eternal "Christmas" you hunger to enjoy.

How loose a thing is *Mercy,* if it be quite devoid of justice! We call it foolish pity. How harsh a thing is justice, if it be not tempered by *Mercy!* We call it tyranny. Separate *Truth* from *Mercy,* and who will trust it? Take *Mercy* from *Truth,* and it condemns rather than delivers. Peace without *Righteousness* is like taking a pain-killer for a broken bone, when the need is to set the bone and restore ease. *All complement each other.* They meet in Christ. He is your answer, lady!

I pray the Holy Spirit will make Christmas real to you this year. I pray you will feel this "kiss" from heaven. The joy it brings is above any other human experience.

HE KNOWETH OUR FRAME

Text: "*Like as a father pitieth his children, so the Lord pitieth them that fear him. For he knoweth our frame; he remembereth that we are dust.*"

Psalm 103:13, 14

THIS element of pity—sympathetic understanding—is incorporated in the universe. I am glad it is. If a Higher Power did not remember me, there could be no personal salvation.

Evidences of God's sovereignty, magnificence, and majesty are abundant, *but the great cry of humanity is for sympathy and love.* Nothing else will satisfy the cravings of the soul. I ask, and I keep asking, "Does He care for me?"

When we study the instincts of animal life, we find *parental affection* predominating over every other instinct. The most timid will become brave, and the instinctive love of life is held in abeyance by the instinctive love of offspring, so that they will expose themselves to death in defense of their young.

This text is a story you will find everywhere. In Greek legend, Laocoon of ancient Troy, when his two sons were enfolded in the deadly coils of a huge serpent, endeavored to rescue them, but failing, he died in the attempt, and one of the most famous pieces of statuary in existence commemorates the event.

After the battle of Gettysburg, a soldier was found dead upon the field holding in his hand the likenesses of his three small children. This evidence of parental love awakened such an echo in the hearts of the nation that it led to the founding of the National Orphan Homestead at Gettysburg, where the children found a home and their mother became a matron. *The element is real.* It is not a synthetic.

Since it belongs to the race, is this not the *impress* God has left of His own nature upon His words? I see no other answer. The impress cannot be erased. It is voiced in David's sorrow for a rebel, ingrate son, Absalom. "Would God I had died for thee, O Absalom, my son!" (2 Samuel 18:33). *The father was superior to the king.* Parental affection lies deeper than regal robes.

God has purposed His concern should be known. It is a part of the record. "I dwell . . . with him also that is of a contrite and humble spirit, to revive the spirit of the humble, and to revive the heart of the contrite ones" (Isaiah 57:15).

The broken heart never bleeds alone. Someone cares. "Can a woman forget her sucking child, that she should not have compassion on the son of her womb? yea, they may forget, yet will I not forget thee" (Isaiah 49:15).

God publicly acknowledges His relationship to me. He is responsible for my being. "Like as a father pitieth his children." It was this responsibility that produced our Saviour. God so felt for me that He sent "his own Son in the likeness of sinful flesh, and for sin, condemned sin in the flesh" (Romans 8:3). The evidence is overwhelming.

I respect God's providence. I see it operate through the laws of nature. It makes possible the satisfaction of my physical wants. But that is cold—*and nature responds only to sacrifice and toil.* But, in Christ, mister, God draws near to me. *God's love warms and embraces me.* I know immediately Somebody wants me. I'm not a digit wandering helplessly and aimlessly in the wilderness of space. Calvary debunks that theory. Jesus Christ is the eternal language of God that says, "You matter. You matter very much."

Take the next step with me, sir. Jesus made this claim and died for it. "I and my Father are one" (John 10:30). The tenderness and sympathy of Jesus are the tenderness and sympathy of God. Jesus is the meticulous, close-up of God. As He loved, pitied, and sympathized with me in the days of His flesh, so does God always.

I'll tell you something, Mister Nature-Lover. No Yosemite, no Mount Everest, no Niagara will ever move your soul as the shadow of a simple cross can. *That hill of shame is the language of love.*

Look at Jesus Christ and you will want to go His way! He comforted and fed the poor. He bore our sicknesses and carried our sorrows. There wasn't one special group He didn't love—the deaf, the contagiously diseased, the bereaved, the immigrant, the black, the blind, the military, the parent, the child, the preacher. *He loved them all.*

When Jesus stood by the grave of Lazarus, He mingled His tears with those of Mary and Martha. *Why did He weep?* He knew that Lazarus would soon be restored to his friends. He knew their sorrow would turn to joy. Christ wept because He saw every open grave, and in those weeping sisters He saw represented every tearful eye, every broken heart, every smitten household. The tears of Jesus, sir, were a genuine outburst of sympathy, human and divine comingled, for human suffering and tragedy.

God gave a Saviour "to give . . . beauty for ashes, the oil of joy for mourning, the garment of praise for the spirit of heaviness" (Isaiah 61:3).

This text says that *the sympathy of God is that of a father.* That is a lot closer than angelic interest. And some of you would gladly settle for some angel guardian. *I'm going to settle for a Father.* Some of you are willing to settle for a lucky star. I want to be a member of the Family.

When a dad looks down toward his child and says, "Remember, we are pals!" that child, in that moment, is ready to go through hell for that man. When I read, "as a father pitieth," I'm examining the strongest possible tie. "He that keepeth thee will not slumber" (Psalm 121:3).

I have sung these words and I believe them: "On the stormy sea, Jesus speaks to me. How the billows cease to roll!"

This divine understanding isn't sloppy sentiment to be merchandised by phonies. *It is guided by infinite wisdom.* "He knoweth our frame." He knows the shock and the stress. He knows the absorption point. He knows just how much I can bear; *and whether I should bear it,* which is even more important. The eternal rule is this. "As thy days, so shall thy strength be" (Deuteronomy 33:25).

Samson knew the promise and the penalty of that rule. When he gave his day to God, his strength was enormous. But when he gave his day to selfish ends, his strength was puny.

I think we ought to come to terms with this fact. If our life were the life of a *beast* merely, no doubt God would speedily relieve us. But there is in man a *soul,* and by *discipline* God designs to make us partakers of His holiness.

"Our *frame*" isn't the last work in God's creativity. So God judges correctly. "He remembereth that we are *dust.*" *Almost all others forget that.* Parents forget that about their children. Educators forget that about their students. Preachers forget that about their members. *We demand too much.* The United Nations could never arrange a "Calvary." *God could* because He *remembers.* There wouldn't be any salvation, any grace, without divine sympathy.

It is something in my own household that hits me the hardest. I feel for my neighbor, but never with the intensity that I feel for my own. God is like this.

We are His creation. He is knit to us. He suffers when we suffer. He is the Head of the Household. "Like as a father pitieth. . . ." It matters to Him. Without that, nothing makes sense.

I've witnessed a lot of human sympathy and nobility toward others in my life. It makes you proud to be a member of the human race. The flow of charity is massive. I have seen the response leap in times of accident or disease or sorrow. And there's more to it than money! I have seen people really *care.* All this compassion makes a sizable entry on the other side, the credit side, of the ledger.

Make no mistake about it, mister! A lot of people do care. You may not think so. Satan may lie to you and tell you that they don't. But, God forbid, let some grief happen in your life, and you will see for yourself that lots of folk care. *That comfort will help you survive.*

If this is true with mankind, *and it is true,* then how much more is it true in another world to which we relate? Heaven is concerned about me. I believe that like I believe two and two make four. If heaven can forget a widow, abandon her, offer her no sympathy, that is a heaven I don't want to enter. If heaven can't shed a tear toward an invalid, bedfast, or so crippled that his or her world is limited to a wheelchair, that is a heaven too frosty, too cold, for me to ever feel at home.

No, sir! *I want to head toward something better than a smoohly operating, profit-making corporation.* This text assures me. It's a heaven that *cares.* Everything else is conditioned by that fact.

That is why Jesus won't disappoint you, lady. Yes, He is a *High Priest*—but not remote and unapproachable—not like that at all. He is a High Priest, with all the authority you will ever need, who is "*touched* with the feeling of our infirmities" (Hebrews 4:15).

He knows my bank balance better than I do. He realizes my obscurity, how little I am known anywhere, better than I do. He spent 30 years at Nazareth. He was born in a stable. God had to supply His groceries. He knows how limited my education may be. He got to the big city one time for less than a week before His 30th birthday. Sorrows, that we wouldn't divulge to our best friends on earth, *are known to God.* That nearness supports me. It makes a difference—believe me!

Your real problem, sinner—more than anything else—is that you are not *family.* That kind of loneliness and pain of the soul is frightening. That can be remedied in seconds. God offers you *family.* You can become as much His child as John Wesley or Catherine Booth or St. Augustine were ever His children. Jesus Christ guarantees it.

Let me read it to you! We are "made nigh by the blood of Christ" (Ephesians 2:13). I want you to feel that closeness at this altar. Then you'll never feel lonely again.

"In all their affliction he was afflicted, and the angel of his presence saved them: in his love and in his pity he redeemed them; and he bare them, and carried them all the days of old" (Isaiah 63:9). That testimony can be yours.